A
MASTER
COURSE
IN
FENG-SHUI

Books by Eva Wong

CULTIVATING STILLNESS

CULTIVATING THE ENERGY OF LIFE

FENG-SHUI

HARMONIZING YIN AND YANG

HOLDING YIN, EMBRACING YANG

LIEH-TZU

A MASTER COURSE IN FENG-SHUI

NOURISHING THE ESSENCE OF LIFE

SEVEN TAOIST MASTERS

TALES OF THE DANCING DRAGON

TALES OF THE TAOIST IMMORTALS

THE TAO OF HEALTH, LONGEVITY, AND IMMORTALITY

TAOISM: AN ESSENTIAL GUIDE

TEACHINGS OF THE TAO

A MASTER COURSE IN
FENG-SHUI

EVA WONG

SHAMBHALA
Boston & London
2001

Shambhala Publications, Inc.
Horticultural Hall
300 Massachusetts Avenue
Boston, Massachusetts 02115
www.shambhala.com

13   12   11   10   9   8   7   6

Book Design by Ruth Kolbert

Printed in the United States of America

♾ *This edition is printed on acid-free paper that meets*
the American National Standards Institute Z39.48 Standard.

♻ *Shambhala Publications makes every effort to print on recycled paper.*
For more information please visit www.shambhala.com.

Distributed in the United States by Penguin Random House LLC
and in Canada by Random House of Canada Ltd

Library of Congress Cataloging-in-Publication Data

Wong, Eva, 1951–
A master course in feng-shui / Eva Wong.—1st ed.
p.   cm.
Includes index.
ISBN 978-1-57062-584-8 (alk. paper)
1. Feng shui.   I. Title.
BF1779.F4   W657 2001
133.3'337—dc21   00-047024

This book is dedicated to my teacher
of yang-domain feng-shui—
Mr. Ma Jen-chou.

CONTENTS

FOREWORD

Having been in the feng-shui industry for over fifty years now, I've seen my fair share of feng-shui masters, authors, and practitioners. I rarely, if ever, recommend feng-shui books. Most of the ones on the market today bank on the fact that while it is a field of growing interest, it is a subject that few people know very much about.

Eva, however, comes from a proud and strong lineage of feng-shui masters, and she has written a book that is in a class of its own. This is the definitive textbook for all genuine feng-shui enthusiasts. It is almost like a how-to manual, successfully condensing authentic feng-shui theories into useful, applicable concepts, with do-it-yourself feng-shui projects. Her skill as an author and her own practical experience have allowed her to clearly explain the Form School theories in conjunction with the Flying Stars (Time Dimension) system, something few authors have ever done before. Her chapters on countermeasures contain recommendations that I am sure many readers will find helpful. The most useful aspect of this excellent book (as I am sure you will realize as you go along) are the exercises.

Eva and I met at a seminar in London. Our immediate friendship stemmed from the fact that we were both ardent Taoists rather than feng-shui practitioners. At that time I had great regard for Eva. She was a trustworthy, loyal, and genuine person. But most importantly, for all her knowledge and fame, she was a modest, affable person. I am glad to note that we have remained great friends ever since, both in the field of Taoism as well as feng-shui.

Read this book. Then read it again. And again. You will find a new nugget of information each time. Congratulations to Eva on a book well written.

Yap Cheng Hai
January 2001
Yap Cheng Hai Feng Shui
Center of Excellence
Kuala Lumpur, Malaysia
www.ychfengshui.com

PREFACE

Feng-shui is the traditional Chinese art and science of living in harmony with the environment. Deeply rooted in Chinese culture and Taoist philosophy, it is a way of seeing and interacting with the energy of the universe. This book shows you how to use the traditional art of feng-shui to choose a home, build a house, select an office, and find a retail space. Structured as a home-study course, the book is divided into three parts.

In part one you will learn how to use the techniques of the Landform school to evaluate the feng-shui of landscapes and the external environment. The Landform school originated in the Han dynasty (206 B.C.E.–219 C.E.), and its theories and methods were systematized by the feng-shui masters of the Chin (265–420 C.E.) and T'ang (618–906 C.E.) dynasties. Next, you will learn how to use the techniques of the Compass school to chart the pattern of energy that flows within a building. The particular method of the Compass school detailed in this book is called the Hsüan-k'ung (mysterious subtleties) technique, or the Flying Stars system. It was developed by the feng-shui master Hsü Jen-wang in the Sung dynasty (960–1279 C.E.), and today it is the most widely practiced form of feng-shui in Hong Kong, Taiwan, and China.

In part two you will learn how to use countermeasures, enhancers, and renovations to improve the feng-shui of a building.

In part three you will learn how to use your knowledge of feng-shui to build a new house, choose an apartment, select an office, and find a retail space.

Readers who are familiar with my *Feng-shui: The Ancient Wisdom of Harmonious Living for Modern Times* will find that this book is very different from the earlier one. While the earlier work focuses on the historical and philosophical background as well as the practical applications of the art, this book is purely a how-to manual with do-it-yourself feng-shui projects. Also, the earlier work adopts a more conservative approach, retaining the flavor of Hsüan-k'ung feng-shui as it was practiced in early-twentieth-century China. In this book, I have revised several rules based on my experience and discussions with fellow Hsüan-k'ung practitioners. The differences are not great, but I believe that the revisions make the principles of Hsüan-k'ung feng-shui more applicable to modern times.

Although this book is written primarily for home owners, renters, and small-business proprietors who want to improve the feng-shui of their homes and workplaces, real estate agents, interior designers, and architects also will find it useful as a reference manual. The book is not meant to replace the kind of training required of professional feng-shui practitioners. Having a working knowledge of feng-shui to take care of your personal needs is different from having the expertise to work on other people's homes and businesses. Understanding the materials presented in this book does not make you a master practitioner of feng-shui, just as knowing the basics of electricity does not make you a licensed electrician. If you encounter problems that you cannot solve, you should consult an expert.

Since the publication of *Feng-shui: The Ancient Wisdom of Harmonious Living for Modern Times,* many readers have asked me how to identify capable feng-shui practitioners. I have a few suggestions, but they are by no means exhaustive. First, I believe that a good feng-shui practitioner should have an appreciation for and understanding of the culture in which feng-shui originated. I don't think you need to be Chinese to practice feng-shui, but you need to be very familiar with Chinese culture to practice it well. Second, a competent feng-shui practitioner should explain the rationale behind every rec-

ommendation. The answer to "why" is just as important as the answer to "what" and "how."

Third, in my experience the proficient practitioners tend to be people who have undergone formal training and apprenticeship and can tell you the origins and history of the school where they were trained. Finally, I think that the best way to judge whether someone is a skilled practitioner is to have an educated view of feng-shui. If you are familiar with the principles of feng-shui, you will be able to ask good questions and evaluate the answers intelligently.

Feng-shui has become very popular in North America and Europe in the past ten years. With so many people claiming to be practitioners, it is often difficult to separate fad from tradition. For me the difference is that fads come and go, but traditions are here to stay. Feng-shui has been integral to Chinese culture for several thousand years. Throughout the centuries, it has helped the Chinese people design cities, build homes, and bury the dead. I am proud and honored to be a practitioner and a carrier of this wisdom tradition of my ancestors, and I hope that in writing this book, I have been able to share a part of that tradition with you.

HOW TO USE THIS BOOK

This is a workbook. You should study the contents, work through the sample problems, and do the exercises.

Part one covers the basics of feng-shui. You need to master the information presented in this section before you go on to parts two and three. Even if you are familiar with the contents of my other book, you should still work through the examples, do the exercises, and reacquaint yourself with the basics of feng-shui. The pace in this part of the course is fairly slow—I assume that most readers are learning the materials for the first time.

Part two covers three advanced topics in feng-shui—countermeasures, enhancers, and renovations. The pace in this part of the course is faster, and the information is more complex. You should not attempt to study this section until you have mastered all the materials covered in part one.

Part three deals with specific projects. This section of the course is modular in structure—you need not study the chapters in sequence. In fact, you can ignore the chapters that do not interest you or skip those that do not address your feng-shui needs. The pace in this section of the course is fast. It is assumed that you have mastered the information covered in parts one and two.

At the end of each chapter are exercises. After you have completed the exercises in the chapter, check your answers against the solutions. Finish all the exercises in a chapter before you look at the answers. Do not hesitate to redo selected exercises or to work through sections in the text for a second or even a third time. Once you feel that you have mastered the materials in a chapter, you should gain field experience on the topic. For example, after you have learned how to choose and design a business suite, you should visit commercial buildings and evaluate the feng-shui of the offices. The more hands-on experience you have, the more competent you will be.

The appendix to this workbook contains the Nine Cycles diagrams that are necessary for setting up the geomantic chart. You may wish to photocopy the appendix and have it in front of you while you are studying the text or trying out the exercises.

I have excluded design topics that I feel are beyond the scope of the do-it-yourself type of feng-shui project. These projects include shopping plazas, business complexes, resorts, college campuses, religious institutions, industrial parks, car dealerships, factories, manufacturing plants, warehouses, transportation terminals (airports, bus stations, freight terminals, and piers), government buildings, and housing projects. These applications require expertise that cannot be learned from a book. If you need feng-shui advice in these areas, you should consult an expert. (See the preface for guidance in choosing a practitioner.) Also, this book deals exclusively with yang-domain feng-shui, which is the feng-shui of residences and businesses. Yin-domain feng-shui, the feng-shui of burial sites and cemeteries, requires a deep understanding of the *lo-p'an* (the traditional Chinese geomantic compass), and learning the lo-p'an is beyond the scope of a home-study course.

I will also be presenting additional material on the Web. For a question-and-answer forum, occasional essays, and analysis of additional landforms with dozens of color examples, please visit my web site at *www.shambhala.com/fengshui.*

A
MASTER
COURSE
IN
FENG-SHUI

THE BASICS OF FENG-SHUI

Part one introduces you to the basics of feng-shui.
Although we will use the example of choosing and designing a house
to illustrate the principles of feng-shui, the information
covered in this part is applicable to every chapter in the book.

The topics covered in part one are these:

1. Evaluating the surrounding environment, including landforms, buildings, and natural and artificial features (chapter 1)

2. Evaluating the internal environment, including the shape of the building, the floor plans, and the interior architectural features (chapter 2)

3. Taking directional readings of the building and setting up the geomantic chart (chapters 3 and 4)

4. Superimposing the chart onto the floor plan (chapter 5)

5. Interpreting the geomantic chart and designing the usage of space (chapters 6 and 7)

6. Matching the occupants to the building (chapter 8)

7. Placing furniture (chapter 9)

1

Evaluating the External Environment

The external environment is an important factor in determining the feng-shui of a building. If the surrounding environment is untenable, we need not go further to examine the floor plan and the architectural details. For example, a house situated at the edge of a cliff with waves crashing in from the sea will be buffeted by destructive energy despite excellent floor plans and a good geomantic chart.

The characteristics of the environment are the strongest determinants of the feng-shui of a place, because they carry the energy of nature. Moreover, they are the most difficult to change. Removing natural features is not integral to the ethics of feng-shui. If the natural features carry too much destructive energy, we should respect that and leave it alone rather than try to compete with it. There are three important factors in evaluating the external environment: finding protection, avoiding destructive energy, and receiving benevolent energy.

FINDING PROTECTION

The building should be located in a protected space. Protection means safety, and people living in a safe place are protected from such calamities as health problems, sudden death, bankruptcy, and disharmonious relationships. There are four desirable protectors in the surrounding environment: the Green Dragon, White Tiger, Red Raven, and Black Tortoise. In rural areas they are the landforms in the vicinity of a house, and in the urban environment they are the neighboring building structures.

Identifying the Four Protectors

The four protective features are identified with reference to the position of the observer and are named after four guardian animals from Chinese mythology. The Black Tortoise is the feature at the back of the house, and the Red Raven is the feature in front. Ideally, the Black Tortoise should be higher and the Red Raven should be lower than the house. To put it simply, the Black Tortoise should be the only feature you can see from the back of the house, and the Red Raven should not block the view from the front. Identifying the Green Dragon and White Tiger is a bit more complicated, because their positions are different in yang-domain (residential and commercial) feng-shui and in yin-domain (burial site) feng-shui.

In yang-domain feng-shui, we identify the Green Dragon and White Tiger by facing the front of the house. To our left is the Green Dragon, and to our right is the White Tiger. In the yin domain, we stand with our backs to the headstone of the grave. To our left is the Green Dragon, and to our right is the White Tiger. Notice that in both cases, the rule is still "left Green Dragon and right White Tiger," but the positions of the two protectors are reversed because the observer's position of reference is different for the two forms of feng-shui (figure 1.1). Many people know the rule "left Green Dragon / right White Tiger" but are unaware that the reference points for recognizing them are different for yin- and yang-domain feng-shui. I have even seen feng-shui texts that identify the Green Dragon and White Tiger of a residence as if it were a burial site. This mistake in designating the Green Dragon and White Tiger can have disastrous consequences in analyzing the feng-shui of a place. Study figure 1.1 carefully, and make sure that you know how to distinguish the Green Dragon and White Tiger. (For a more detailed discussion of the four protection landforms, see box 1.1. See also figure 1.2 for examples of the Green Dragon, White Tiger, Black Tortoise, and Red Raven formations.)

In a rural environment, it is ideal for the Green Dragon formation to be covered with vegetation and the White Tiger formation to be an outcrop of whitish-colored rock. The Black Tortoise and Red Raven should have smooth slopes and ridges.

In an urban environment, the ideal Green Dragon formation is a building with a greenish or bluish tint. A building with a green stone facade or windows tinted with the appropriate color will serve the purpose. Buildings with trees or hedges on their sides or with ivy clinging to the walls are also viable Green Dragons. An effective White Tiger is a building that has a white stone facade. The next in order of preference is a building simply painted white.

The Black Tortoise should be a building taller than yours, but not too close. In a suburb, your backyard should provide enough distance between your house and the Black Tortoise. In the city, you would want to have a parking lot or even an alley between your building and the one behind you. The Red Raven in front should be lower than your house.

If the surrounding buildings are not effective protectors, you can build a fence or plant hedges and trees around your house. You can use trees for the Black Tortoise, hedges and bushes for the Green Dragon, a white stone or granite wall as the White Tiger, and a low brick wall or redwood fence as the Red Raven.

Here are key points to consider when you look for protection:

- The best site for a house is one that is surrounded by all four guardian landforms.
- The next best is one that has the Black Tortoise, Green Dragon, and White Tiger.
- If there is only one protection feature, it should be the Black Tortoise.
- Never position a house on the Green Dragon, White Tiger, or Black Tortoise formations. These landforms are meant

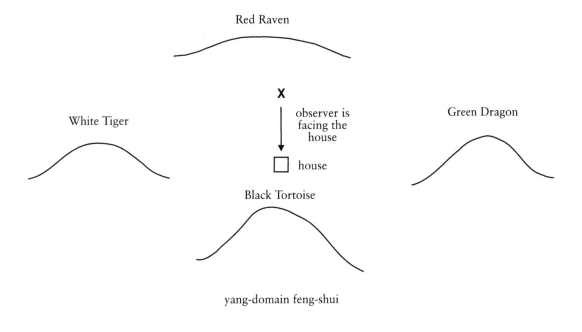

yang-domain feng-shui

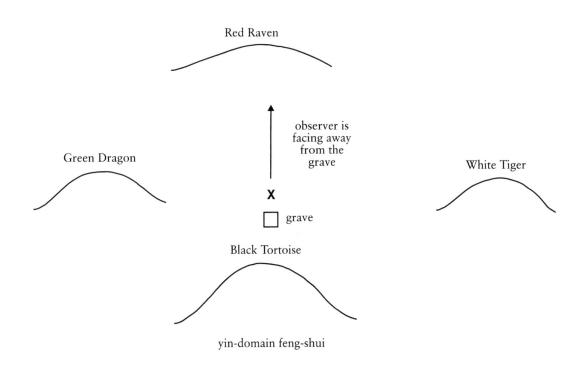

yin-domain feng-shui

Figure 1.1 The Green Dragon and White Tiger in yang- and yin-domain feng-shui. Note the different points of observer reference (**X**) in these two forms of feng-shui.

Figure 1.2a Black Tortoise, Green Dragon, and White Tiger landforms. Assuming that we are considering the feng-shui of a residential site, the White Tiger is the mound with the exposed rock on the right side of the photograph (*arrow*). The Green Dragon is the mound with trees and bushes on the left side. The Black Tortoise is the ridge in the center of the picture. Notice that it slopes gently down into a valley.

to shield the house from the onslaught of destructive energy. Should you build a house on top of them, the occupants will bear the full brunt of the destructive forces (figure 1.3a).

- The Red Raven formation should not block the view from the front of the house.
- The Black Tortoise should not be too close to the house.

- Do not live in a house on a slope without vegetation, because vegetation is a form of protection (figure 1.3b).
- Do not live in a house that is situated on top of a ridge or a mountain. These sites have no protection on any side (figure 1.3c). Similarly, a high-rise apartment that is the tallest building in the immediate area also is unprotected from destructive energy.

Figure 1.2b A Red Raven formation. An opening in the branches reveals layers of ridges.

- Land should slope gently down in front of the house and should not slope away from the back of the house. (Box 1.2 shows you how to evaluate the steepness of slopes.) The site should have the feel of "security," as if there is something for it to lean against. Sites without this feel are shown in figure 1.3c and d.

Figure 1.3a–d Houses built on landforms associated with bad feng-shui.

Figure 1.3a House on the head of a White Tiger.

Figure 1.3b Houses on bare slopes.

Figure 1.3c House on a ridge.

Figure 1.3d Houses on the edge of a steep slope.

BOX 1.1

THE ORIGINS OF IDENTIFYING THE GREEN DRAGON AND WHITE TIGER FORMATIONS

In ancient China, it was believed that benevolent energy came from the south. In a culture that originated in the Northern Hemisphere, south-facing houses received more sun and warmth and were sheltered from the cold north winds. For this reason, it was customary for towns to be laid on a north–south axis, with the windows and doors of the houses facing south. When the kings built their dynasties and their palaces, they, too, oriented the seat of government toward the south. The emperors sat with their backs to the north and received their ministers and subjects facing south.

In the Chinese geomantic compass, the direction south is always located at the top. Since the Chinese always have oriented themselves facing south, the direction east would be to the left, and west would be to the right. The four protector animals— Green Dragon, White Tiger, Red Raven, and Black Tortoise—are associated with the four cardinal directions of the original Chinese compass, and each direction and the center are associated with specific elements. Thus, Green Dragon is the wood element of the east, White Tiger is the metal element of the west, Red Raven is the fire element of the south, Black Tortoise is the water element of the north. The center is associated with the element earth.

When the early Chinese emperors built their palaces four thousand years ago, their shaman advisers planned the layout of the palaces so that the four protector animals surrounded the seat of government. When the emperor sat with his back to the north and faced south, the Green Dragon (east) would be to his left, and the White Tiger (west) would be to his right. The Black Tortoise (north) would be at his back, and the Red Raven (south) would be in front (figure B1.1).

During the Chin dynasty (265–420 C.E.), the great feng-shui master Kuo-p'u laid down the principles of selecting burial sites to benefit the descendants of a family. The idea behind yin-domain feng-shui (the feng-shui of burial sites) is that if an ancestor were buried in a spot where the land carried the energy of prosperity and fame, the descendants would benefit and would become high-ranking officials or even founders of dynasties. The most auspicious grave site is one in which the land to the back of the grave resembles the back of the emperor's chair. The auspiciousness of the site is enhanced further when this formation is directly to the north of the headstone. Completing the ideal landform of burial sites are the "arms" of hills to the east and west of the chair and a small tablelike formation in front (the south). When an ancestor is buried at the site, it is said that he or she "sits" in the emperor's chair, with his or her

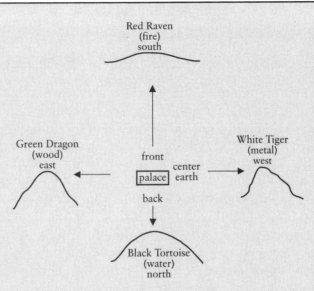

Red Raven
(fire)
south

Green Dragon
(wood)
east

front

center
earth

palace

back

White Tiger
(metal)
west

Black Tortoise
(water)
north

Figure B1.1 The four protector animals with reference to the position of the palace of the ancient Chinese emperors.

back to the Black Tortoise formation to the north, and faces south (the Red Raven formation). The Green Dragon hills would be to the left (east), and the White Tiger rocks would be to the right (west). This is the origin of the feng-shui principle "left Green Dragon and right White Tiger." This principle is still used in the selection of burial sites.

When yang-domain feng-shui (the feng-shui of residences and businesses) began to flourish, especially in the Sung dynasty (tenth through thirteenth centuries), the great feng-shui master and founder of the Hsüan-k'ung school, Hsü Jen-wang, discovered that the feng-shui of the domain of the living is different from the feng-shui of the domain of the dead when it comes to identifying the ideal landforms surrounding a site. Specifically, the reference points for designating the Green Dragon and White Tiger for yin- and yang-domain feng-shui should be reversed. Instead of facing away from the house, the observer should face toward the site of the house when he or she is evaluating the landforms around the residential site. Although the rule is still "left Green Dragon and right White Tiger," notice that the two formations are transposed (figure 1.1 in the text).

Many feng-shui practitioners do not understand this principle and apply the rule blindly, treating houses in the same way as burial sites and vice versa. This mistake is dangerous, because the residential house is viewed as a grave, and the occupants are considered dead people. The evaluations are incorrect, and people can suffer much harm when their houses are mistaken for graves.

BOX 1.2

HOW STEEP IS STEEP?

The steepness of a slope is measured by its gradient. The gradient describes the altitude we gain by the distance we walk. On flat land, for example, we traverse horizontal distance without gaining any vertical distance. For cliffs, we gain vertical distance without traversing horizontal distance. To get an idea of the steepness of a slope, or its gradient, we can measure the gain in altitude over a section of ten feet. If you want to estimate the gradient over a greater distance, you can measure several ten-foot sections and average the measurements.

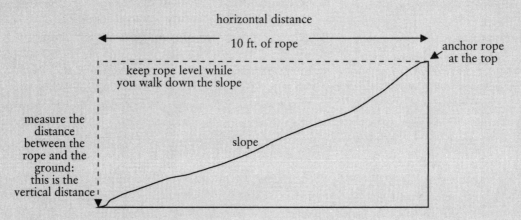

Figure B1.2 *How to measure the gradient (or steepness) of a slope.*

Here is the procedure for measuring the gradient of a slope. (Refer to figure B1.2 for clarification.)

1. Take a coil of rope or string and walk down the slope, uncoiling the rope as you go.
2. Have someone hold one end of the string at the top of the section you wish to measure.
3. While walking down the slope, try to keep the string horizontal. A level should help you do the job.
4. When you have uncoiled ten feet of rope, have another person measure the distance between the rope and the ground. This is the altitude, or the vertical distance you have gained in ten feet.

5. If you find that somewhere within the distance of ten feet the rope is higher than your own height, the slope is too steep.
6. Once you have the measurement of the distance between the rope and the ground, you can calculate the gradient. To do this, divide the vertical distance by the horizontal distance (ten feet). The result is a fraction that tells you the gradient of the slope.

Let's work through some examples. Suppose the vertical distance is one foot. Since we have the horizontal distance set at ten feet, the resulting fraction is one-tenth, which is the gradient. This means that for every ten horizontal feet, we gain one vertical foot. The gradient, read as 1 in 10, tells us that this is a fairly steep slope.

Suppose the vertical distance is three inches (one-fourth foot). Three inches divided by 120 inches (ten feet) is 0.025, which is 25/1,000, or 1/40. This means that for every forty horizontal feet, we gain an altitude of one foot. The gradient, 1 in 40, tells us that this is a very gentle slope.

Now suppose that the vertical distance is eight inches (two-thirds foot). Eight inches divided by 120 inches (ten feet) is 0.066, which is 66/1,000, or approximately 1/15. This means that for every fifteen horizontal feet, we gain an altitude of one foot. The gradient, 1 in 15, tells us that this is a moderate slope. Thus, the smaller the denominator (the number at the bottom of the fraction), the steeper the slope. Sometimes the slope is not uniform in steepness. In this situation, you may wish to measure several ten-foot sections and take an average of the gradient.

The guidelines for evaluating the suitability of the gradient of a slope for building a house are these:

1. Inappropriate: gradients of 1 in 8 or steeper
2. Viable: gradients between 1 in 9 and 1 in 14
3. Desirable: gradients of 1 in 15 or gentler

AVOIDING DESTRUCTIVE ENERGY

Some types of natural landforms and human-made structures carry destructive energy, which can bring ill health, disharmony in relationships, financial problems, accidents, and even death. In considering the feng-shui of a place, it is therefore important to see whether there are any features in the surrounding area that may hold such energy.

Landforms and Building Structures That Carry Destructive Energy

Destructive energy is harbored in landforms and building structures that have a sharp discontinuity with the surrounding environment. (See figures 1.4a–e and 1.5a–e for examples. See also box 1.3.)

CLIFFS

Cliffs, steep canyon walls, and gorges carry destructive energy. Do not live in a house perched on the edge of these landforms. A house at the bottom of a steep canyon also receives the onslaught of negative forces, because the canyon acts as a tunnel for explosive energy to rush through. It is not desirable to set a house against a cliff. It imparts the feeling that the house and occupants are being pushed against a wall with nowhere to go.

Figure 1.4a–e *Examples of destructive landforms.*

Figure 1.4a Rocky slopes with jagged rocks.

ROCK OVERHANGS AND LARGE BOULDERS

Do not live in a house under a rock overhang or beneath large, precariously balanced boulders. These landforms impart the sense that the house and the occupants will be crushed.

GULLIES AND LOOSE ROCKS

Do not live near gullies and slopes with loose rocks. These landforms hold harmful and unstable energy.

Figure 1.4b Rocky escarpment with cliff face.

Figure 1.4d Canyons surrounded by steep cliffs.

Figure 1.4c Scree—a slope with loose rocks.

Figure 1.4e Jagged rocks.

TALL BUILDINGS

Skyscrapers act like cliffs. For this reason, it is not desirable to build a house next to a tall building.

BUILDINGS WITH SHARP EDGES

Buildings with sharp edges or roofs (for example, pyramidal buildings) carry destructive energy. Their sides are like knives cutting into the adjacent buildings. (See box 1.3 for one example.)

IRREGULARLY SHAPED BUILDINGS

Irregular shapes are associated with the unpredictable flow of destructive energy. Thus, a house next to an irregularly shaped building will be buffeted by erratic spurts of harmful energy.

POWER PLANTS

Do not live near power plants, because they carry as well as churn up negative energy (figure 1.5e).

LAND AND BUILDINGS ASSOCIATED WITH DEATH AND ILLNESS

Do not live near land or buildings associated with death and illness. Such places include cemeteries, ancient graves, morgues, mortuaries, slaughterhouses, battlefields, sites of massacres and murders, and any business associated with death and dying (such as hospitals, hospices, and manufacturers of caskets and headstones). These sites gather the forces of death and are very destructive to life energy.

LAND AND BUILDINGS ASSOCIATED WITH DECAY

Do not live near land and buildings associated with decay, including garbage dumps, wastewater-treatment plants, junkyards, and even recycling centers. Energy from decaying matter is also destructive to life forces.

Figure 1.5a–e Examples of destructive structures.

Figure 1.5a Building with sharp edges.

Figure 1.5b Building with a pointed roof (*left*).

Figure 1.5c Arrowlike dormer windows.

Figure 1.5d Building with irregular surfaces.

Figure 1.5e Power plant.

BOX 1.3

BUILDINGS WITH AGGRESSIVE FENG-SHUI

Some buildings have aggressive feng-shui, among them, those that have pointed structures and jagged, knifelike edges directed at neighboring buildings (figure B1.3a and b). Examples of buildings intentionally designed to carry aggressive feng-shui can be found especially in Hong Kong, where feng-shui is used as a tool to enhance one's own enterprise and ruin a competitor's business. Figure B1.3 shows three commercial buildings found in the downtown area of Hong Kong. The feng-shui philosophy behind the architecture of these buildings is "kill or be killed," or "conquer your neighbors." Buildings with hostile feng-shui may bring prosperity to the company, but the gains in wealth are made at the expense of the employees and those who work in the neighboring buildings. I believe that these kinds of architecture are antithetical to the practice of feng-shui, because feng-shui is an art of living in harmony with the environment and those who inhabit it. I hope you will not consider designing such buildings or situating your company's offices inside them.

Figure B1.3a A building with aggressive feng-shui. Notice the two structures at the top that resemble machine guns (left).

Figure B1.3b "Dueling" feng-shui. The building on the left is shaped like an ax with bladelike edges. The building on the right has a structure resembling a machine gun mounted on top (above).

Objects That Carry Destructive Energy

Harmful energy can be carried in objects. There are several classes of such objects that should be avoided or neutralized by countermeasures (see chapter 10). Examples of objects that harbor destructive energy are shown in figures 1.6, 1.7, and 1.8.

SHARP AND POINTED OBJECTS

Sharp objects comprise jagged rocks, tree branches, television antennas, transmitters, electrical transformers, and even sculpture (figure 1.6a–g). It is worst to have these objects point directly at your house.

LARGE OBJECTS THAT DWARF THE HOUSE

Gnarly tree trunks, pits, deep pools, and piles of rocks all can dominate a house. The worst possibility is to have such objects blocking your front door.

Figure 1.6a–g Examples of sharp and pointed objects.

Figure 1.6a Branches of a dead tree.

Figure 1.6b Construction crane.

Figure 1.6c Power transmitter.

Figure 1.6d Utility poles.

Figure 1.6e Satellite transmitters and receivers on communications tower.

Figure 1.6f Sculpture resembling spears.

Figure 1.6g Architectural feature resembling pointing blades.

SHINY AND REFLECTING OBJECTS

Large glass windows and doors, metal roofs, and solar panels represent destructive reflecting objects. Satellite dishes are especially dangerous. They are considered poten- tially harmful because they have a bowl-like structure as well as an antenna, which is a pointed object. They have the capacity to col- lect adverse energy and focus it (figure 1.7a–d).

Figure 1.7a–d *Examples of reflective objects.*

Figure 1.7a Satellite dishes (*above*).

Figure 1.7b Reflective windows (*above*).

Figure 1.7c Reflections of sunlight on a building, making the building appear to be on fire (*left*).

Figure 1.7d Transformers and utility poles imaged on a building with reflective windows.

OBJECTS OF DESTRUCTION

Weapons, objects that resemble weapons, and images of such items carry destructive energy and are to be shunned (figure 1.8a–f).

Waterways and Road Patterns That Carry Destructive Energy

Destructive energy, associated with bad feng-shui, can be conveyed by certain configurations of water pathways and roads. Examples of destructive water formations are shown in figure 1.9a–c.

FAST-FLOWING RIVERS

Rapids, water dropping over great heights, narrow and fast-flowing streams, and water rushing through such obstacles as branches and boulders impart powerful negative energy. Fast-flowing water also can sweep away positive energy.

STAGNANT WATERS

Swamps, large stagnant ponds, lakes covered with growth, river deltas, and floodplains transmit stagnant energy. These are places where negative and decaying energy gathers and cannot dissipate.

STEEP ROADS

Steep, narrow roads also carry harmful energy. The situation is worsened when there is heavy traffic along these streets.

ROADS WITH FAST-FLOWING TRAFFIC

These roads have negative effects similar to those of fast-flowing rivers.

MAZELIKE ROADS

The flow of energy is blocked in roads that resemble a maze. Usually, many dead ends and one-way streets are associated with mazelike road patterns. The best way to determine whether a section of town has mazelike roads is to drive through it diagonally from corner to corner. If your route is convoluted, you have encountered a mazelike road pattern. The other way to ascertain whether an area has mazelike roads is to examine a street map (figure 1.10).

ENTRANCES TO HIGH-SPEED THRUWAYS

Entrances and exits on highways also carry destructive energy. The situation is worsened when traffic is heavy on these ramps.

BRIDGES AND ELEVATED ROADS

A house located near such structures as bridges and elevated roads not only receives deleterious energy carried by the fast-flowing traffic but also has the feel of being crushed by steel girders and concrete slabs.

TRAIN TRACKS AND AIRPORT RUNWAYS

Do not live in a house near a train track or at the end of a runway. Trains and airplanes carry more destructive power than the ordinary vehicle, making the energy traveling in these pathways more dangerous than that on roads.

SPECIFIC RIVER AND ROAD PATTERNS

Some river and road patterns are especially damaging. Figure 1.11 illustrates the worst cases. For the special case of the cul-de-sac, see box 1.4.

Figure 1.8a–f Objects of destruction.

Figure 1.8a A "shooting" sculpture. Notice the gun and the arrows.

Figure 1.8b Sculpture that resembles pointing rifles.

Figure 1.8c Display of a missile.

Figure 1.8d Sculpture with a pointed gun.

Figure 1.8e A building structure that resembles a machine gun.

Figure 1.8f A building structure that resembles a missile launcher.

Figure 1.9a–c Destructive water formations.

Figure 1.9b Frozen lake (stagnant water) next to cliffs.

Figure 1.9a Fast-flowing water next to cliffs.

Figure 1.9c White water.

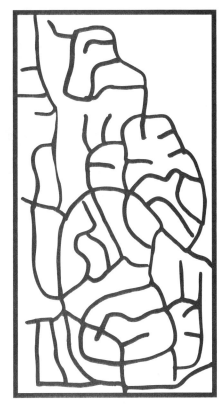

Figure 1.10 Mazelike streets form a bad road pattern.

Figure 1.11a Destructive river patterns.

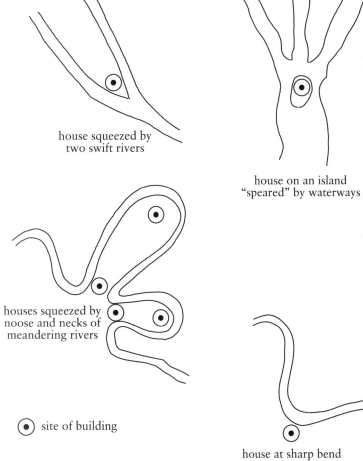

house squeezed by
two swift rivers

house on an island
"speared" by waterways

houses squeezed by
noose and necks of
meandering rivers

• site of building

house at sharp bend
in the river

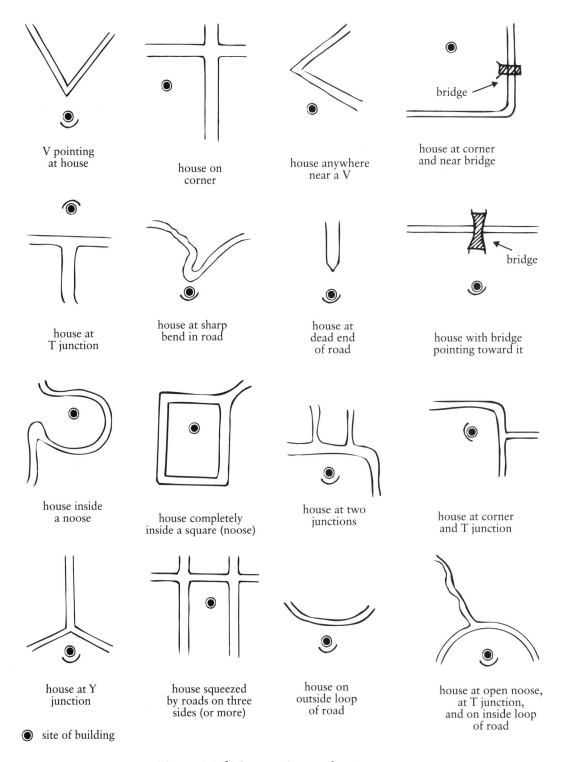

V pointing
at house

house on
corner

house anywhere
near a V

house at corner
and near bridge

bridge

house at
T junction

house at sharp
bend in road

house at
dead end
of road

bridge

house with bridge
pointing toward it

house inside
a noose

house completely
inside a square (noose)

house at two
junctions

house at corner
and T junction

house at Y
junction

house squeezed
by roads on three
sides (or more)

house on
outside loop
of road

house at open noose,
at T junction,
and on inside loop
of road

⦿ site of building

Figure 1.11b Destructive road patterns.

BOX 1.4

THE CUL-DE-SAC

The cul-de-sac is a common road pattern in many residential areas. While the cul-de-sac itself is circular and thus can tame wild energy and gather benevolent forces, some sections along the cul-de-sac are undesirable as building sites. Look at figure B1.4. Houses located at the neck of the road entering the cul-de-sac are in a zone of "discontinuity," where energy from a straight path meets energy from a circular area. The meeting of two different kinds of energy usually creates turmoil, and houses in the vicinity of the turmoil will be buffeted by the destructive energy collected in the area.

A house positioned directly opposite the entrance to the cul-de-sac will receive the brunt of harmful energy from the road pointing straight toward it. Placing a house in this location is similar to building a house at the end of a T junction. The best sites along the cul-de-sac are those located away from the entrance and not opposite the access road. Houses on these sites will gain the benefits of energy tamed and collected in the cul-de-sac.

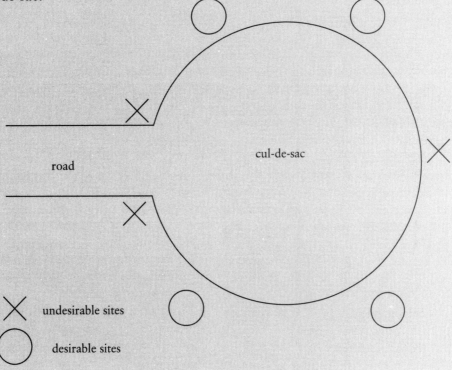

road

cul-de-sac

✕ undesirable sites

◯ desirable sites

Figure B1.4 The cul-de-sac.

RECEIVING BENEVOLENT ENERGY

Benevolent energy brings health, prosperity, harmony, and success in endeavors. For this reason, it is desirable to live in a house in an environment that harbors benevolent energy.

Landforms and Building Structures That Carry Benevolent Energy

GENTLY ROLLING HILLS

Hills with gentle and vegetated slopes carry positive energy. While it is advantageous to live in a house in such areas, it is not advisable to situate the house on a hilltop. Without protection, the positive energy of the hill cannot accumulate and benefit the occupants.

GENTLE WATER

Water that flows in tranquil streams and laps gently onto a sandy beach conveys benevolent energy. Houses overlooking these water environments have good feng-shui. The house should not be situated near the meeting place between land and sea. A rift of energy exists where land and water meet, and a house in the area of the rift does not benefit from the positive energy of that environment but instead may be engulfed by the rift. You should make sure that there is a buffer of flat land between the house and the water.

GROVES AND FORESTS

Plants carry beneficial energy. A house situated near or in the midst of a grove of trees or a forest will receive positive energy from the plant life. Make sure that there is a small clearing between the trees and the house. Otherwise, the trees will compete with the house for energy from the land.

PARKS AND GARDENS

In an urban environment, parks and gardens serve the same function as groves and forests, though the positive energy they carry is weaker than that of a forest. Examples of benevolent landforms are shown in figure 1.12.

ROUND BUILDINGS

Buildings with circular shapes and domed roofs hold positive energy. (In general, round structures impart benevolent energy, and rough structures transmit destructive energy.) Some geodesic domes are not true round structures, because the dome is punctured with spikes (figure 1.13). Such structures carry detrimental energy and should not be confused with domes that have a smooth, round surface.

LAND AND BUILDINGS THAT BRING LIFE ENERGY

Playgrounds, nurseries, preschools, and other areas where children are present bring life energy. The effect of the playground is enhanced when it is also a park and not simply a concrete enclosure. Spiritual retreats and healing centers dedicated to improving health in a wholesome manner also impart nourishing energy, as do places where there are harmonious interactions among people, such as community centers, friendly shopping plazas, churches, temples, and town squares. Farms, orchards, and ranches where livestock is not raised for slaughter also are associated with the forces of life and growth.

Figure 1.12a, b *Benevolent landforms.*

Figure 1.12a Gently rolling hills. The mist is a bonus, because it is a meeting of earth (mountain) and sky (vapor) energies.

Figure 1.12b Vegetative patterns resembling a dragon. The dark, snakelike pattern in the center of the picture is called the Green Water Dragon. This formation typically is found in areas with a stream or subsurface runoff that makes some plants more lush than the ones farther away from this water source.

Figure 1.13 A spiked dome on a building with a deceptively round top. The geodesic top is highlighted with points. Such spiked roofs do not have good feng-shui.

Objects That Carry Benevolent Energy

FOUNTAINS AND SMALL PONDS

Fountains, miniature waterfalls, and small ponds carry positive energy. When designing these features, make sure that the fountain and pond do not dwarf the house. Any object that is larger than the house and too near to it will take energy away from the land, leaving very little for the occupants. Moreover, the water from the fountain or miniature waterfall should flow toward the house, not away from it. If the water flows alongside the house, a barrier should be built to pool the water, so that the energy is gathered and not swept away (figure 1.14).

GAZEBOS, HOT TUBS, DECKS

Gazebos, hot tubs, and decks can bring benevolent energy if they are round in shape. Again, make sure that these features are not too large compared with the house.

SUNDIALS, BIRD FEEDERS, BIRDBATHS, AND GARDEN ORNAMENTS

Garden ornaments, bird feeders, birdbaths, and sundials can foster positive energy if they are round in shape. When positioning these objects, make sure that you do not clutter the garden or the yard. Otherwise, the objects will block positive energy rather than conduct it.

Waterways and Road Patterns That Carry Benevolent Energy

Beneficial forces, associated with good feng-shui, can be carried by certain configurations of water pathways and roads.

SERENE, SMOOTH-FLOWING STREAMS

Peaceful rivers and streams carry benevolent energy, especially if their banks are gentle and there are no obstacles along the course. Irrigation ditches and canals serve the same purpose. The positive effect is enhanced if the

Figure 1.14a,b Waterfalls.

Figure 1.14a A waterfall with good feng-shui. The water collects in a pool and is prevented from running away from the building.

Figure 1.14b A waterfall with bad feng-shui. The water runs away from the building. The waterfall is indicated by the black arrows.

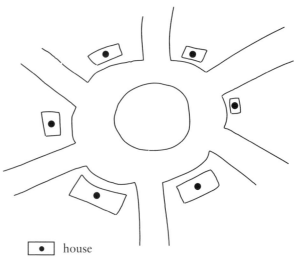

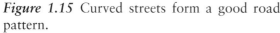

Figure 1.15 Curved streets form a good road pattern.

Figure 1.16 Traffic circle. Houses adjacent to the circle are buffeted by energy churned up by the traffic. Houses that are slightly removed from the circle receive beneficial energy from the circular road pattern.

stream meanders. If the winding of the stream is severe, it will act as a noose strangling the house. (See examples in figure 1.11.)

GENTLY WINDING STREETS

Streets that wind gently have the same effect as serenely flowing streams. These types of streets also can smooth out wild, rushing energy in an area. It is desirable to live in a house where streets are curved rather than set in a square grid (figure 1.15).

TRAFFIC CIRCLES

Traffic circles are beneficial road patterns, because they do not have the sharpness of intersections. Moreover, traffic enters and exits with the flow of the circle, enhancing the positive effects of the circular structure. You do

not want to live in a house adjacent to the entrances of the circle, because the merging traffic churns up too much energy (figure 1.16).

SPECIFIC RIVER AND ROAD PATTERNS

Figures 1.17 and 1.18 illustrate river and road patterns that best foster benevolent energy. Gently winding rivers and roads carry positive energy, pools at the confluence of quiet streams gather beneficial energy, and circular driveways tame wild energy.

Now that you have an idea of benevolent river and road patterns, complete exercises 1.1 and 1.2. Sometimes good and bad sites are found side by side, and you need to examine the road patterns carefully before you can discriminate the good ones from the bad.

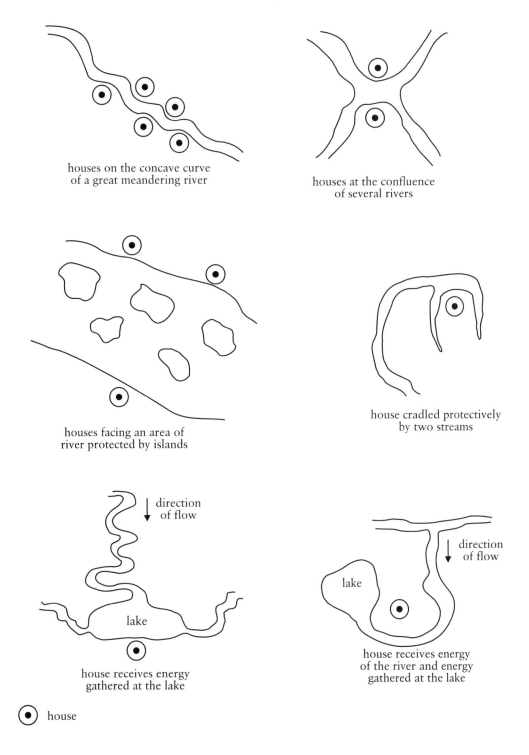

houses on the concave curve
of a great meandering river

houses at the confluence
of several rivers

houses facing an area of
river protected by islands

house cradled protectively
by two streams

direction
of flow

lake

house receives energy
gathered at the lake

direction
of flow

lake

house receives energy
of the river and energy
gathered at the lake

house

Figure 1.17 River patterns associated with benevolent energy.

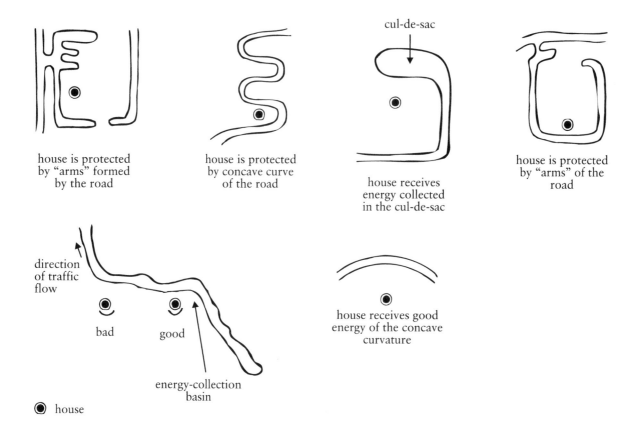

house is protected
by "arms" formed
by the road

house is protected
by concave curve
of the road

cul-de-sac

house receives
energy collected
in the cul-de-sac

house is protected
by "arms" of the
road

direction
of traffic
flow

bad   good

energy-collection
basin

house

house receives good
energy of the concave
curvature

Figure 1.18 Road patterns associated with benevolent energy.

When you have understood the material covered in this chapter and have completed the exercises, you should take field trips into urban, suburban, and rural environments. The more field experience you have, the more competent you will be at evaluating the feng-shui of the external environment. Remember, if the surrounding environment is not tenable, there is no point in going forward with further analysis of the place.

EXERCISES

EXERCISE 1.1

In this exercise, evaluate the feng-shui of sites (good or bad) marked 2 to 16 in figure 1.19, giving reasons for your choice. No. 1 is a worked example.

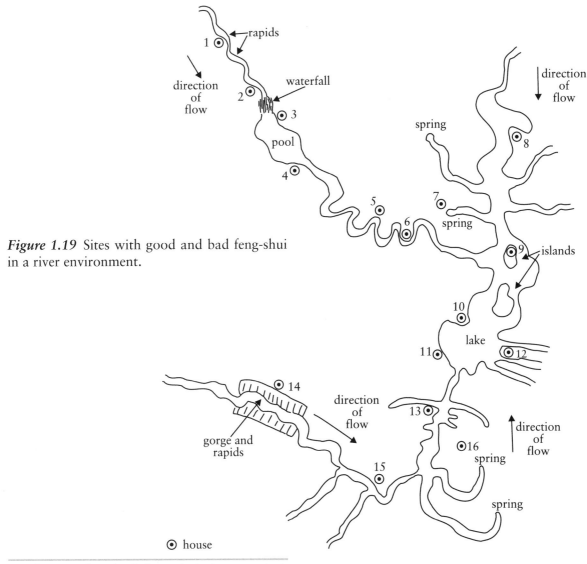

Figure 1.19 Sites with good and bad feng-shui in a river environment.

1. This site has bad feng-shui, because it is close to rapids and rapids carry destructive energy.

EXERCISE 1.2

In this exercise, evaluate the feng-shui of sites (good or bad) marked 2 to 20 in figure 1.20, giving reasons for your choice. No. 1 is a worked example.

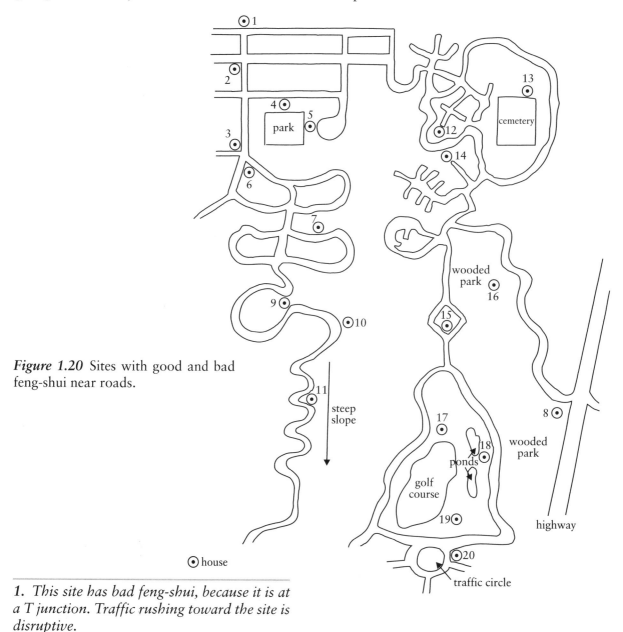

Figure 1.20 Sites with good and bad feng-shui near roads.

1. *This site has bad feng-shui, because it is at a T junction. Traffic rushing toward the site is disruptive.*

ANSWERS

EXERCISE 1.1

2. Bad: The site is at the edge of a waterfall and close to a steep drop in the slope.
3. Bad: The site is at the bottom of a waterfall, with water rushing down toward it.
4. Good: The site is adjacent to a pool that collects and tames wild energy.
5. Bad: The river bend is pressing against the site.
6. Good: The site is cradled by two arms of the river.
7. Good: The site is near a spring. Springs are associated with life energy.
8. Good: The site receives energy flowing from the river into the small bay.
9. Bad: The river is running straight toward the site. This situation is similar to placing a house at the end of a road.
10. Good: The site is situated on the shores of a lake that collects energy from the rivers flowing into it.
11. Good: This site has the same positive aspects as site 10. In addition, it is sheltered by a cove.
12. Bad: The site is squeezed by two rivers.
13. Good: The site lies at the confluence of three rivers but has no waterway running directly toward it.
14. Bad: The site is at the top of a cliff above a gorge.
15. Bad: A waterway is running directly toward the site.
16. Extremely good: The site is cradled by two arms of the river and has sufficient land around it to collect the benevolent energy from the rivers.

EXERCISE 1.2

2. Bad: The site is located at an intersection.
3. Bad: The site is located at an intersection, and there is a road running directly toward it.
4. Good: The site is adjacent to a park, where plant life fosters benevolent energy.
5. Good: The site is sheltered inside a cul-de-sac.
6. Bad: The site is squeezed by two roads, and there is another road running directly toward it.
7. Good: The site is along the concave bend of a road.
8. Bad: The site is near a high-speed road and the entrance to a highway.
9. Bad: The site is squeezed by a noose formed by the road.
10. Bad: The site is along the convex bend of a road.
11. Bad: The site is along a steep, winding road.
12. Bad: The site is at the end of a road.
13. Bad: The site is adjacent to a cemetery. Cemeteries harbor decaying and dying energy.
14. Bad: The site is at the end of a road.
15. Bad: The site is surrounded by a triangular road pattern, and there is a road running directly toward it.
16. Good: The site is located near a wooded park, where plant life imparts positive energy.
17. Good: The site is located near a golf course, which is equivalent to a park.

18. Good: The site is near ponds and a wooded park.

19. Good: The site is near a golf course, which has the positive energy of a park. It also receives benevolent energy from the traffic circle without being buffeted by traffic running toward it.

20. Bad: The site is squeezed by two arms of a traffic circle, and it is too close to the circle.

2

Evaluating the Internal Environment

Once you are satisfied with the feng-shui of the environment surrounding the house, the next step is to examine the internal environment of the building, that is, the shape of the house, its general appearance, the floor plan, and the interior architectural features.

In assessing the internal environment, we will start with the aspects that are the most difficult to change—the shape and general appearance of the house. If these features are untenable, there is no point in proceeding further.

SHAPE OF A BUILDING

The choice of the shape for a house is guided by three principles—stability, balance, and smoothness. A house with these three characteristics brings harmony, health, prosperity, and good luck.

Stability

A house is said to have a stable shape if the parts of the building are held up in a sturdy way and none of the levels are significantly larger than the others. Also, a house is stable if the upper levels rest on a solid foundation. The corollary is that houses built on stilts and pillars are unstable in feng-shui terms even though they may be structurally safe.

Balance

A house is thought to be balanced if it does not have an irregular shape.

Smoothness

The smoothness of a house is determined by an absence of harsh and protruding structures, including rooms jutting out from the upper floors, steep triangular roofs, dormer windows, and tall towers and chimneys. Small alcoves, bay windows, and enclosed window planters are excluded, because the volume of space they occupy relative to the house is small. Protruding sections trap negative energy and contain it inside the house.

Figures 2.1a–d and 2.2a–j show examples of shapes of houses that are associated with bad feng-shui. Shapes associated with good feng-shui are depicted in figure 2.3a–d. Some-times the shape of a house may not be obvi-ous at the time you are walking through it. You should look at the floor plan of the house and, if possible, view it from a high point nearby.

Figure 2.1a–d Examples of shapes of houses that are associated with bad feng-shui.

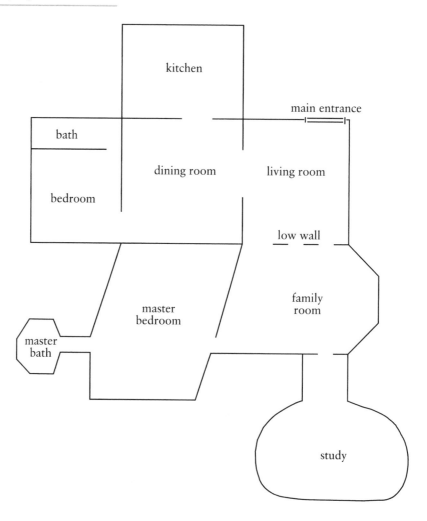

Figure 2.1a This house has an irregular floor plan and bottleneck corridors.

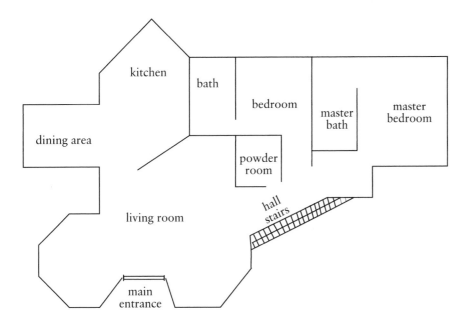

Figure 2.1b This house has an irregular outline and many triangularly shaped rooms.

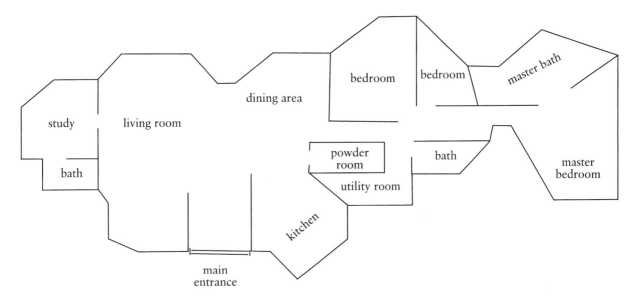

Figure 2.1c This house has an irregular outline, triangularly shaped rooms, and many apexes.

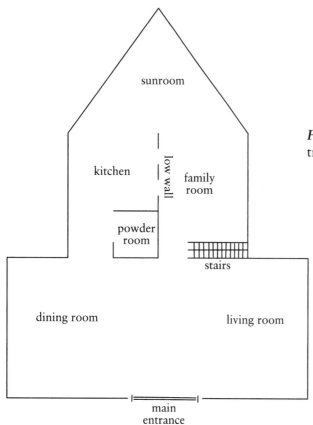

sunroom

kitchen

low wall

family
room

powder
room

dining room

stairs

living room

main
entrance

Figure 2.1d This house has a pronounced triangular room.

Figure 2.2a–j More examples of houses with undesirable shapes.

Figure 2.2a A top-heavy house.

Figure 2.2b Triangular houses.

Figure 2.2c A chopped-up house. Notice that the house is made up of three distinct sections—the triangular section on the left, the pagoda-like section in the middle, and the rectangular section on the right.

Figure 2.2d A house with an irregular shape. Notice also that it is set against a cliff.

Figure 2.2e A house with a protruding section on the roof.

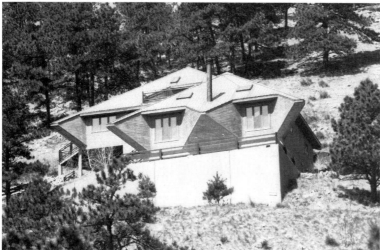

Figure 2.2f A house with an irregular shape and protruding sections. Notice also the triangular and pointed walls.

Figure 2.2g A house with a complex roofline and dormers has not only an irregular shape but also many protruding sections.

Figure 2.2h A house with a zig-zag floor plan.

Figure 2.2i A house with overhanging sections.

Figure 2.2j A house with one section perched on pillars.

Figure 2.3a–d *Examples of houses with shapes that are associated with good feng-shui.*

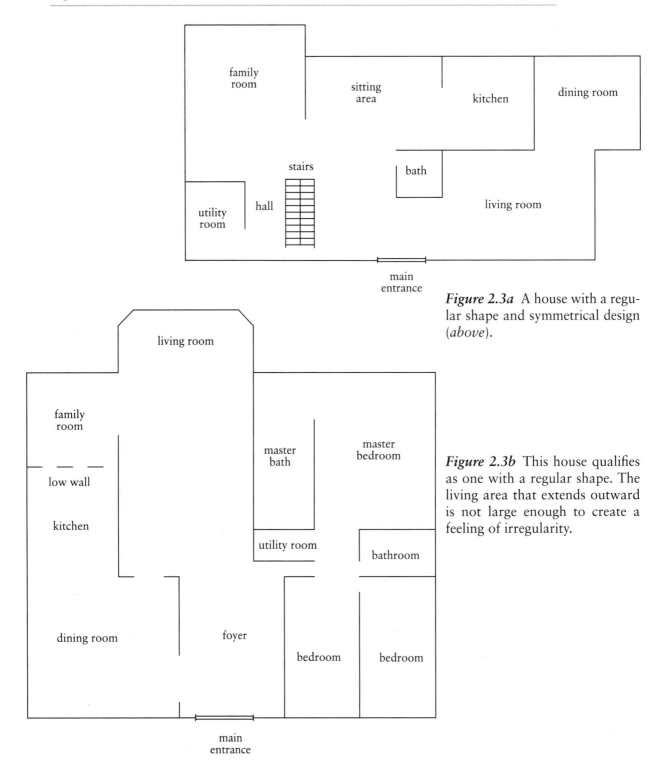

Figure 2.3a A house with a regular shape and symmetrical design (*above*).

Figure 2.3b This house qualifies as one with a regular shape. The living area that extends outward is not large enough to create a feeling of irregularity.

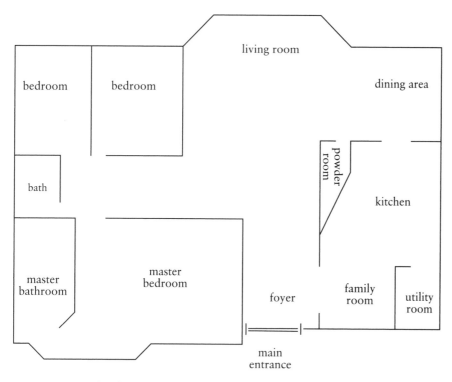

Figure 2.3c This house also has a regular shape. The small areas extending outward from the living area and master bedroom are not large enough to impart a sense of irregularity. The only triangular space in the house is the powder room, and this room is not important enough to introduce negativity.

Figure 2.3d This house has a regular shape. The small areas extending outward in the breakfast nook and the master bath are not large enough to produce an irregular effect.

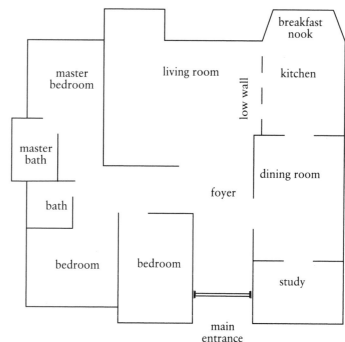

GENERAL APPEARANCE OF A BUILDING

The general appearance of a house can affect its feng-shui. For example, houses that look like military installations, forts, and implements of destruction are associated with violence and death. Houses surrounded by pillars give the impression that they and the occupants are constrained and jailed. Such houses usually generate financial problems and obstacles in business enterprises.

Houses that seem to be weighed down by a large object or capped by a lid are associated with difficulties in realizing business and personal goals. The occupants will be dominated by other people, and their projects will never get started. Houses that appear to be chopped up into sections can dispose to separations in relationships. They also have a tendency to isolate occupants from each other. Figure 2.4a–g shows examples of houses with shapes that impart bad feng-shui.

In my experience, houses with a conservative shape and architectural design tend to be the most stable and balanced, and houses that sport fancy nouveau architecture tend to have shapes associated with bad feng-shui. At this point, you should begin to examine houses and their general appearances. Look at houses in your town and peruse books on house design. Such books are illustrated lavishly and will give you information on perspective, floor plans, side elevations, and detailed architectural features. See if you can identify houses with good and bad feng-shui based on their shapes and general appearance. By the time you have gone through one or two of these books, you should be able to determine the feng-shui of a house, given its shape and appearance.

Figure 2.4a–g *Examples of houses with troublesome appearances.*

Figure 2.4a The upper section of this house looks as if it is falling down.

Figure 2.4b A different perspective of the house shown in figure 2.4a. It appears to be capped by a lid.

Figure 2.4c A house resembling a castle. Notice the battlements.

Figure 2.4d A house chopped into two sections.

Figure 2.4e Another example of a chopped-up house. This one looks as if it is cut in two by a blade (the brick wall).

Figure 2.4f A house that resembles a prison tower.

Figure 2.4g An untidy patchwork brick facade.

FLOOR PLAN

The floor plan is the arrangement of rooms, hallways, doors, windows, and stairs. When evaluating the floor plan, you must first look at the arrangement of the rooms. Are rooms partitioned in an irregular manner? Do the levels of the house overlap, making it difficult to determine which level you are on? If so, this is enough reason to reject the house in question.

Second, you need to have an idea of the frequency of usage of each area of the house. Entranceways, stairs, and corridors tend to be used often, because they are passageways. In typical households, bedrooms, the kitchen, and the family room are also frequently used. Make sure that these high-traffic areas have positive feng-shui.

The floor plan should be the first thing you consider when you evaluate the interior of a house. Here are guidelines for choosing a beneficial arrangement for the layout of the rooms in a building:

- The front and back doors should not be lined up. Otherwise, any benevolent energy entering the front door will go straight out the back.
- Levels within the building should be well defined. Uneven levels generate unbalanced circulation of energy.
- The arrangement of rooms should not be too irregular, because irregular space turns positive energy into harsh, destructive energy.
- There should be no long, dark corridors. This type of passageway carries negative forces.

- Windows should not be too big. Large windows allow harmful energy to enter a house and beneficial energy to leak out.
- Flat or domed ceilings are ideal, because they allow smooth circulation of energy. Uneven ceilings, on the other hand, restrict the flow of positive energy and gather destructive energy.
- Ceilings should not be too high. Nourishing energy is thinned in a room with a high ceiling.
- Rooms that are used frequently should have good natural lighting.
- The doors of bedrooms, home offices, and studies should not face the stairway or a door that exits the house.
- Preferably, the stairway should not be aligned with the front door.
- Roof levels in different parts of the house should not be too uneven.

Entrances

Energy enters and exits through entrances. Entrances that have positive feng-shui will circulate benevolent energy and dampen, dissipate, or block destructive energy. As a result, they can enhance the health, fortunes, and interpersonal relationships of the occupants. Figure 2.5a and b shows examples of such entrances.

Entrances that transmit bad feng-shui can block the circulation of benevolent energy, turn it into negative energy, and let it escape. Likewise, they can trap destructive energy in an area. As a result, occupants can suffer from bad health, bankruptcy, and the breakup of

Figure 2.5a,b Examples of entrances with good feng-shui.

Figure 2.5a In a good entrance, the doorway does not dominate the house.

Figure 2.5b In a good entrance, the doorway is not blocked by architectural features.

relationships. Figure 2.6a–e shows examples of such entryways.

Some houses have entranceways with ceilings that extend to the upper levels of the building. This kind of entrance tends to thin out benevolent energy, leaving insufficient amounts of positive energy for the rest of the house. It also renders the upper floors (where the bedrooms usually are located) unprotected, because negative forces from outside the house can flow directly to the upper levels.

Figure 2.6a–e Examples of entrances with bad feng-shui.

Figure 2.6a An entrance capped by a sloping roof.

Figure 2.6b An entrance that dominates the house. Also, the triangular roof accumulates negative energy.

Figure 2.6c This entrance is oppressed by an overhanging section of the house.

Figure 2.6d The architectural feature above the entrance resembles a guillotine.

Corridors

Corridors are conduits of energy, because they connect different parts of the house. Corridors with good feng-shui can distribute positive forces and disperse destructive forces. On the other hand, corridors with bad feng-shui can neutralize positive energy or even turn it into negative energy and can trap destructive energy inside the house. Figure 2.7 shows an example of corridors with good feng-shui, and figure 2.8 shows an example of corridors with bad feng-shui.

Figure 2.6e An entrance jailed by pillars.

Stairways

Stairways are also conduits of energy, because they connect the different levels of a house. Staircases with good feng-shui can enhance beneficial energy and neutralize adverse energy, while staircases with bad feng-shui can restrict the flow of positive forces and transform them into damaging energy. The following is a summary of types of staircases associated with bad feng-shui:

- Spiral staircases turn positive energy into negative energy, because they force it to funnel and twist as it rises and falls. A spiral staircase is one in which the stairs curl around themselves at least once. The narrower the stairs, the more destructive they are.
- Narrow stairs also can transform positive into negative forces. When energy is

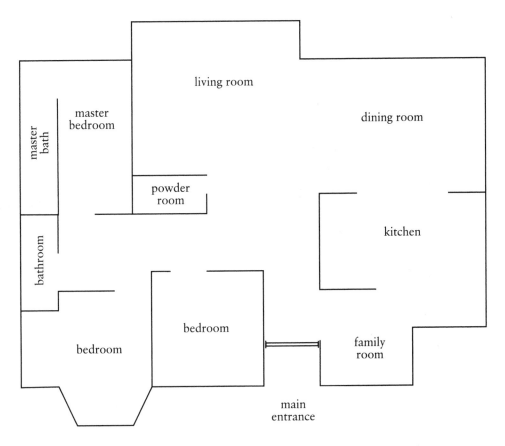

Figure 2.7 Example of corridors with good feng-shui. Notice that the passageways are wide and spacious.

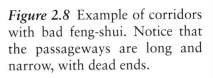

Figure 2.8 Example of corridors with bad feng-shui. Notice that the passageways are long and narrow, with dead ends.

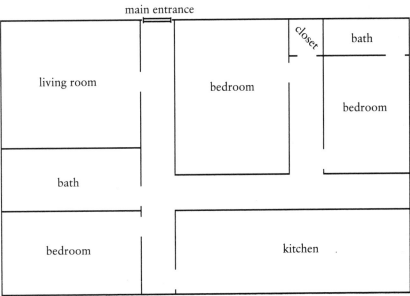

squeezed through a narrow space, it is churned up, like water flowing into a narrow gorge.

- Long, steep stairways also carry destructive energy. In this case, energy rolls down at tremendous speeds to swamp the lower levels. Because of the steepness, it is also difficult for positive energy to reach the upper floor.
- Stairs that are lined up with an entrance will allow harmful energy entering the house to move to the upper floors without obstruction. (It is a special case when the stairs occupy an extremely good spot in the Nine Palaces. The term *Nine Palaces* refers to a grid of nine squares laid over the floor plan of a house, which depicts the flow of energy in the house. The procedure for generating this grid is described in chapter 4.)
- Stairs that are dark accumulate decaying and deleterious energy.

The following list summarizes types of staircases that contribute to good feng-shui:

- Stairs that are wide and shallow allow gentle movement of energy between different levels of the house.
- Stairs that are well lit permit positive energy carried by sunlight to enter the house.
- Stairs that open onto wide landings allow energy to slow down before entering various rooms. They also can help dissipate and weaken destructive energy and gather positive energy into the rooms.

Garage

The garage is associated with travel. A well-positioned garage is conducive to safety in transit for the occupants. Moreover, energy brought to the home by cars can affect the health and fortunes of the occupants. Figure 2.9a shows positions of garages in their order of preference from the best to the worst, and figure 2.9b shows an example of a house perched on top of a garage. Cars driving into the garage destabilize energy in the rooms above. Moreover, the vehicles may pick up harmful energy on the roads and bring it into the garage, where it can travel upward into the living quarters.

Kitchen

The kitchen is associated with health and livelihood (i.e., having enough money). A kitchen with bad feng-shui can bring on illness associated with food regardless of whether the food is consumed at home or in a restaurant. A kitchen with good feng-shui, on the other hand, will favor well-fed and healthy occupants. The following list is a set of guidelines for evaluating the feng-shui of the kitchen in the floor plan of a house:

- The kitchen should be shielded from the front door. When you enter a house, you should not have an unobstructed view of the kitchen.
- The cooking area of the kitchen should be protected and should not be exposed on more than two sides. Ceiling-to-floor windows are not appropriate for kitchens.

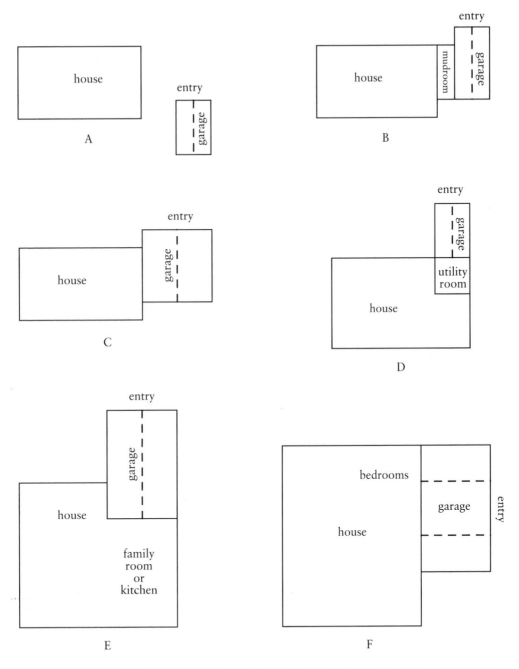

Figure 2.9a The location of the garage. Panel A shows the optimal location of the garage, followed by panels B, C, and D. Panels E and F show undesirable locations of the garage, where the vehicles drive toward living space in the house.

Figure 2.9b A house with living areas over the garage.

- The entrance should not be a narrow, dark hallway.
- The cooking area should be symmetrical and regular, so that energy can circulate freely.

Bedroom

The bedroom is where people spend the largest part of their time, since most of us sleep at least six hours a day. Because we are particularly vulnerable to the loss of energy during sleeping and because, in sleeping, we gather and replenish energy, the bedroom should be very protected. Here are guidelines for evaluating the feng-shui of the bedroom in the floor plan of a house:

- The bedroom should not have more than one doorway. If it does, positive energy inside the room will not be contained.
- If the bedroom has a door that opens out to a balcony, this door should be closed at night. You also should hang curtains over the door to cut down exposure.
- The bedroom door should not face a stairway.
- There should be no exposed beams in the bedroom.
- The ceiling should be flat or domed.
- The shape of the room should be symmetrical and regular.

Other Rooms

Rooms used for home offices and studies also should be symmetrical and regular and not too exposed. Preferably, the doors to these rooms should not be lined up with the front door.

Family rooms and recreation areas do not require the kind of protection that is demanded by bedrooms, kitchens, and home offices. They can be situated anywhere in the house as long as the rooms do not have irregular shapes and exposed beams.

The bathroom and utility room are of secondary importance. They can be located anywhere and are best used as buffer spaces between the residential portion of the house and a garage. (See figure 2.9a.) After you have familiarized yourself with evaluating the feng-shui of the floor plan of a house, complete exercises 2.1 and 2.2.

(See figure 2.9a.)

ARCHITECTURAL FEATURES

Frontage and Driveway

The frontage and driveway act as buffers between the outside world and the house. Depending on the layout of the frontage, the feng-shui of a house can be enhanced or ruined. Here is a list of guidelines for evaluating the frontage of a property:

- The backyard should be larger than the front lawn.
- The driveway should not run straight toward the living quarters of the house.
- The driveway of the house across the street should not point at your front door.
- Do not have a long, narrow path leading up to the front door.
- Do not build fences with sharp points.
- Do not place trees blocking the front door.
- Fountains, gazebos, and ponds should not dwarf the house.
- Trellised walks, gardens, and porches are desirable, because they create a buffer between the house and the outside world.

Bridges, Landings, Verandas, and Decks

Bridges, landings, verandas, and decks affect the kind of energy that flows in the vicinity of a house. Exterior structures with good feng-shui can bring positive energy into the area, and ones with bad feng-shui can build up negative energy. Here is a list of guidelines for evaluating exterior structures:

- A bridge or covered walkway should not connect two houses or two sections of a house.
- Verandas and decks should be supported by strong, thick pillars.
- Structures on the deck, such as gazebos or hot tubs, should be round.

Interior Structures

Interior structures affect the type of energy that flows within the house. Depending on their design, interior structures can generate positive or negative energy or neutralize benevolent or malevolent forces. The following is a list of guidelines for evaluating interior structures:

- There should be no exposed beams in the house.
- Fireplaces and woodstoves should not dwarf a room.
- Wooden doors, floors, and wall panels should not have excessively knotty, harsh-looking patterns.
- Do not use vertical blinds, because when

they are opened, they resemble knives cutting into the room.

- Do not suspend lights low from the ceiling. They are called *hanging lights* and are extremely harmful.
- Crystal lights and lamps that cast spotty shadows on the walls should be avoided.
- Do not have a wall with a sharp, jagged, rocklike facade inside the house.

Building Materials

Building materials also can affect the feng-shui of a house. Some materials introduce positive energy, while others can draw in destructive energy. Here is a list of guidelines for evaluating building materials:

- Bright-red bricks belong to the element of fire and will attract hazards associated with fire.
- Materials that reflect are bad. Aluminum sidings are acceptable as long as they do not create reflections.
- Rock facades are acceptable on an outside wall if the rocks do not protrude. (See figure 2.10 for an example of an acceptable rock facade.) An untidy patchwork facade is associated with irregular energy (figure 2.4g).
- Large glass windows that form a wall provide very little protection for the house. (See figure 2.11 for an example of a house with sets of windows forming a wall.)

- The best kinds of materials for the outside walls are greenish bricks, adobe, and wood.
- Dirt or gravel driveways are preferable to concrete or tar, because they do not block positive energy from rising and benefiting the house. A concrete driveway with colors that resemble the surrounding landscape is better than a black tar driveway.

When you feel comfortable with the materials presented so far, you should test yourself by looking at floor plans and architectural designs in books. You also may want to visit model homes and look at architectural plans. The more experience you have, the better you will be able to evaluate the floor plan and the interior design of a house.

This completes the introduction to the basics of the Landform school of feng-shui. Landform feng-shui works with the visible world, because it is concerned with features we can see, whether they are outside or inside a house. These features carry energy, and the goal of Landform feng-shui is to recognize which features (natural or human-made) are associated with destructive energy and which features draw benevolent energy. In the next chapter, we will examine the world of "invisible" energy, the energy that moves within a place at a particular time. The tools that make this invisible energy visible are the geomantic compass and the geomantic chart.

Figure 2.10 A wall made of smooth rocks.

Figure 2.11 A wall composed of windows.

EXERCISES

EXERCISE 2.1

List everything wrong with the floor plans shown in figure 2.12 and give your reasons. No. 1 is a partially worked example.

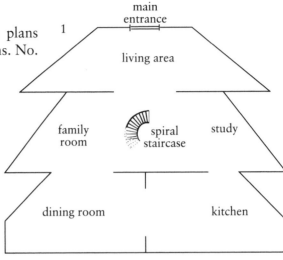

Figure 2.12 What is wrong with these floor plans?

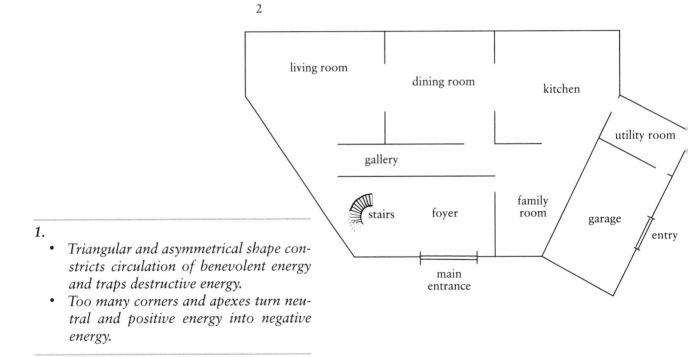

1.
- *Triangular and asymmetrical shape constricts circulation of benevolent energy and traps destructive energy.*
- *Too many corners and apexes turn neutral and positive energy into negative energy.*

(Continue with the analysis.)

EXERCISE 2.2

List everything that is correct about the floor plans shown in figure 2.13 and give your reasons. No. 1 is a partially worked example.

1.

- *House is symmetrical, allowing benevolent energy to circulate freely. Destructive energy cannot accumulate.*
- *There are no apexes and triangular spaces to trap harmful energy.*

(Continue with the analysis.)

Figure 2.13 What is correct about these floor plans?

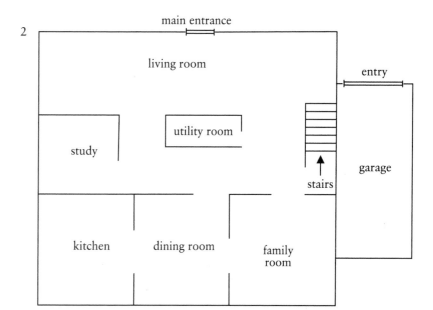

ANSWERS

EXERCISE 2.1

1.
- Spiral staircase creates a vortex of twisted and malevolent energy.

2.
- The house is wedge-shaped, squeezing energy as it flows from the larger area into the smaller area.
- Long corridor (the gallery) traps and constricts energy.
- Garage is against family room; vehicles drive toward living area, carrying disruptive and unpredictable energy.

EXERCISE 2.2

1.
- Kitchen and study are buffered from the front entrance by a foyer.
- Stairs are located away from the main entrance.

2.
- House is symmetrical, with good feng-shui for the reasons specified in no. 1.
- Garage is to the side of house; traffic does not "drive" toward any living space.

3

Taking Readings with the Geomantic Compass

The Chinese geomantic compass (lo-p'an) has twenty-four directions and concentric rings (figure 3.1). Most of the rings are used for evaluating the feng-shui of burial sites. The only ring in the compass with which you will need to be familiar when you are working on the feng-shui of your home or business is the one representing the Twenty-four Directions. Since the traditional lo-p'an is not easily obtainable in non-Chinese communities, I have worked out a procedure by which you can convert a Western compass to the Twenty-four Directions compass.

Before you proceed, you need to obtain a compass. I recommend one that is used for trail finding and orienteering. This type of compass is sometimes called a protractor compass and can be purchased in stores that sell camping and hiking supplies (figure 3.2). Look for a compass that is graduated in two-degree steps. North is zero. Clockwise, east is 90 degrees, south is 180 degrees, west is 270 degrees, and north is 360 degrees. The compass should have a rotating capsule or dial. The capsule itself should sit on a rectangular base plate, which allows you to align the magnetic needle with the bar underneath it simply by turning the capsule. The line of sight, which is a line or a notch on the base plate, is a very useful feature. Use a compass that is easy to read. The simplest models are the best. At the time of writing this book, I found suitable compasses costing between ten and fifteen dollars.

When you have obtained your compass, you are ready to proceed to the materials covered in this chapter. To convert the 360-degree regular compass to the Chinese geomantic compass, make a cardboard ring locating the Twenty-four Directions (figure 3.3). When it is attached to your compass, you can read off the Twenty-four Directions for any given compass bearing.

To prepare the ring, photocopy the template shown in figure 3.3 and paste it onto a piece of cardboard. This is the Twenty-four Directions ring of the geomantic compass. The marker that bisects the segment *tzu* indicates due north. Next, cut a hole in the center of your cardboard disc so that it fits the capsule of your compass. The inner circle in the template provided in figure 3.3 should fit the largest models of an orienteering compass. If the capsule is smaller than the inner circle of the template, you can draw a smaller circle that matches the diameter of the compass capsule. Notice that in the geomantic compass, south (*wu*) is located on top and north (tzu) is

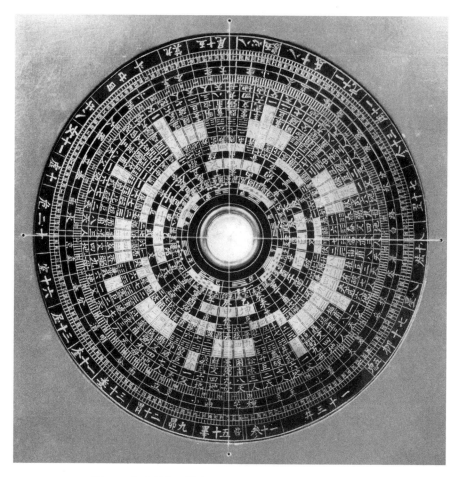

Figure 3.1 The Chinese geomantic compass.

at the bottom. You should familiarize yourself with this orientation of the compass. Learn to think and work with the Twenty-four Directions using their romanized Chinese names until you don't have to convert them back to the Western directional equivalents.

The geomantic compass is used to determine the front and back orientations of a building. The front of the building is its "facing direction," and the back of the building is its "mountain direction." Before you start to use the compass, you need to ascertain which side of the building is the front. Here are the working rules for identifying the front of a building:

1. Landforms in the immediate area around the building are the most important determinant. If the house is located on a slope, the front of the building, regardless of the position of doors, is the side with the unblocked view of the downward slope. Consequently, the back of the building is the side that faces the upward slope (see figure 3.4).

2. If the land around the building is flat but there are trees planted on the property, the

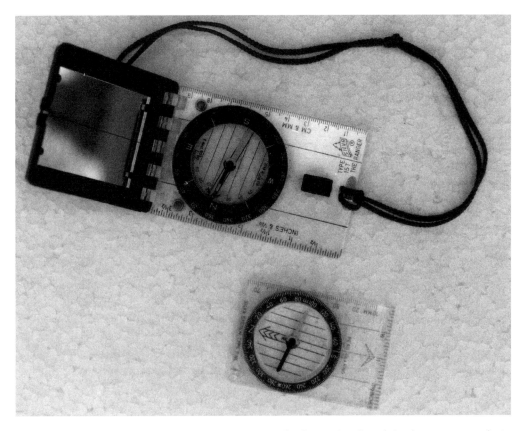

Figure 3.2 Two models of an orienteering compass. The line of sight of the larger example is marked by a notch in the dark bezel. In the bottom example, it is indicated by an arrow. Both models are made by Silva and can be obtained easily from camping and hiking equipment stores.

side of the building that faces the tallest trees constitutes the back, and the side that has an open view is the front, regardless of the position of doors.

3. If there are no defining features in the surrounding environment, the side of the house with the most open view is the front.

4. If the shape and floor plan of the house are so irregular that you cannot determine which side is the front, you should use the front door as the facing direction. Because there is no definite front orientation, however,

the predictive power of the geomantic chart is weakened. This is one reason why you don't want a building with an irregular floor plan.

If you cannot fix the facing direction of a building, you should obtain the services of a feng-shui expert. In many houses, the main entrance is not necessarily located in the front. Moreover, it does not have to be there for a house to have good feng-shui (see box 3.1). Determining the front of a building is not easy. Even professional feng-shui practitioners sometimes get it wrong. The rules

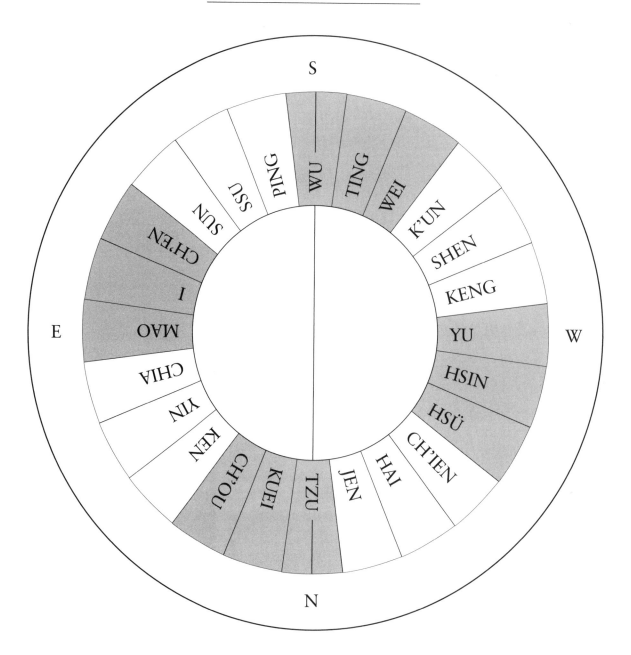

Figure 3.3 Template of the Twenty-four Directions of the Chinese geomantic compass. When this template is fitted to the regular compass, you can convert the reading in degrees to the Twenty-four Directions (see text for instructions). S, south; W, west; N, north; E, east. Note that south is at the top.

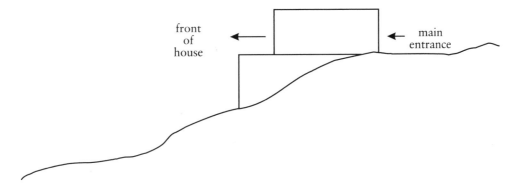

Figure 3.4 Determining the front of a building.

cited here will help, but they are not meant to be set in stone. Competence in figuring out the front of a building requires experience. I find that the best way to determine the facing direction of a building is by "feel." Imagine the building as a chair. Where is the backrest of the chair? The back of the chair will be the back of the building. Which way are you facing when you are sitting in the chair? Your facing direction in the chair will be the front of the building.

Sometimes a house has competing facing directions. Ambiguous facing directions can cause many problems in sorting out the feng-shui of a building. Usually, these houses are not desirable dwellings until a front facing direction has been identified.

Now do exercise 3.1. After you have completed the exercise, you should drive around town, examining as many buildings as you can, and see if you can figure out which side of a building constitutes its front.

LEARNING HOW TO USE YOUR HOMEMADE GEOMANTIC COMPASS

When you feel that you are competent in identifying the front of a building, you are ready to learn how to use your homemade geomantic compass. Here are the steps to follow in finding the facing direction of a building using the Twenty-four Directions compass, after you have determined its front:

1. Set the base plate of the compass on the ground parallel to the front wall of the building. The arrow indicating the line of sight should point away from the building. Make sure the compass is not placed near metal fittings, because they can distort the magnetic sensor.

2. Rotate the capsule on the compass so that the needle aligns with the parallel bars on the faceplate. Make sure the arrow of the magnetic needle is pointing north (zero degree).

3. Do not move the compass. To convert degrees into the Twenty-four Directions, care-

BOX 3.1

WHY THE FACING DIRECTION IS NOT DETERMINED BY THE MAIN ENTRANCE

Energy enters a house from its facing direction. This energy is expansive and is the dominant force in the building. Expansive energy is called *facing direction energy,* and it enters through the side of the house with the most unblocked exposure, that is, the side with the most unobstructed view. A good way to determine which side of the house has the most open exposure is to go inside and find the side with the farthest horizon.

The side of the house with the most unobstructed view is its front facing. Sometimes the main entrance is not necessarily positioned there. Look at figure B3.1a. In houses where the main entrance is on the side with the unobstructed view (house A), the front door usually opens into the living room or great room, where the scenic windows are found. Facing direction energy comes into the house through the scenic windows and the front entrance.

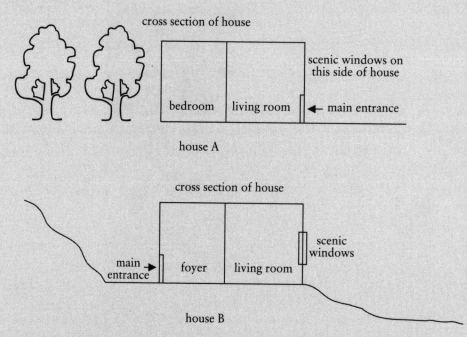

Figure B3.1a Comparison of the facing directions of two buildings and the positions of the main entrances.

In houses where the main entrance is not on the side with the unobstructed view (house B), the door usually opens into the back of the house, where the storage, utility room, and garage are located. In this type of house, the incoming energy does not enter through the main entrance but through the scenic windows on the side with the unobstructed view. The main entrance by itself does not have enough exposure to admit the expansive energy.

If a house is situated on a slope, the building's facing direction should be toward the downward slope, because it is the side that has the farthest horizon and the most unobstructed view. The appropriate floor plan would be one in which the living room and its scenic windows face the downward slope. If the direction of the unobstructed views is incongruent with the direction of the farthest horizon, the amount of expansive energy entering the house is diminished severely, and the benevolent effects are minimized.

Some houses have unobstructed views on several sides. These houses are said to have "competing facings" (figure B3.1b). The feng-shui of such houses is very difficult to evaluate, because the expansive forces from one or more directions vie for dominance in the house. Moreover, the energies that flow in the house tend to be unstable, making it difficult to predict the locations of positive and negative forces.

Figure B3.1b *This house has three competing facing directions. Located at an intersection, the house can face either street (both sides have equal exposure). It also can face diagonally into the intersection, because the entranceway on that side of the house has a dominating appearance. The three competing facing directions are denoted by the three dark arrows.*

fully fit the cardboard template onto the compass so that due north (zero) on the compass is lined up with the mark that bisects the tzu segment. After the ring is in place, make sure the needle is still aligned with the bar underneath. This is very important. Any misalignment will give you an erroneous reading.

4. To determine the facing direction of the building, simply look at where the line of sight lies in the Twenty-four Directions. To ascertain the back of the building, which is the mountain direction, simply find the segment directly opposite the facing direction. For example, if the facing direction is tzu, the back (or mountain direction) is wu; if the front is *mao*, the back is *yu;* if the front is *jen,* the back is *ping;* and so on.

Let's go through some examples. After lining up the needle with the bar, the line of sight is at 320 degrees. Place the ring template over the capsule of the compass so that the marker of the segment tzu is aligned with zero (north). You will find that the line of sight goes through the segment *ch'ien.* This is the facing direction. The segment opposite ch'ien is *sun,* which is the mountain direction. In another scenario, the line of sight is at 230 degrees. With the ring in place, you will find that the corresponding segment in the Twenty-four Directions is *k'un* (which is the facing direction) and the mountain direction, opposite k'un, is *ken.*

Now you need to practice determining the facing direction of buildings with your compass. Ask your friends, relatives, and neighbors to let you practice on their homes. Try out examples until you do not have to refer to the book.

Using a regular compass, you have now learned how to obtain the most important piece of information required in a feng-shui reading. Of course, there is much more information in the traditional Chinese lo-p'an than the Twenty-four Directions, but for the purposes of learning the basics of feng-shui for your personal needs, this is all you need.

MULTIPLE ORIENTATIONS AND READINGS

Traditionally, if we find that the main door is not located at the front of the house, we should take readings for both the main door and the front of the house. After a year or so of observation, the facing direction that gives the best prediction is chosen. Although this rule is used by some professional feng-shui practitioners, in my experience, we need to take only the reading based on the facing direction of the house.

EXERCISES

EXERCISE 3.1

In this exercise, identify the facing direction of the houses marked with an **X** in examples 2 through 12 in figure 3.5. For each house, draw an arrow pointing toward the facing direction of the building. Then briefly give reasons for your choice of the facing direction. No. 1 is a worked example.

Figure 3.5 Which side of the building is the front of the house? (The house in question is marked by an **X**.) (Figure continues on next page.)

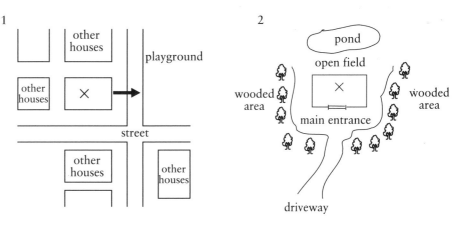

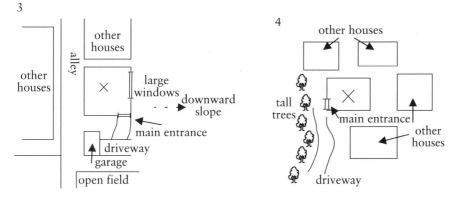

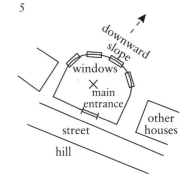

1. *The house faces the playground, because that side has the unblocked or most open view. Views from all the other sides are blocked by buildings.*

Hint: Look for the side of the house that has the least obstructed view. Also look at the surrounding landform for clues.

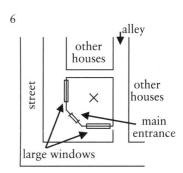

7

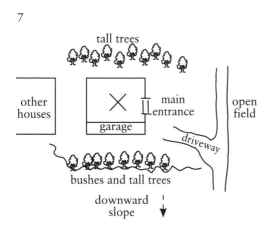

8

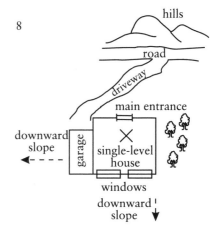

9

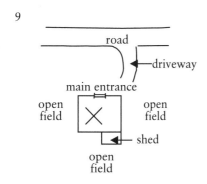

10

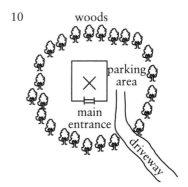

11

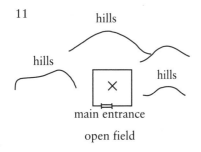

12

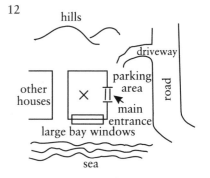

ANSWERS

EXERCISE 3.1

See figure 3.6.

Figure 3.6 Answers to exercise 3.1.

2

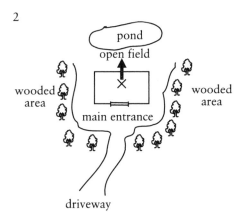

3

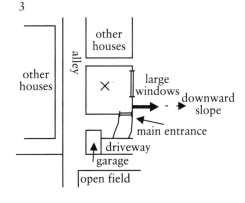

4

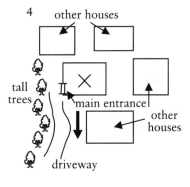

5

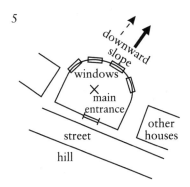

2. The house faces the open field and the pond, because that side has the most unblocked view. All the other sides are surrounded by trees.

3. The house faces the side overlooking the downward slope because that side has the large windows giving the most open views. The facing direction is confirmed further by the direction of the downward slope.

4. The house faces the driveway, because that side is least obstructed by surrounding structures.

5. The house faces the direction of the downward slope, because that side has the most windows giving an unobstructed view. The facing direction is confirmed further by the direction of the downward slope.

6. This house has two competing facing di-

6

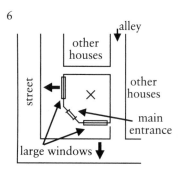

alley

other houses

street

other houses

main entrance

large windows

7

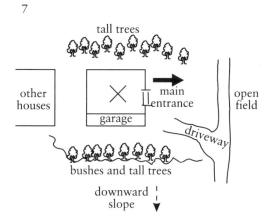

tall trees

other houses

garage

main entrance

open field

driveway

bushes and tall trees

downward slope

8

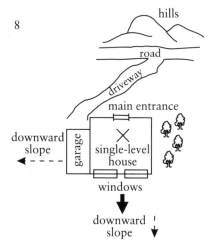

hills

road

driveway

main entrance

downward slope

garage

single-level house

windows

downward slope

9

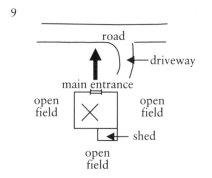

road

driveway

main entrance

open field

open field

shed

open field

10

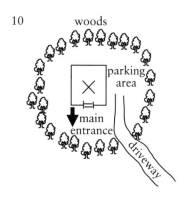

woods

parking area

main entrance

driveway

11

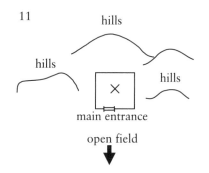

hills

hills

hills

main entrance

open field

12

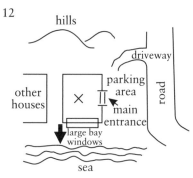

hills

driveway

parking area

road

main entrance

other houses

large bay windows

sea

rections, because there are large windows on both sides that give equally unobstructed views.

7. The house faces the open field, because the other three sides have blocked views. The downward slope is not sufficient to determine the front of the house, because the view toward that direction is blocked by bushes and tall trees.

8. The house faces the downward slope, because that side has the most unobstructed view. The hills help to distinguish the back of the house, thus confirming the facing direction.

9. With open fields on all sides of the house and no significant differences in exposure along three sides of the building, the fac-

ing direction is determined by the position of the main entrance.

10. When the views from all sides of a house are equally blocked and there is no significant difference in exposure along all sides of the building, the facing direction is fixed by the position of the main entrance.

11. The house faces the open field, because that side has the unblocked view. The facing is differentiated further by the hills surrounding the other sides of the building.

12. The house faces the sea, because the large windows on that side offer the most unobstructed view. The hills help determine the back of the house, thus confirming the facing direction.

4

Setting Up the Geomantic Chart

We are now ready to set up the geomantic chart. The chart tells us about the pattern of energy that flows within a house. When a building is erected, the energy of the space is captured inside it. The Hsüan-k'ung school of feng-shui has devised a system called the Nine Palaces to make this invisible energy visible. This is the geomantic chart.

The geomantic chart is constructed using three pieces of information: the year the house was built, the facing direction, and the back-facing (or mountain) direction. You can find out when a house was built by looking at the deed. If you are renting a house, ask the owner. In many North American cities you generally can get this information from the city's buildings department or the county offices. The other two pieces of information that you need are obtained with the geomantic compass.

CONSTRUCTING A GEOMANTIC CHART

Step 1: *Find the year (and cycle) a house was built.*

The energy of a place changes with time. The Chinese calendar system is cyclic and is designed to chart the cycles of time and the changes that accompany each cycle. In feng-shui, the most important set of cycles is the Nine Cycles. There are twenty years in each cycle, and it is important to pinpoint the cycle in which a house was completed. To ascertain the year and the cycle in which the house was built, simply look at figure 4.1. For example, let's say the house was built in 1972. Look at the figure. We find that 1972 lies in the sixth cycle. Try another example. Suppose the house was built in 1942. This puts it in the fourth cycle. To go back before 1864, subtract twenty years for each cycle. For example, a house built between 1844 and 1863 is a ninth-cycle house, a house built between 1824 and 1843 is an eighth-cycle house, and so on.

If the house was completed in January or February of the year that a cycle changes (for example, in 1984), you will need to find out whether it was completed in the Chinese year before or after the Western New Year. For example, let's consider a house that was completed on January 24, 1984. Looking at figure

ERA	CYCLE	STARTING YEAR
Upper Era		
	first cycle	1864
	second cycle	1884
	third cycle	1904
Middle Era		
	fourth cycle	1924
	fifth cycle	1944
	sixth cycle	1964
Lower Era		
	seventh cycle	1984
	eighth cycle	2004
	ninth cycle	2024

Figure 4.1 The Three Eras, the Nine Cycles, and their starting years.

4.2, we find that in 1984, January 24 occurred before the Chinese New Year (which fell on February 2, 1984). Therefore, we use the year 1983 (the previous year) instead of 1984 to determine the cycle in which the house was completed. This puts the house in the sixth cycle instead of the seventh. How about a house completed on February 18, 1964? Again, looking at the figure, we find that in 1964, February 18 occurred after the Chinese New Year (which fell on February 13). This house, therefore, belongs to the sixth cycle.

To summarize, if a house was completed in the month of January or February during the year when a cycle changed, find out whether the date of completion fell before or after the Chinese New Year. If it occurred before, the house belongs to the previous cycle; if it was after, the house belongs to the new cycle.

What about the circumstance in which the acquisition of land and completion of building take place in different cycles? Suppose you purchased the plot of land in 1963 and did

not build the house until 1965? Which cycle should you use for the geomantic chart? In this case, we use the cycle in which the house was completed. Energy in the land roams freely if there are no structures to capture it. Once a structure is finished, the energy is encapsulated in that space and time. Regardless of when the land is purchased, we use the year that the house is completed to construct the geomantic chart.

Now do exercise 4.1 and familiarize yourself with cross-referencing between the Chinese year and the Western year. After you are comfortable with determining the cycle in which a house was built, you are ready to set up the geomantic chart.

Step 2: *Set up the Earth Base of the geomantic chart.*

The geomantic chart, a 3 × 3 grid of nine squares, is the key to understanding the pattern of energy that flows within a building. The squares are called the Nine Palaces (figure 4.3). The Earth Base stars represent energy associated with the cycle in which a house was completed. To obtain the Earth Base stars, you need to start with the year the house was built. For example, let's say the house was built in 1980. This puts the house in the sixth cycle (figure 4.1).

For a house built in the sixth cycle, the number 6 goes into the center square of the Nine Palaces grid. The rest of the numbers entered into the grid of the Nine Palaces are (in sequence) 7, 8, 9, 1, 2, 3, 4, and 5. Notice that there are a total of nine numbers. The sequence of the numbers of the Earth Base is filled according to a set pattern, beginning in the center. Look at figure 4.4. The boxes represent the squares of the Nine Palaces. The arrows represent the sequence of number

1905	Feb. 4	1942	Feb. 15	1979	Jan. 28
1906	Jan. 25	1943	Feb. 5	1980	Feb. 16
1907	Feb. 13	1944	Jan. 25	1981	Feb. 5
1908	Feb. 2	1945	Feb. 13	1982	Jan. 25
1909	Jan. 22	1946	Feb. 2	1983	Feb. 13
1910	Feb. 10	1947	Jan. 22	1984	Feb. 2
1911	Jan. 30	1948	Feb. 10	1985	Feb. 20
1912	Feb. 18	1949	Jan. 29	1986	Feb. 9
1913	Feb. 6	1950	Feb. 17	1987	Jan. 29
1914	Jan. 26	1951	Feb. 6	1988	Feb. 17
1915	Feb. 14	1952	Jan. 27	1989	Feb. 6
1916	Feb. 4	1953	Feb. 14	1990	Jan. 27
1917	Jan. 23	1954	Feb. 3	1991	Feb. 15
1918	Feb. 11	1955	Jan. 24	1992	Feb. 4
1919	Feb. 1	1956	Feb. 12	1993	Jan. 23
1920	Feb. 20	1957	Jan. 31	1994	Feb. 10
1921	Feb. 8	1958	Feb. 18	1995	Jan. 31
1922	Jan. 28	1959	Feb. 8	1996	Feb. 19
1923	Feb. 16	1960	Jan. 28	1997	Feb. 7
1924	Feb. 5	1961	Feb. 15	1998	Jan. 28
1925	Jan. 24	1962	Feb. 5	1999	Feb. 16
1926	Feb. 13	1963	Jan. 25	2000	Feb. 5
1927	Feb. 2	1964	Feb. 13	2001	Jan. 24
1928	Jan. 23	1965	Feb. 2	2002	Feb. 12
1929	Feb. 10	1966	Jan. 21	2003	Feb. 1
1930	Jan. 30	1967	Feb. 9	2004	Jan. 22
1931	Feb. 17	1968	Jan. 30	2005	Feb. 9
1932	Feb. 6	1969	Feb. 17	2006	Jan. 29
1933	Jan. 26	1970	Feb. 6	2007	Feb. 18
1934	Feb. 14	1971	Jan. 27	2008	Feb. 7
1935	Feb. 4	1972	Feb. 15	2009	Jan. 26
1936	Jan. 24	1973	Feb. 3	2010	Feb. 14
1937	Feb. 11	1974	Jan. 23	2011	Feb. 3
1938	Jan. 31	1975	Feb. 11	2012	Jan. 23
1939	Feb. 19	1976	Jan. 31	2013	Feb. 10
1940	Feb. 8	1977	Feb. 18	2014	Jan. 31
1941	Jan. 27	1978	Feb. 7	2015	Feb. 19

Figure 4.2 The Chinese New Year and the equivalent dates in the Western calendar. To find out on which day the Chinese New Year fell in a particular year in the Western calendar, simply locate the year (for example, 1942) and read off the date next to that year (February 15).

```
7 4        2 9        9 2
  9          5          7


           M F
8 3        6 5        4 7
  8          1          3


3 8        1 1        5 6
  4          6          2
```

Figure 4.3 The geomantic chart consists of a 3 × 3 grid called the Nine Palaces. (See text for more complete discussion.) M, Mountain Star; F, Facing Star.

placement. We call this the *pathway of the Nine Palaces.*

Let's now return to our example, a house built in 1980. Because the house was built in the sixth cycle, we enter the number 6 in the center of the Nine Palaces grid. Following the pathway of the Nine Palaces in figure 4.4, we place the next number, which is 7, in the lower right corner. The next number, which is 8, is entered above the 7. Then we enter 9 in the lower left corner, and so on, until all nine numbers are placed in the grid. The completed Earth Base numbers are shown here:

```
5   1   3
4   6   8
9   2   7
```

Let's try another example. Suppose the house was built in 1941, in the fourth cycle. To enter the Earth Base numbers in the grid of the Nine Palaces, we first place 4 in the center. The next number, 5, will occupy the lower

right corner, and the following number, 6, will be above 5. The next number, 7, will occupy the lower left corner. After all the numbers are entered according to the path described in figure 4.4, we have the following set of completed Earth Base numbers:

```
3   8   1
2   4   6
7   9   5
```

Notice that the cycle in which the house was built determines which number goes into the center square. After that, the sequence of numbers is entered in the remaining squares using the pathway outlined in figure 4.4.

Now complete exercise 4.2. It is designed to familiarize you with the procedure of setting up the Earth Base stars (or numbers) of a geomantic chart.

Step 3: *Fill in the Mountain stars of the geomantic chart.*

Once you have entered all the Earth Base numbers into the Nine Palaces, your next step is to enter the Mountain stars. The Mountain stars represent energy associated with the mountain direction (back) of a house. To determine the Mountain stars in the Nine Palaces, we must first obtain the mountain direction of the building using the geomantic compass. Let's say, for example, that the mountain direction for the house is tzu (due north), because its facing direction is wu (due south), and the house was built in 1980.

Now turn to the appendix. You may wish to photocopy the nine circular diagrams so that you can have them in front of you. You will be referring to these diagrams often as you learn how to set up the geomantic chart for a building. Because the house was built in

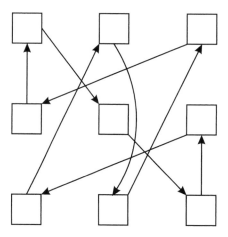

path of movement in the Nine Palaces

4	9	2
3	5	7
8	1	6

clockwise
sequence

6	1	8
7	5	3
2	9	4

counterclockwise
sequence

Figure 4.4 The sequence of numbering in the Nine Palaces (top). The numbers in clockwise and counterclockwise sequence (bottom). Regardless of which number occupies the center, the square in the center is filled first, then the square in the lower right corner, then the one above it, and so on. Whether the numbers run in a clockwise or a counterclockwise sequence will depend on the cycle in which a building was erected and its facing and mountain directions. (See text for further explanation.)

1980, we will be using the diagram for the sixth cycle, the one with the large number 6 in the center. We already have entered the Earth Base numbers in the Nine Palaces, as shown in figure 4.5. Now we will fill in the numbers of the Mountain stars.

Look at the diagram for the sixth cycle. Locate the inner ring of numbers and find the position tzu. You will notice that it lies in the segment one-white. If you work your way outward from this position, you will find the segment two-black in the outer ring. Two-

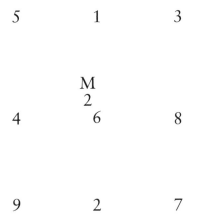

Figure 4.5 The geomantic chart with all the Earth Base numbers and the center Mountain Star (M).

black is the Mountain Star that will go into the center of the Nine Palaces in the Mountain Star position at the upper left (figure 4.5).

Now you are ready to fill in the other Mountain stars in the rest of the Nine Palaces. Look at the sixth cycle diagram again. Directly lined up with tzu (the mountain direction) is k'un (in the two-black segment). Next to k'un is an open circle. Open circles indicate yang movement. In this situation, yang movement will determine the positions of the rest of the Mountain Star numbers in the Nine Palaces. For yang movement, we count the numbers of the Mountain stars in a forward sequence. In our example, the first Mountain Star, which was placed in the central square, is 2 (two-black). The next number in the forward sequence is 3 and then 4, 5, 6, 7, 8, 9, and 1. Following the path of yang movement shown in figure 4.4, we get the pattern of the Mountain stars depicted in figure 4.6.

Let's try another example. Suppose that the mountain direction is *chia* and the house was completed in 1996. Looking at the seventh cycle diagram in the appendix, we enter the

Earth Base numbers in the Nine Palaces (figure 4.7). Using the same diagram, we locate chia in the three-jade segment of the inner ring. Working outward, we find the segment five-yellow. Thus, the number 5 will take the Mountain Star position in the center of the Nine Palaces (in the upper left). Because chia is lined up with wu, which is next to an open circle, the numbering of the Mountain stars, starting with 5, will follow a forward sequence. Counting forward from 5 and following the pathway of the Nine Palaces, we place 6 in the lower right corner, 7 above it, 8 in the square in the lower left corner, and so on, until all nine numbers of the Mountain Star are in place (figure 4.7).

Here is one more example. How about a mountain direction of yu in a house built in 1961? Using the fifth cycle diagram, we enter the Earth Base stars shown in figure 4.8. Next, we put in the Mountain stars in the Nine Palaces. Look at the fifth cycle diagram again. Directly lined up with yu (the mountain direction) is also yu (in the seven-red seg-

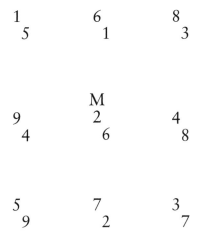

Figure 4.6 The geomantic chart with all the Earth Base and Mountain Star (M) numbers filled in.

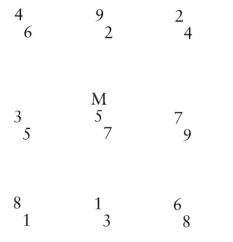

4	9	2
6	2	4
M		
3	5	7
5	7	9
8	1	6
1	3	8

Figure 4.7 The geomantic chart with all the Earth Base and Mountain Star (M) numbers filled in.

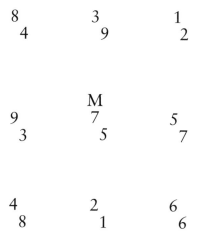

8	3	1
4	9	2
	M	
9	7	5
3	5	7
4	2	6
8	1	6

Figure 4.8 The geomantic chart with all the Earth Base and Mountain Star (M) numbers filled in.

ment). Next to yu is a filled circle. Filled circles indicate yin movement. In this situation, yin movement will determine the locations of the rest of the Mountain Star numbers in the Nine Palaces. For yin movement, we count the numbers of the Mountain stars in a backward sequence.

In this example, the first Mountain Star, which was placed in the central square, is 7. The next number in the backward sequence is 6, followed by 5, 4, 3, 2, 1, 9, and 8. Counting backward from 7, we place the number 6 in the Mountain Star position in the lower right, the number 5 above it, the number 4 in the lower left, and so on until we form the pattern of the Mountain stars shown in figure 4.8. Notice that the pathway (shown by the arrow sequence in figure 4.4) is the same for both the forward and the reverse sequences of numbering in the Nine Palaces. The only difference is whether you count the numbers forward or backward.

Now complete exercise 4.3. It will familiarize you with filling in the Mountain stars in the geomantic chart.

Step 4: *Fill in the Facing stars of the geomantic chart.*

Next, we will enter the Facing stars in each square of the Nine Palaces. The Facing stars represent energy associated with the facing direction of a house. We first need to find the facing direction of the house with the geomantic compass. Let's say that the facing direction is wu, or due south, and the house was built in 1977. Locate wu in the inner ring of the sixth cycle diagram. You will see that it is in the segment nine-purple. Working your way outward, you will find the segment one-white in the outer ring. The number 1 is therefore the Facing Star that will fill the center of the Nine Palaces grid at the upper right.

Now we put in the rest of the Facing Star numbers in the Nine Palaces. Look at the sixth cycle diagram again. Directly lined up with wu (the facing direction) is tzu (in the one-white segment). Next to tzu is a filled circle. Remember that filled circles indicate yin movement. Yin movement determines the placement of the Facing Star numbers in the Nine Palaces. We count the numbers of the Facing stars backward. In our example, the first Facing Star, which was placed in the central square, is 1. The next number in the backward sequence is 9, followed by 8, 7, 6, 5, 4, 3, and 2. Counting backward from 1, we get the pattern of Facing stars depicted in figure 4.9. Again, notice that the pathway (shown by the arrow sequence in figure 4.4) is the same for both the forward and the reverse sequences of numbering in the Nine Palaces. The only difference is whether you count the numbers forward or backward.

Let's work through another example. Suppose the facing direction is ken and the house was built in 1908. Using the third cycle diagram, we put in the Earth Base numbers shown in figure 4.10. Next, locate ken in the inner ring of the diagram. You will see that it is in the segment eight-white. Working your way outward, you will find the segment six-white in the outer ring. The number 6 is therefore the Facing Star that will take the center position of the Nine Palaces grid in the upper right (figure 4.10).

Now we put the rest of the Facing Star numbers in the Nine Palaces. Look at the third cycle diagram again. Directly lined up with ken (the facing direction) is ch'ien (which is in the six-white segment). Next to ch'ien is an open circle, which indicates yang movement. Here yang movement will determine the layout of the Facing Star numbers in the Nine Palaces. We count the numbers of the Facing stars in a forward sequence starting from 6 to form the pattern of the Facing stars shown in figure 4.10.

Now do exercise 4.4, which is designed to familiarize you with filling in the Facing stars of the geomantic chart. Generating the geomantic chart is one of the most important steps in a feng-shui reading of a building.

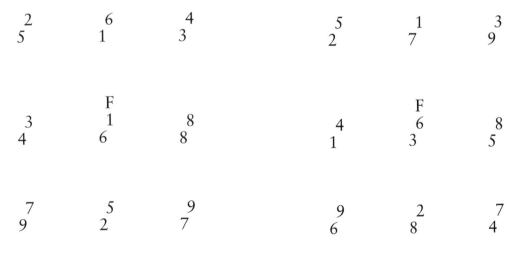

Figure 4.9 The geomantic chart with all the Earth Base and Facing Star (F) numbers filled in.

Figure 4.10 The geomantic chart with all the Earth Base and Facing Star (F) numbers filled in.

To review, here is a summary of the steps so far:

1. To find out which Earth Base Star occupies the center of the Nine Palaces, you need to know the year (and therefore the cycle) in which the house was built.

2. To fill in the rest of the Earth Base stars, follow the movement pathway of the Nine Palaces. Earth Base stars always run in a forward sequence.

3. To determine which Mountain Star occupies the center of the Nine Palaces, you need to ascertain the mountain direction of the house from the geomantic compass. Then refer to the circular diagram from the appropriate cycle to figure out the correct number. To fill in the rest of the Mountain stars, follow the movement pathway of the Nine Palaces, referring to the circular diagram to ascertain whether the numbers run in a forward or a backward sequence.

4. To find out which Facing Star occupies the center of the Nine Palaces, you need to assess the facing direction of the house using the geomantic compass and figure out the appropriate number from the circular diagram from the appropriate cycle. To fill in the rest of the Facing stars, follow the movement pathway of the Nine Palaces, being sure to determine from the circular diagram whether the numbers run in a forward or a backward sequence.

In exercise 4.5, your task is to work out the full geomantic chart—Earth Base, Mountain, and Facing stars. Before you proceed to exercise 4.5, here is an example of the way in which all the numbers of the three stars—Earth Base, Mountain, and Facing—are generated in the geomantic chart.

Suppose the mountain direction is *ssu*, the facing direction is *hai*, and the house was completed in 1942. Using the fourth cycle diagram, we enter the numbers of the Earth Base in the Nine Palaces shown in figure 4.11. Next, locate ssu (the Mountain Star) in the inner ring of the diagram. You will see that it is in the segment four-green. Work your way outward, and you will find the segment three-jade in the outer ring. The number 3 is therefore the Mountain Star that will fill the center of the Nine Palaces grid at the upper left (figure 4.11).

Now we put the rest of the Mountain Star numbers in the Nine Palaces. Look at the fourth cycle diagram again. Directly lined up with ssu (the mountain direction) is *i* (in the three-jade segment). Next to i is a filled circle, indicating yin movement. Yin movement will determine the locations of the rest of the Mountain Star numbers in the Nine Palaces. Counting the numbers of the Mountain stars backward from 3, we form the pattern of the Mountain stars shown in figure 4.11.

To fill in the Facing stars, we first locate hai (the Facing Star) in the segment six-white of the inner ring of the fourth cycle diagram. Moving outward, you will find the segment five-yellow in the outer ring. The number 5 is therefore the Facing Star that is placed in the center of the Nine Palaces grid at the upper right (figure 4.11).

Next, we add the other Facing Star numbers to the Nine Palaces. Look at the fourth cycle diagram again. Directly lined up with hai (the facing direction) is wu (in the five-yellow segment). Next to wu is an open circle, representing yang movement. Yang movement will determine the layout of the rest of the Facing stars in the Nine Palaces. We count the numbers of the Facing stars in a forward sequence starting with 5 and obtain the pattern shown in figure 4.11.

4 4 3	8 9 8	6 2 1
5 3 2	M F 3 5 4	1 7 6
9 8 7	7 1 9	2 6 5

Figure 4.11 The full geomantic chart. M, Mountain Star; F, Facing Star.

wu facing

1 2 5	6 6 1 Facing Palace	8 4 3
9 3 4	M F 2 1 6	4 8 8
5 7 9	7 5 2	3 9 7

tzu mountain

Figure 4.12 Finding the front facing of the geomantic chart and identifying the Facing Palace. M, Mountain Star; F, Facing Star.

Now try exercise 4.5 and practice generating the full geomantic chart.

Step 5: *Orient the geomantic chart and identify the Facing Palace.*

When the geomantic chart is completed, we need to orient it and identify the Facing Palace, the square representing the facing direction. Figure 4.12 depicts the geomantic chart of a house finished in the sixth cycle, with tzu as the mountain direction and wu as the facing direction. We identify the facing direction of the geomantic chart by placing the name of the facing direction on that side.

In this example, we ascertained the orientation of the chart by looking at the inner ring of the sixth cycle diagram. Find wu, the facing direction of the house, in the segment nine-purple. Working outward, we locate one-white in the outer ring. Now find the Earth

Base number 1 in the geomantic chart depicted in figure 4.12. You will see that the words *wu facing* are placed above that square, showing the front facing of the geomantic chart and identifying the square with the Earth Base one-white as the Facing Palace. The Facing Palace always lies at the front of the building and is the square representing the facing direction (in this case wu). The location of the Facing Palace helps us superimpose the chart correctly onto the building, so that the front of the geomantic chart is lined up with the front of the building.

Let's try another example. Look at the geomantic chart in figure 4.13. It shows a house built in the seventh cycle, with chia as the mountain direction and *keng* as the facing direction. Looking at the seventh cycle diagram, we find that the facing direction keng is lined up with the outer ring segment nine-purple. The Facing Palace is thus the

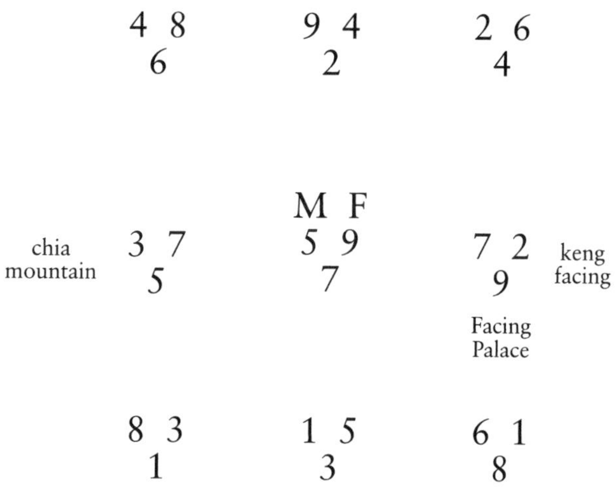

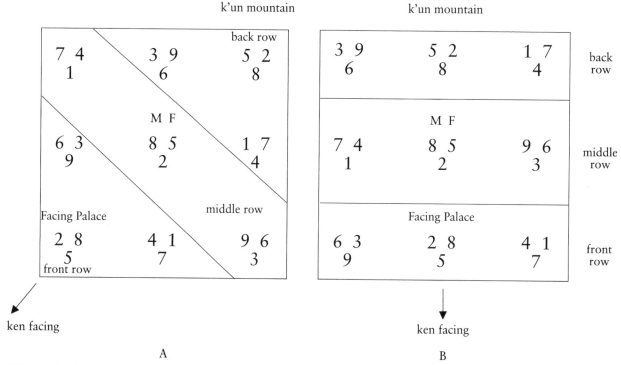

4 8   9 4   2 6
  6   2   4

                M F
chia   3 7   5 9   7 2   keng
mountain   5   7   9   facing

                              Facing
                              Palace

8 3   1 5   6 1
  1   3   8

Figure 4.13 Finding the front facing of
the geomantic chart and identifying the
Facing Palace. M, Mountain Star; F,
Facing Star.

Figure 4.14 How to adjust a geomantic chart when the Facing Palace is in a corner. The Facing Palace in panel A is in the lower left corner. Panel B shows the adjusted grid. In the adjustment, the lower triangle becomes the front row, the diagonal in the middle becomes the middle row, and the upper triangle becomes the back row. Note that the Facing Palace is now in the center of the front row. M, Mountain Star; F, Facing Star.

square with the number 9 as the Earth Base (figure 4.13).

Now look at Figure 4.14. We have a circumstance in which the Facing Palace is in the corner of the chart (panel A). Do not let this confuse you. When we encounter this type of situation, we simply reorient the chart so that the Facing Palace is on the side of the Nine Palaces grid and not at the corner. Panel B of figure 4.14 shows you how to reorient the Facing Palace.

Try exercise 4.6 and see if you can identify the Facing Palace of the geomantic charts and adjust them if necessary.

TYPES OF GEOMANTIC CHARTS

The typical geomantic charts are divided into four types:

- Forward mountain / backward facing
- Backward mountain / forward facing
- Forward mountain / forward facing
- Backward mountain / backward facing

In the forward mountain / backward facing type of chart, called the Descending Water condition, the Mountain stars run in a forward sequence when they are entered into the Nine Palaces, and the Facing stars run in reverse. The fortunes of a house with this combination will be enhanced if there is water in front.

In the backward mountain / forward facing chart, called the Ascending Mountain condition, the Mountain stars run in a reverse sequence, while the Facing stars run in a forward sequence in the Nine Palaces. The fortunes of such a house will be enhanced if there is a mountain at the back.

In the forward mountain / forward facing type of chart, called the Ascending Mountain and Descending Water condition, both the Mountain and Facing stars run in a forward sequence in the Nine Palaces. The fortunes of this house will be enhanced if water lies in front and mountains are at the back.

In the backward mountain / backward facing condition, called the Reverse Mountain and Reverse Water condition, both the Mountain and Facing stars run in a reverse sequence in the Nine Palaces. A house with this combination will have good fortune regardless of its position relative to mountains and water.

Now that you have become familiar with these four types of geomantic charts, try doing exercise 4.7.

SPECIAL GEOMANTIC CHARTS

There are two types of special geomantic charts. The conditions they represent are rare; if they occur, their auspiciousness overrides all other interpretations. If you come across a house with one of these charts, you are very lucky.

Three Combinations Chart

The "Three Combinations chart" refers to the combinations of three sets of numbers: one, four, seven; two, five, eight; and three, six, nine. If any of these combinations is present in all Nine Palaces, the chart qualifies as a Three Combinations chart. It does not matter which number is the Earth Base and which is the Facing Star or Mountain Star. As long as these numbers are present, the geomantic chart fits the condition of the Three Combinations. Figure 4.15 shows examples of this chart.

The Three Combinations chart is associated with good health, great fortune, fame, respect, familial harmony, and descendants. This chart does not occur in the first, third, seventh, or ninth cycle, but it appears three times each in the second, fifth, and eighth cycles, in the following combinations: ken mountain / k'un facing, *yin* mountain / *shen* facing, k'un mountain / ken facing, and shen mountain / yin facing. In the fourth and sixth cycles, there are two occurrences each, in the combinations *ch'ou* mountain / *wei* facing and wei mountain / ch'ou facing. Thus, there are sixteen instances of the Three Combinations throughout the 180 years of the Nine Cycles.

Combination of Ten Chart

The "Combination of Ten" refers to the condition in which the sum of the numbers of the Earth Base and Facing Star or Mountain Star in all Nine Palaces adds up to ten. This, too, is an auspicious chart and has the same benefits as the Three Combinations chart. Figure 4.16 shows examples of the Combination of Ten chart.

There are twenty occurrences of the Combination of Ten in the Nine Cycles. In the first and ninth cycles, it is found when ch'ien, sun, ssu, or hai is either the facing or the mountain direction. In the second and eighth cycles, it pertains when ch'ou or wei is either the facing or the mountain direction. In the third and seventh cycles, it occurs when tzu, wu, *kuei*, or *ting* is either the facing or the mountain direction. In the fourth and sixth cycles, it takes effect when keng or chia is either the facing or the mountain direction.

The special auspiciousness of the Three Combinations and the Combination of Ten overrides all interpretations of the interactions of the Earth Base, Facing, and Mountain stars (see chapter 6). If at any level one or more squares lie outside the building, however, the Three Combinations and the Combination of Ten do not apply (see box 4.1).

You have learned how to generate the geomantic chart of a building. The next steps involve superimposing the chart onto the floor plan, interpreting its meaning, and planning the usage of space. Make sure you are competent in generating the geomantic chart before proceeding to the next chapter. The discussions in the remaining chapters of part one assume that you have mastered the materials covered in the first four chapters.

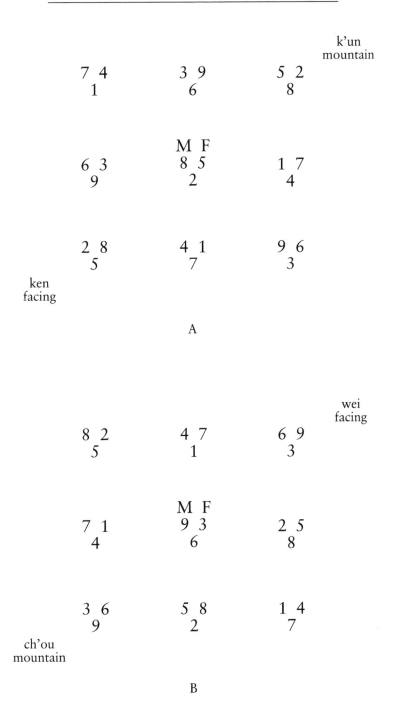

Figure 4.15 Two examples of the Three Combinations chart. A: Ken facing in the second cycle.
B: Wei facing in the sixth cycle. M, Mountain Star; F, Facing Star.

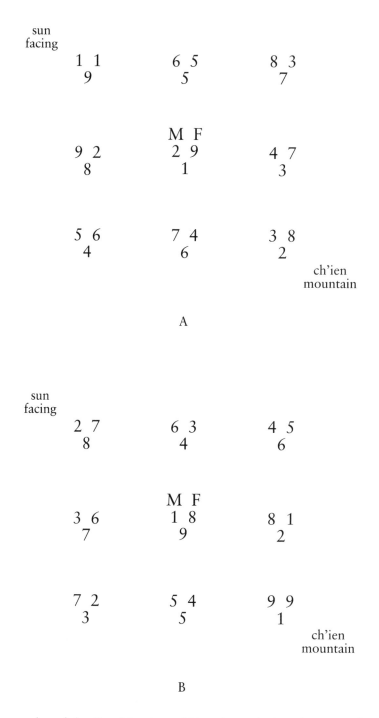

Figure 4.16 Two examples of the Combination of Ten chart. A: Sun facing in the first cycle. B: Sun facing in the second cycle. M, Mountain Star; F, Facing Star.

BOX 4.1

THE THREE COMBINATIONS AND THE COMBINATION OF TEN CHARTS AND IRREGULAR FLOOR PLANS

The benevolent effects of the Three Combinations and the Combination of Ten charts manifest only when all the Nine Palaces are situated inside the building. The corollary, of course, is that when one or more of the Nine Palaces lie outside the house, the benefits of these charts do not apply (figure B4.1). In this situation, the interactions of the stars of the Nine Palaces are treated in the same way as those of normal charts. The Three Combinations and the Combination of Ten charts describe the perfect flow of energy. All Nine Palaces must be present inside a building for this perfection to take effect. When one or more are missing because they lie outside the house, this state of perfection is lost.

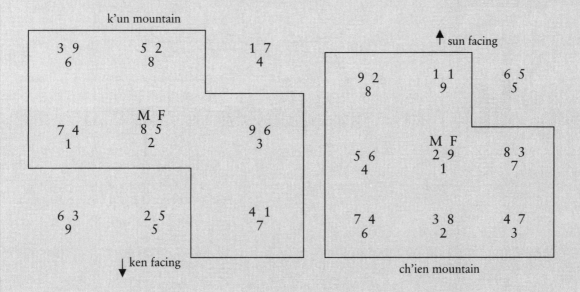

Figure B4.1 *Examples of the Three Combinations and the Combination of Ten charts. Their auspiciousness is lost when at least one palace lies outside the house.*

EXERCISES

EXERCISE 4.1

Specify the cycle that should be used for houses completed on these dates:

1. Feb. 1, 1984
2. Jan. 26, 1981
3. Jan. 1, 1949

4. Feb. 18, 1984
5. Jan. 29, 1924

EXERCISE 4.2

Set up the Earth Base stars of the Nine Palaces for houses completed on the dates given. No. 1 is a worked example.

1. Sept. 12, 1966

5	1	3
4	6	8
9	2	7

2. Jan. 14, 1921
3. April 20, 1992
4. July 6, 1887
5. Jan. 22, 1964

EXERCISE 4.3

Set up the Earth Base and Mountain stars of houses that have the listed completion dates and mountain directions. No. 1 is a worked example.

1. Jan. 14, 1998; mountain direction ting

1		6		8	
	6		2		4
		M			
9		2		4	
	5		7		9
5		7		3	
	1		3		8

2. Aug. 21, 1993; mountain direction hai
3. May 21, 1967; mountain direction kuei

EXERCISE 4.4

Set up the Earth Base and Facing stars of houses that have the cited completion dates and facing directions. No. 1 is a worked example.

1. Sept. 1, 1955; facing direction jen

9	5	7
4	9	2
	F	
8	1	3
3	5	7
4	6	2
8	1	6

2. Jan. 4, 1906; facing direction mao
3. Nov. 1, 1996; facing direction sun

EXERCISE 4.5

Set up the Earth Base, Mountain, and Facing stars of houses that have the completion dates and facing directions listed here. No. 1 is a worked example.

1. Jan. 6, 1999; facing direction wu

4	1	8	6	6	8
	6		2		4
		M	*F*		
5	9	3	2	1	4
	5		7		9
9	5	7	7	2	3
	1		3		8

2. Aug. 1, 1888; facing direction sun
3. Sept. 1, 1997; facing direction k'un

EXERCISE 4.7

Identify the type of each geomantic chart that you have generated in exercise 4.5. No. 1 is a worked example.

1. Backward mountain / forward facing: Ascending Mountain

EXERCISE 4.6

Identify the Facing Palace and front facing of each of the geomantic charts you have generated in exercise 4.5 and adjust the orientation if necessary.

ANSWERS

EXERCISE 4.1

1. Sixth cycle
2. Sixth cycle
3. Fifth cycle
4. Seventh cycle
5. Third cycle

EXERCISE 4.2

2.

2	7	9
1	3	5
6	8	4

3.

6	2	4
5	7	9
1	3	8

4.

1	6	8
9	2	4
5	7	3

5.

4	9	2
3	5	7
8	1	6

EXERCISE 4.3

2.

7 6	3 2	5 4
6 5	M 8 7	1 9
2 1	4 3	9 8

3.

1 5	6 1	8 3
9 4	M 2 6	4 8
5 9	7 2	3 7

EXERCISE 4.4

2.

2 2	6 7	4 9
3 1	F 1 3	8 5
7 6	5 8	9 4

3.

5 6	1 2	3 4
4 5	F 6 7	8 9
9 1	2 3	7 8

EXERCISES 4.5 AND 4.6

2.

sun
facing

4 2	8 6	6 4
1	6	8

	M F	
5 3	3 1	1 8
9	2	4

9 7	7 5	2 9
5	7	3

ch'ien
mountain

3.

k'un
facing

2 3	6 8	4 1
6	2	4

	M F	
3 2	1 4	8 6
5	7	9

7 7	5 9	9 5
1	3	8

ken
mountain

Reoriented chart

sun facing

5 3	4 2	8 6
9	1	6
	Facing Palace	

	M F	
9 7	3 1	6 4
5	2	8

7 5	2 9	1 8
7	3	4

ch'ien
mountain

Reoriented chart

k'un facing

6 8	4 1	8 6
2	4	9
	Facing Palace	

	M F	
2 3	1 4	9 5
6	7	8

3 2	7 7	5 9
5	1	3

ken mountain

EXERCISE 4.7

2. Backward mountain / backward facing: Reverse Mountain / Reverse Water
3. Backward mountain / forward facing: Ascending Mountain

5

Superimposing the Geomantic Chart
onto a Floor Plan

When the geomantic chart is superimposed onto the floor plan of a building, it describes the flow of energy, benevolent and malevolent, in that place. The chart is laid first over the entire building (the macrocosm), floor by floor, and then over each room (the microcosm).

SUPERIMPOSING THE GEOMANTIC CHART ONTO AN ENTIRE BUILDING

Floor Plans with Regular Shapes

It is easiest to work with floor plans that have regular shapes. You simply fit the grid of the Nine Palaces over it (figure 5.1).* Most houses are rectangular, so the square shape of the Nine Palaces has to be "stretched" to fit the floor plan. I use the general rule that if a room occupies more than half a square, I assign it one square. Similarly, if a room occupies more than a square and a half, I assign it two squares (figure 5.2).

Floor Plans with Irregular or Nonrectangular Shapes

Laying geomantic charts over floor plans that have triangular or irregular shapes requires more care. Figure 5.3 shows how the geomantic chart is fitted to two irregularly shaped floor plans. Notice that in the floor plans shown here, some of the squares of the Nine Palaces lie outside the house and therefore have no influence at all on the energy inside the house. If a house has a very irregular floor plan, it will be difficult to accommodate a geomantic chart to its floor plan. This is another reason why you don't want a house with such irregular floor plans.

*As in the figures to chapter 4, the abbreviation M refers to the Mountain Star, and the abbreviation F means Facing Star in all remaining figures in this book.

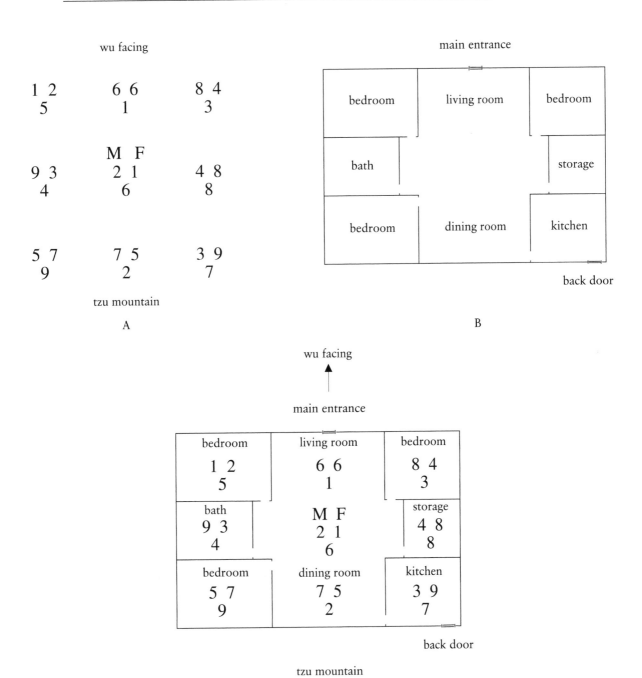

Figure 5.1 Superimposing a geomantic chart onto a floor plan. A: The geomantic chart. B: The floor plan. C: The chart superimposed on the floor plan.

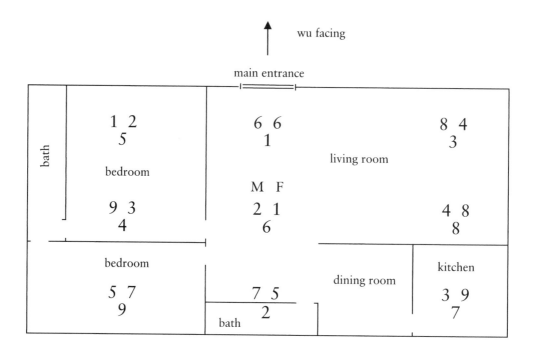

Figure 5.2 Stretching a geomantic chart to fit a rectangular floor plan. Notice that the larger bedroom occupies two squares in the Nine Palaces and the living room occupies four squares.

HOUSES DIVIDED INTO DISTINCT SECTIONS

Some houses are divided in such a way that areas appear to be independent of each other. Usually, this situation occurs in buildings that have wings or new sections added to them. Look at the floor plan of the house in figure 5.4. This house clearly is divided into two distinct segments. How would we reconcile a geomantic chart with this kind of house? Here we need to generate two charts, one for each segment of the house. Since the two sections have different facing directions, two compass readings must be taken. The building is treated as two separate houses with different Facing and Mountain stars, even if the two segments were completed within the same cycle. If the segments were finished in different cycles, the Earth Base as well as the Facing and Mountain stars will be different for the two sections of the house. Because the house is chopped into two segments, the flow of energy within the building will be erratic and unpredictable. Moreover, energy near the border of the divided segments tends to be stormy and destructive. This is not a desirable type of house to live in.

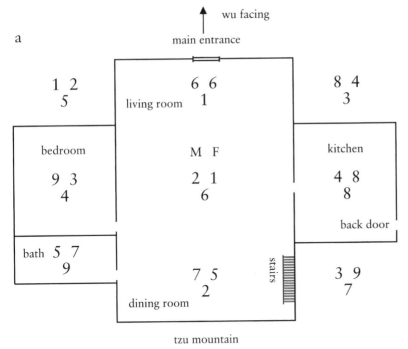

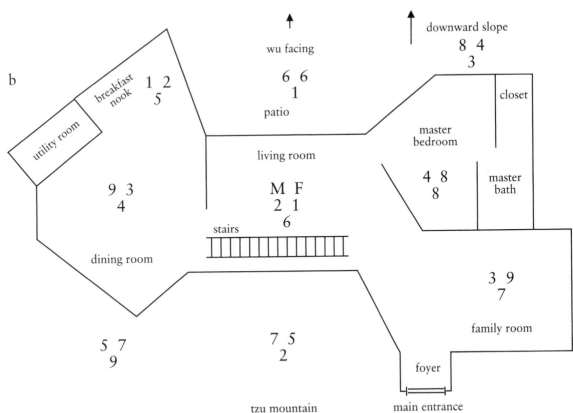

Figure 5.3a,b Fitting the geomantic chart onto irregular floor plans. Notice that some squares of the Nine Palaces fall outside the buildings.

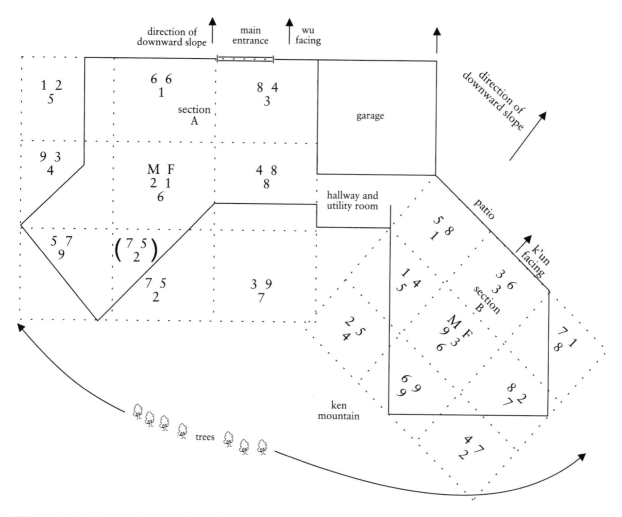

Figure 5.4 A house that is divided into two segments (sections A and B). Two separate geomantic charts are generated and superimposed onto the segments as if they were separate houses.

Split-Level Houses

In split-level houses, one section occupies only a portion of the house (figure 5.5). This type of house is treated like a two-story house in which one level is missing some of the palaces of the geomantic chart.

Multistory Houses

If a house has multiple levels, the geomantic chart is superimposed onto each level separately. If all the levels are neatly stacked on top of each other, the chart applies uniformly to every level (figure 5.6). If the levels differ,

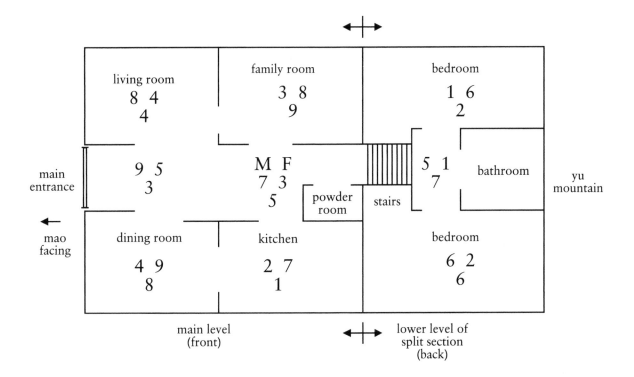

main level
(front)

lower level of
split section
(back)

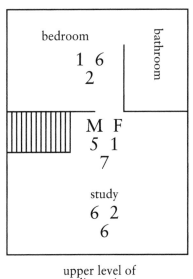

Figure 5.5 Fitting the geomantic chart onto the floor plan of a split-level house. Notice that one of the sections is included in the main area of the house while the other is treated as a smaller upper level.

upper level of
split section
(back)

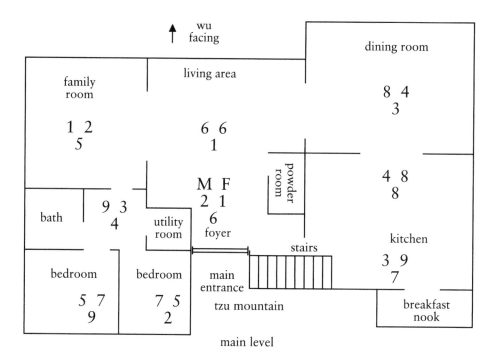

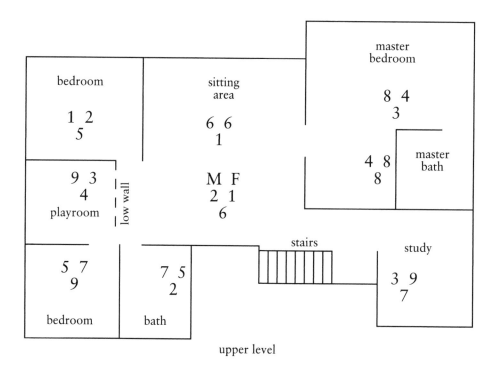

Figure 5.6 Superimposing the geomantic chart onto the floor plan of a multistory house whose levels are similar.

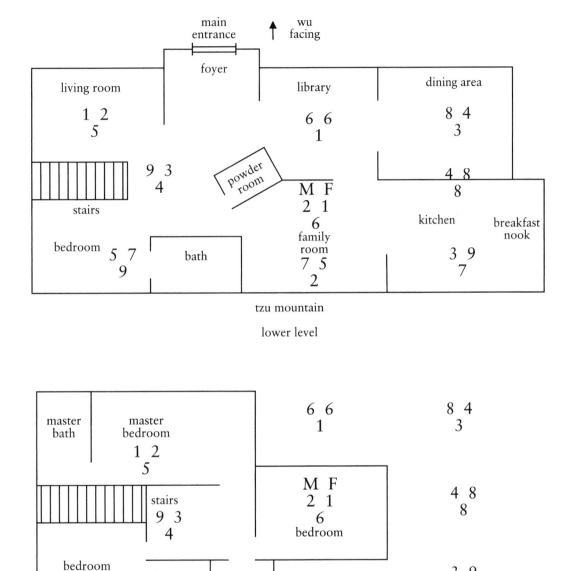

Figure 5.7 Superimposing the geomantic chart onto the floor plan of a house in which the upper level is smaller.

the chart will have to be applied differently on each level. (See examples in figures 5.7 and 5.8. See also box 5.1 for a discussion of the walkout basement.)

Look at the example shown in figure 5.7. This is the floor plan of a two-story house in which the upper level covers only a fraction of the entire footprint of a house. (The footprint

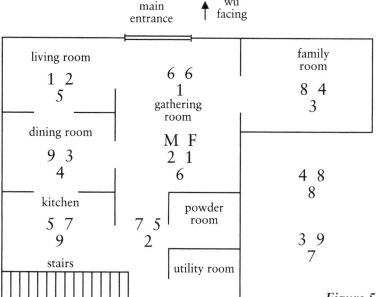

lower level

Figure 5.8 Superimposing the geomantic chart onto the floor plan of a house in which the lower level is smaller.

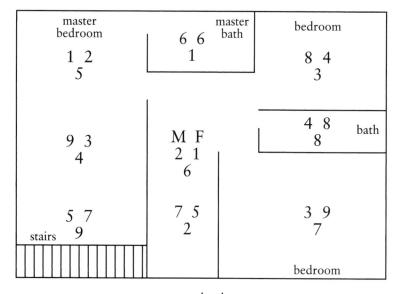

upper level

of a house is the extent of its foundation.) When superimposing the geomantic chart onto the upper level of the house, we find that we have lost five of the Nine Palaces.

In the house plan depicted in figure 5.8, the lower level has lost two squares, while the upper level has all the Nine Palaces. In the floor plan pictured in figure 5.9, an attic has been

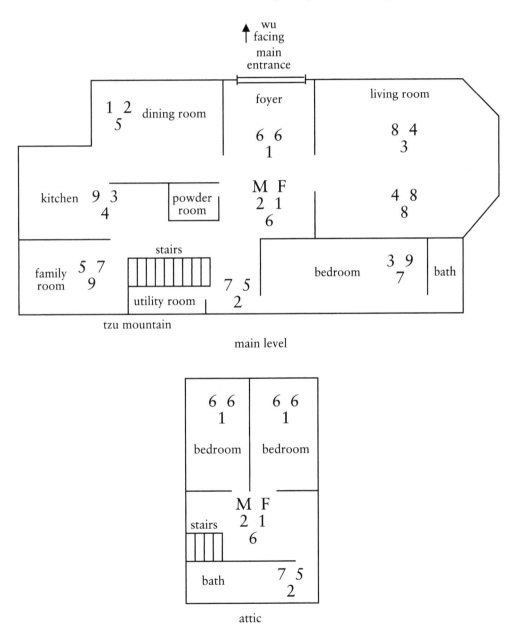

Figure 5.9 Superimposing the geomantic chart onto the floor plan of a house with a lived-in attic.

converted into living space. This is quite common in older, smaller houses. Notice that the attic occupies only the center column of the Nine Palaces.

In the example shown in figure 5.10, the floor plan is even more complex. The entranceway stretches all the way up to the second level, and there are areas of high ceilings in the living room. Notice that in this case, the lower level has lost the palace square that lies outside the house. In the upper level, three squares of the Nine Palaces are lost—one outside the house and two above the living room.

In general, when superimposing the geomantic chart onto houses in which the levels are unequal in area, you must first apply the entire geomantic chart to the level with the largest area. Using that level as a reference, work out which squares of the Nine Palaces are missing in the other areas. Overall, it is best when all the squares of the Nine Palaces

are represented in a house. The circulation of energy is smoother and more regular. If there is an area with an inauspicious combination of palace stars, it may be better to exclude that area from the building (see chapter 12).

Now do exercise 5.1 and familiarize yourself with fitting geomantic charts onto floor plans. After you have completed exercise 5.1, you should get a book on house designs. You can find such books in bookstores together with books on architectural styles and building design. Make up facing directions, generate charts from different cycles, and fit them onto the floor plans in the book. The more you practice, the better you will become at matching geomantic charts to the floor plans of buildings. Finally, if you have problems figuring out the levels of a house, it is time to call in an expert feng-shui practitioner.

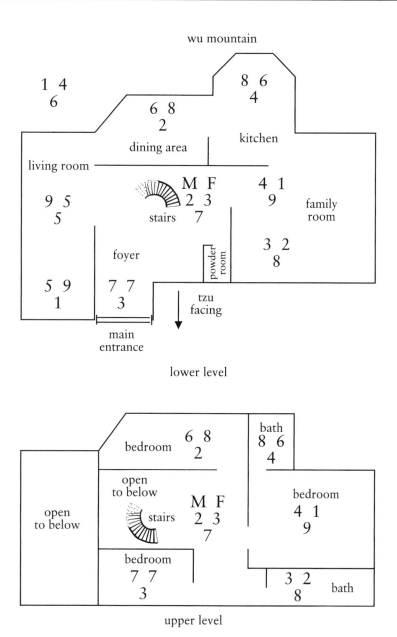

Figure 5.10 Superimposing the geomantic chart onto the floor plan of a house with uneven ceilings.

BOX 5.1

THE WALKOUT BASEMENT

A house built on a slope with a walkout basement is treated in the same way as a house with two levels. When parts of the lower level are excavated out of the slope and the upper level is situated directly on top of the lower level, the house is treated as a two-story building. The geomantic chart is simply superimposed onto each level, with some squares missing in the lower level (figure B5.1).

If the upper and lower levels are not directly on top of each other, and if both levels have similar square footage, the chart is superimposed independently on each story of the building, as if the two levels are bungalows on top of each other (figure B5.1).

The front facing of the walkout basement is not necessarily the same as that for the upper level. For example, while the walkout basement usually faces the downward slope, the most unobstructed side of the upper level may face a different direction. If the upper level and the walkout basement have different facing directions, two compass directions must be taken and two geomantic charts generated—one for the walkout basement and one for the upper level.

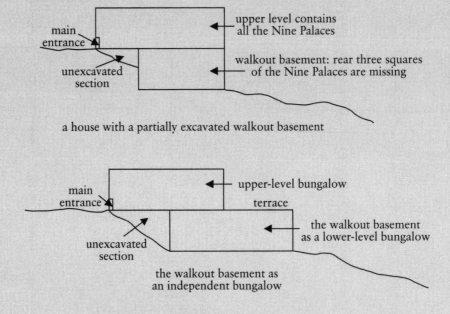

Figure B5.1 Types of walkout basements.

EXERCISES

EXERCISE 5.1

Generate the geomantic charts and superimpose them onto the floor plans shown in figure 5.11. The facing direction and the cycle in which the house was completed are specified. No. 1 is a worked example.

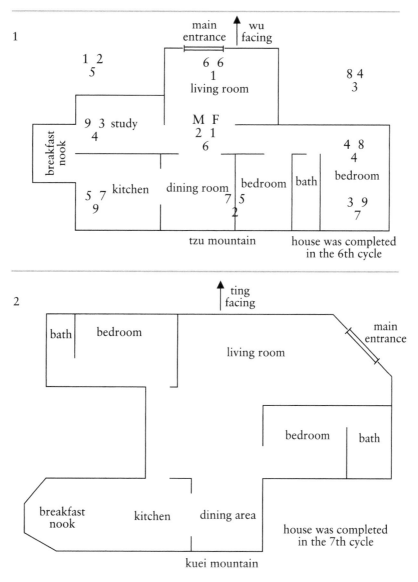

Figure 5.11 Generating the geomantic charts and superimposing them onto four sample houses (continued on next page).

3

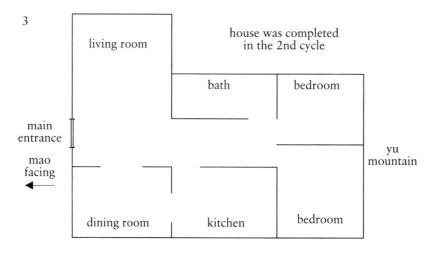

living room

house was completed
in the 2nd cycle

bath   bedroom

main
entrance

mao
facing

yu
mountain

dining room   kitchen   bedroom

wu mountain

4

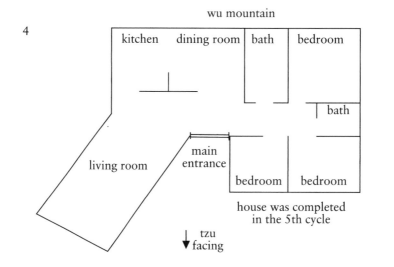

kitchen   dining room   bath   bedroom

bath

living room

main
entrance

bedroom   bedroom

house was completed
in the 5th cycle

tzu
facing

ANSWERS

EXERCISE 5.1

See figure 5.12.

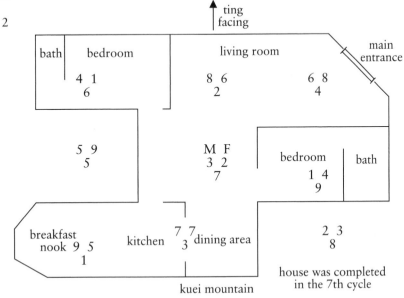

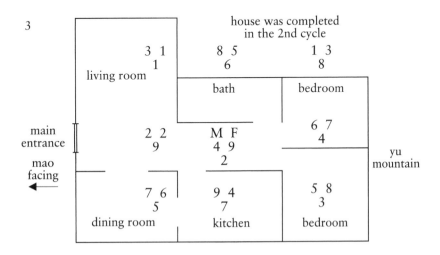

Figure 5.12 Answers to exercise 5.1

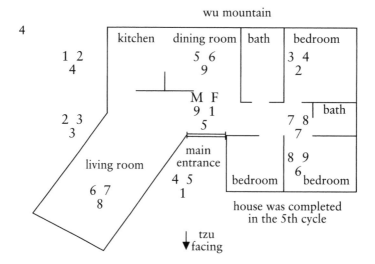

6

Interpreting the Geomantic Chart

Your goal in this chapter is to learn how to interpret the three numbers (Earth Base, Facing Star, Mountain Star) of the Nine Palaces. The numbers tell us about the kinds of energy that flow in each area of the house. In evaluating the flow of energy within a house, we first look at the conditional interaction between the Earth Base and Facing Star in the Facing Palace, then at the unconditional interactions between the Earth Base and the Facing Star in the rest of the palaces, and, last, at the additive interactions among the three stars.

CONDITIONAL INTERACTIONS

The conditional interaction refers to the interaction of the Earth Base and the Facing Star only in the Facing Palace. The Facing Palace is the square that represents the facing direction of the building. (See figure 6.1a and b; if you need a review, refer to chapter 4.) We evaluate the effects of the conditional interaction first, because they have priority over the unconditional interaction in that square. The effects of the conditional interaction differ depending on whether the combination of the Earth Base and Facing Star is waxing, strong, or malevolent. These conditions themselves are dependent on their directional location within the compass.

Figure 6.2 shows a listing of the nature of the numerical combinations (waxing, strong, and malevolent) and their compass positions. These combinations are effective as long as the pairs of numbers are present. It does not matter which number is the Earth Base and which is the Facing Star. When the combination of the Earth Base and the Facing Star is in its waxing or strong phase:

- A one-six combination yields successful scholarly pursuits. Children will be intelligent and talented.
- A two-seven combination makes for financial success, but seedy connections may be involved.
- A three-eight combination fosters success in politics or in producing caring and responsible children.

wu facing

5 6 / 9	1 1 / 5 — Facing Palace	3 8 / 7
4 7 / 8	M F / 6 5 / 1	8 3 / 3
9 2 / 4	2 9 / 6	7 4 / 2

tzu mountain

Figure 6.1a The Facing Palace is the square with the combination five-one-one (*left*).

k'un mountain

7 4 / 1	3 9 / 6	5 2 / 8
6 3 / 9	M F / 8 5 / 2	1 7 / 4
2 8 / 5 — Facing Palace	4 1 / 7	9 6 / 3

ken facing

The ken-facing chart reoriented

k'un mountain

3 9 / 6	5 2 / 8	1 7 / 4
7 4 / 1	M F / 8 5 / 2	9 6 / 3
6 3 / 9	2 8 / 5 — Facing Palace	4 1 / 7

ken facing

Figure 6.1b The Facing Palace is located in the lower corner, because the chart has a ken facing. In this case, we simply reorient the chart so that the Facing Palace is on the side instead of at the corner of the grid.

COMBINATION	NATURE OF COMBINATION	DIRECTIONS
1/6	waxing	chia, mao, i (east) ch'en, sun, ssu (southeast)
1/6	strong	jen, tzu, kuei (north)
1/6	malevolent	ping, wu, ting (south)
2/7	waxing	wei, k'un, shen (southwest) ch'ou, ken, yin (northeast)
2/7	strong	ping, wu, ting (south)
2/7	malevolent	hsü, ch'ien, hai (northwest) keng, yu, hsin (west)
3/8	waxing	ping, wu, ting (south)
3/8	strong	chia, mao, i (east) ch'en, sun, ssu (southeast)
3/8	malevolent	wei, k'un, shen (southwest)
4/9	waxing	jen, tzu, kuei (north)
	strong	keng, yu, hsin (west) hsü, ch'ien, hai (northwest)
	malevolent	chia, mao, i (east)

Figure 6.2 Table of conditional interactions.

- A four-nine combination promotes tremendous success in business through ethical means.

When the combination of the Earth Base and Facing Star is in its malevolent phase:

- A one-six combination means that the head of the family will be injured in accidents. Children may be uncaring toward their parents, and descendants may become thieves and bring harm to family members.
- A two-seven combination indicates infant death, illness, and accidents.

- A three-eight combination suggests suicide. Children may die young.
- A four-nine combination denotes injury or death in war. Children will become orphans.

Let's try to evaluate an example of a conditional interaction.

1. First, we identify and examine the Facing Palace of the geomantic chart and see if any of the combinations one-six, two-seven, three-eight, or four-nine is present. Let's say that we find the combination one-six in the Facing Palace.

2. Next, we find out whether the one-six combination is in the waxing, strong, or malevolent phase. To do this, we need to identify the facing direction of the house. Suppose in this example that the facing direction is mao.

3. Consulting figure 6.2, we find that for the direction mao, one-six is in its waxing phase.

4. Finally, we look up the interpretation of one-six in its waxing phase, and we find that one-six fosters success in scholarly pursuits and intelligent and talented children.

If the Facing Palace lies outside the house, the effects of the conditional interaction do not occur.

To familiarize yourself with evaluating the conditional interaction of the Earth Base and Facing Star in the Facing Palace, do exercise 6.1.

UNCONDITIONAL INTERACTIONS

Unconditional interactions do not depend on special circumstances and will occur whenever specific numerical combinations of the Earth Base and Facing Star appear. Interactions in the Central Palace (the center square of the Nine Palaces) affect everyone in the household. Interactions in specific rooms affect activities in those rooms and the individuals using them.

Unconditional interactions always take place between the Earth Base and the Facing Star. In unconditional interactions, we need to identify the Earth Base and the Facing Star numbers, because the numerical combinations are not reciprocal. In the interpretations of unconditional interactions listed here, the first number refers to the Earth Base, and the second number refers to the Facing Star.

Auspicious Combinations

- A one-four or four-one combination encourages success in scholarly pursuits.
- A six-eight combination contributes to success in business or the military arts.

- An eight-six combination supports success in scholarly or artistic endeavors.
- A four-six combination brings talent and fame.
- An eight-nine combination fosters many happy occasions in family life.
- A nine-eight combination enhances fame.
- A two-eight combination in the northwest (hsü, ch'ien, or hai in the Twenty-four Directions) generates great wealth.
- A three-one combination in the western position (keng, yu, or hsin in the Twenty-four Directions) engenders many descendants.
- Combinations of one, four, six, and eight, regardless of whether they are in the Earth Base or Facing Star, all bring good fortune and good health (except for eight-four, where eight is the Earth Base and four is the Facing Star).

Destructive Combinations

- A seven-nine combination forebodes problems associated with politics.

- A two-five or five-two combination presages severe illness.
- A nine-seven combination promotes fire caused by human activity, for example, a child playing with matches.
- A two-seven combination augurs fire caused by natural circumstances, for example, lightning.
- A five-five combination brings about severe illness or death.
- Combinations of five-nine and nine-five signify accidents that lead to injury or death.
- Combinations of seven-six and six-seven portend armed robbery and loss of fortunes. There is also the possibility of injuries.
- A three-two or two-three combination leads to quarrels and disharmony in relationships. If this combination is located in the kitchen, it signifies having too many mouths to feed, that is, financial hard times for the family.
- A seven-three combination supports unexpected gains in business, but these gains will invite robbery and trickery.
- A three-seven combination brings about illness associated with worries and anxieties. There is also the possibility of being victimized by politics or being embroiled in legal disputes.
- A six-nine combination promotes illness involving the failure of internal organs. The eldest member of the family has the highest risk.
- A seven-nine-five triple combination foreshadows terminal illness.
- An eight-four combination means that children will be unhealthy.
- A two-nine combination suggests obstacles in business ventures.
- A seven-nine combination in a bedroom contributes to serious illness in those occupying the bedroom.
- In general, two-black is associated with minor illness and five-yellow with major illness.

A three-eight combination traditionally is considered to be associated with illness in children. In my experience, however, this combination is really a neutral interaction and is not hazardous. Any combination not specified has no special effects. If the palace lies outside the house, the unconditional interaction does not affect the occupants of the house. To familiarize yourself with evaluating the unconditional interactions, try exercise 6.2.

ADDITIVE EFFECTS

In the palaces of the geomantic chart where there are no specific conditional and unconditional interactions (as listed earlier), we need to evaluate the additive effects of the Earth Base, Facing Star, and Mountain Star. The Facing Star carries the highest level of energy, the Earth Base imparts a medium level of energy, and the Mountain Star transmits a low level of energy.

The general rules for evaluating the additive effects of the three stars are these:

- A benevolent Earth Base can neutralize a malevolent Mountain Star.

- A benevolent Facing Star can neutralize a malevolent Mountain Star with residual benefits.
- A benevolent Facing Star can neutralize a malevolent Earth Base.
- Both a benevolent Earth Base and a benevolent Mountain Star are needed to neutralize a malevolent Facing Star.
- Stars that are neutral do not have influence on other stars.
- When stars are not used to neutralize the effects of other stars, their benefits are additive.
- If a star is used to neutralize a malevolent star in the same palace, its energy is tied up and cannot be used for other purposes, such as protecting the occupant (see chapter 7).

Figure 6.3 lists the nine stars and their effects.

PALACE STAR	EFFECT
one-white	benevolent
two-black	malevolent
three-jade	neutral
four-green	benevolent
five-yellow	malevolent
six-white	benevolent
seven-red	neutral
eight-white	benevolent
nine-purple	neutral in the company of neutral and benevolent stars malevolent in the company of malevolent stars

Figure 6.3 The stars of the Nine Palaces and their effects.

Let's look at several examples of how the additive interactions of the Earth Base, Facing Star, and Mountain Star work. (The numbers are cited in the order Earth Base / Facing Star / Mountain Star.)

Example 1: Four-Three-Nine

In this example, four-green (the Earth Base) is a benevolent star, and three-jade (the Facing Star) is neutral. The effect of nine-purple (the Mountain Star) is also neutral, because it is not in the company of malevolent stars (such as two-black and five-yellow). In this situation, the benevolent effect of four-green is not affected by the other two stars. Because the Earth Base carries a medium level of energy, we have a residual medium level of good energy.

Example 2: Two-Six-Six

In this instance, two-black (the Earth Base) is a malevolent star associated with illness; six-white (the Facing and Mountain stars) is an extremely auspicious star. In this situation, the six-white of the Facing Star can neutralize the two-black of the Earth Base. Because the Mountain Star carries a low level of energy, we have some positive energy left over when the effects of the three stars are added up.

Example 3: One-Five-Six

In this circumstance, both one-white in the Earth Base and six-white in the Mountain Star are required to neutralize the malevolent five-yellow in the Facing Star. There are no residual benefits, because both benevolent stars of the Earth Base and Mountain Star are used up to counter five-yellow.

Now do exercise 6.3 and evaluate the additive interactions of the Earth Base, Facing Star, and Mountain Star. When you feel that you have a firm grasp of the conditional, unconditional, and additive interactions, try exercise 6.4. Do not skip this exercise. Knowing how to evaluate the interactions of the numbers in the Nine Palaces is crucial to understanding the feng-shui of a building. Remember, the sequence of evaluating the numbers in the Nine Palaces is this:

1. Look for conditional interactions in the Facing Palace. The conditional interaction takes precedence over the unconditional interaction only in the Facing Palace.

2. Look for unconditional interactions in all the palaces, including the Facing Palace if there is no conditional interaction there.

3. In squares where there are no conditional or unconditional interactions, evaluate the additive effects of the Earth Base, Facing Star, and Mountain Star.

Information covered in this chapter is critical to planning the usage of space in a house. Make sure you are very comfortable with the materials here before you proceed to the next chapter.

EXERCISES

EXERCISE 6.1

Evaluate the following conditional interactions. It does not matter which number is the Earth Base and which the Facing Star. No. 1 is a worked example.

---

1. 3/8 located in k'un
This combination is malevolent. It forebodes suicidal death and/or the death of young children.

2. 1/6 located in *ch'en*
3. 4/9 located in kuei
4. 2/7 located in wu

EXERCISE 6.2

Evaluate the following unconditional interactions. The first number is the Earth Base, and the second number is the Facing Star. No. 1 is a worked example.

---

1. 2/7
This combination forebodes the threat of fire from natural causes.

2. 2/3
3. 7/6
4. 1/6
5. 5/2

EXERCISE 6.3

Evaluate the following additive interactions. The first number is the Earth Base, the second is the Facing Star, and the third is the Mountain Star. No. 1 is a worked example.

---

1. 3/1/5
The Facing Star one-white counters the Mountain Star five-yellow, leaving residual benefits. The Earth Base three-jade is neutral and does not contribute to the interaction.

2. 4/2/6
3. 5/3/7
4. 3/4/1
5. 5/1/4

EXERCISE 6.4

Evaluate the stars of the Nine Palaces in the following geomantic charts. Identify the conditional, unconditional, and additive interactions and interpret their meanings. No. 1 is a partially worked example.

1.

ting facing

7 8	3 3	5 1
2	7	9

M F

6 9	8 7	1 5
1	3	5

2 4	4 2	9 6
6	8	4

kuei mountain

There are no conditional interactions. The unconditional interactions are these:
- *3/7—legal problems, political intrigues, or illness associated with anxieties and worries*
- *4/6—talent and fame*

(Continue with the analysis.)

2.

shen
facing

1 4	5 8	3 6
5	1	3

M F

2 5	9 3	7 1
4	6	8

6 9	4 7	8 2
9	2	7

yin
mountain

ANSWERS

EXERCISE 6.1

2. 1/6 in ch'en is waxing and benevolent. It indicates successful scholarly pursuits. Children will be talented.
3. 4/9 in kuei is waxing and benevolent. It portends great success in business through ethical means.
4. 2/7 in wu is strong. It brings about financial success, but seedy connections may be involved.

EXERCISE 6.2

2. 2/3 contributes to quarrels and disharmony.
3. 7/6 indicates robbery that may lead to injuries.
4. 1/6 fosters health, prosperity, and good fortune.
5. 5/2 leads to illness.

EXERCISE 6.3

2. 4/2/6

The Earth Base four-green and the Mountain Star six-white are both needed to neutralize the negative two-black in the Facing Star. There are no residual effects.

3. 5/3/7

The Facing Star three-jade and the Mountain Star seven-red are both neutral and cannot neutralize the negative five-yellow in the Earth Base. This has a residual negative effect.

4. 3/4/1

The Facing Star four-green and the Mountain Star one-white are both benevolent, and the Earth Base three-jade is neutral. This results in a substantial benevolent effect coming from the Facing and Mountain stars.

5. 5/1/4

The Facing Star one-white is used up to counter the negative five-yellow of the Earth Base, leaving a small benevolent effect carried by the Mountain Star four-green.

EXERCISE 6.4

1.

The remaining unconditional interactions are these:

- 5/5—severe illness or death
- 7/3—unexpected gains that lead to robbery and trickery
- 6/4—health, prosperity, and good fortune

The additive interactions are these:

- 2/8/7—There is no net effect. Eight-white completely neutralizes two-black, and seven-red is itself neutral.
- 9/1/5—One-white neutralizes nine-purple, leaving a small negative effect carried by the Mountain Star five-yellow.
- 1/9/6—A substantial positive effect is carried by one-white and six-white.
- 8/2/4—There is no net effect. Eight-white and four-green are used up to neutralize two-black.

2.

There are no conditional interactions. The unconditional interactions are these:

- 1/8—health, prosperity, and good fortune

- 8/1—health, prosperity, and good fortune
- 2/7—fire hazard associated with natural causes

The additive interactions are these:

- 5/4/1—Four-green is used up to neutralize five-yellow, leaving a small benevolent effect carried by one-white.
- 3/6/3—There is a sizable benevolent effect carried by six-white.
- 4/5/2—Four-green is used up to neutralize two-black, leaving a sizable negative effect carried by five-yellow.
- 6/3/9—There is a moderate benevolent effect carried by six-white.
- 9/9/6—There is a small benevolent effect carried by six-white.
- 7/2/8—A moderate negative effect is left after eight-white is used to counter two-black.

7

Evaluating and Planning the Usage of Space

Once you have set up the geomantic chart and interpreted the meanings of the stars of the Nine Palaces, you can begin to evaluate the usage of space in the house. To do this, we look at the conditional, unconditional, and additive interactions of the stars of the Nine Palaces in each area of the building. In the following discussion, the first number refers to the Earth Base, the second to the Facing Star, and the third to the Mountain Star.

ENTRANCES, HALLWAYS, AND STAIRS

Entrances, hallways, and stairs are conduits that channel energy to the rest of the house. If they are located in areas occupied by auspicious stars of the Nine Palaces, they can enhance benevolent energy, neutralize destructive energy, and facilitate the flow of positive energy in the house. If they are located in areas occupied by inauspicious stars, they can bring harm to the occupants.

These are the points to remember when evaluating the feng-shui of entrances, hallways, and stairs:

- Auspicious Earth Base and Facing stars for these areas are combinations of one-white, four-green, six-white, and eight-white. It does not matter if the number is the Earth Base or the Facing Star. (The exception is eight-four, where eight is the Earth Base and four is the Facing Star.)
- The worst combinations are two-two, two-five, five-five, two-nine, and five-nine or the reverse (that is, either number can be the Earth Base or the Facing Star).
- The combinations two-three and three-two forebode disharmony and quarrels with neighbors.
- The combinations two-seven and seven-nine are associated with fire.
- The combinations seven-six and six-seven are associated with robbery and break-in.

In general, two-black, five-yellow, and nine-purple are not good stars for the entrance, hallways, or stairs, whether the numbers represent the Earth Base, the Facing Star, or even the Mountain Star. If these numbers are accompanied by the combinations one-white, six-white, and eight-white, their destructive influence is lessened.

Figures 7.1, 7.2, and 7.3 show examples of how to assess entrances, hallways, and stairs. In the floor plan shown in figure 7.1, the stars of the Nine Palaces are evaluated as a regular geomantic chart. Although the Earth Base and Facing Star add up to ten, making this a Combination of Ten chart, the chart has no auspicious effect, because one palace (three-seven-seven) is missing.

Looking at the lower level of the house, we find that the main entrance, the stairs, and the

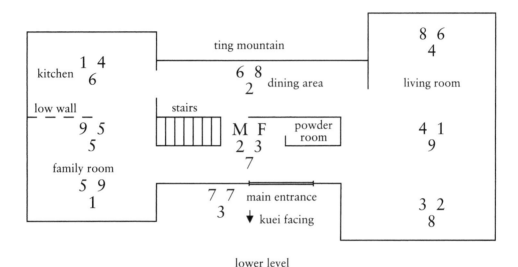

lower level

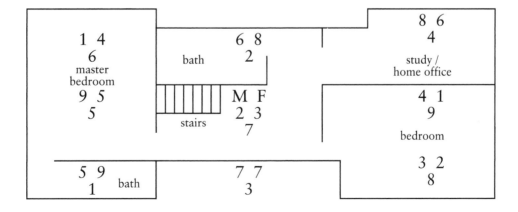

upper level

Figure 7.1 Evaluating the usage of space.

hallway are occupied by the combination seven-three-two. The unconditional interaction of seven-three presages gains in business, but the wealth will invite robbery. Since this combination is found in the area of the main entrance and the stairs, where movement amplifies the strength of the malevolent stars, the risk of robbery through the front door is enhanced. In the upper level, the combination seven-three-two also is located in the stairway and hallway. This, too, heightens the danger of theft and robbery.

Taking the floor plan shown in figure 7.2, we need to treat the stars as a regular geomantic chart instead of a Combination of Ten chart, because one palace (six-four-one) is outside the house. Looking at the lower level, we find that the main entrance is occupied by the combination three-seven-seven. The unconditional interaction of three-seven fosters legal disputes, political intrigues, or illness associated with worries and anxieties. Situated at the front door, where the effects are magnified by movement in and out of the house, these risks are enhanced.

The stairs are positioned in the area occupied by the combination eight-two-three. Evaluating the additive effects of these three stars (because there is no unconditional interaction), we find that the malevolent Facing Star two-black cannot be neutralized by the benevolent Earth Base Star eight-white. Being neutral, three-jade in the Mountain Star position cannot help counter two-black. Therefore, we have a residual negative effect in this area.

In the upper level, there are two sections of hallway—one with the combination three-seven-seven and the other with the combination seven-three-two. The combination three-seven portends legal troubles, political intrigues, or mental illness associated with

anxiety and worries. The negative effect of three-seven is enhanced by usage and movement. The combination seven-three promotes success in business, but the wealth invites robbery. Because this combination is located in a hallway, the risk of robbery is amplified by usage and movement.

In the floor plan shown in figure 7.3, the main entrance is occupied by the combination five-seven-two. Gauging the additive effects of these three stars, we find that seven-red, the neutral Facing Star, cannot neutralize the malevolent aspects of five-yellow and two-black. Therefore, we have a considerable negative effect in this area. The stars five-yellow (Earth Base) and two-black (Facing Star) are associated with illness, and their negative potential is enhanced by movement in the area of the front door. Because neither five-yellow nor two-black is the Facing Star, however, the illness will not be fatal.

The stairs are located in the area occupied by the combination seven-five-nine. Looking at the additive effects of these stars, we find that seven-red, the neutral Earth Base, cannot neutralize the five-yellow in the Facing Star. Moreover, because nine-purple is in the presence of a malevolent star, the negative power of the Facing Star five-yellow is enhanced. The problem is exacerbated by the fact that the stairway is a frequently used area and that it conducts energy between the two levels of the house. All these factors add up to a very undesirable situation, where the occupants of the house will be constantly threatened by illness. Furthermore, because the Facing Star five-yellow is strengthened by nine-purple, some of the health problems may be life-threatening. The combination seven-five-nine also is found in the hallways around the stairs, which reinforces the risk of serious and fatal illness.

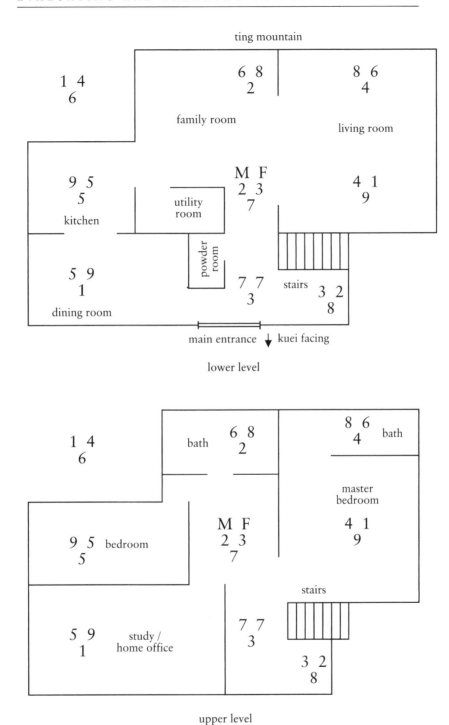

Figure 7.2 Evaluating the usage of space.

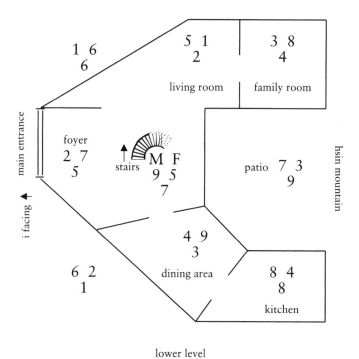

Figure 7.3 Evaluating the usage of space.

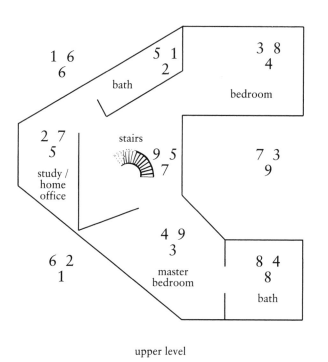

If you find that the entrance, hallways, and stairs are occupied by inauspicious stars, the first thing you should do is see whether the destructive effect is lessened by the other stars in the palace (as shown in the examples in figures 7.1, 7.2, and 7.3). Should you find that these areas still cause problems after the influences of the other stars are taken into account, you will need to install objects to neutralize the inauspicious stars. Chapter 10 shows you how to install the necessary countermeasures.

BEDROOMS

The stars of the Nine Palaces in the bedrooms affect the health of the individuals sleeping there. For this reason, rooms with two or more stars associated with illness—five-yellow and two-black—should not be used as bedrooms, unless the individual has two-black or five-yellow as his or her guardian star (see chapter 8). Bedrooms should not be chosen until the guardian stars of the occupants have been determined. Chapter 8 takes up the discussion of how to choose the appropriate bedroom for each occupant of the house.

KITCHEN

The kitchen is associated with health, livelihood, and harmony. These are the points to remember when you are evaluating the feng-shui of the kitchen:

- The combinations three-seven, seven-three, six-seven, and seven-six forebode unemployment and not having enough to eat (that is, hardships in making a living).
- Combinations of one-white, four-green, six-white, and eight-white, regardless of whether the number is the Earth Base or the Facing Star, suggest that the occupants will be healthy and always will have enough to eat. The exception is the combination eight-four, which is associated with ill health in children.

- The combinations two-seven and seven-nine portend fire and injury associated with fire. They are very undesirable stars for the kitchen.
- Combinations of two-black and five-yellow, regardless of which one is the Earth Base and which the Facing Star, foreshadow food poisoning and illness associated with food. If nine-purple is also present, the illness may be fatal.
- Combinations of two-three and three-two contribute to disharmony and quarrels in the kitchen. When seven-red is also present, the quarrels may lead to fights and injuries.

Look again at figures 7.1, 7.2, and 7.3. In figure 7.1, the kitchen is occupied by the combination six-four-one, the stars of prosperity and health. These are extremely auspicious stars for a kitchen. The kitchen in figure 7.2 is in a troublesome area. The combination five-five-nine presages severe and fatal illnesses. When stars of illness are located in the kitchen, the occupants will become sick from eating food at home or in restaurants. In figure 7.3, the kitchen is located in an undesirable area (eight-four-eight) if there are children in the household. The combination eight-four is associated with illness in children. If there are no children in the household, this is a good spot for the kitchen.

It is usually difficult to relocate a kitchen within a house. If you find that the kitchen is situated in an area that can cause problems, you will need to install countermeasures to neutralize the destructive stars. Chapter 10 shows you how to do this.

FAMILY ROOM

The stars of the Nine Palaces affect all the members of the family who use the family room. These are the points to remember when you are evaluating the feng-shui of this room, especially when the room is used frequently:

- Do not situate a family room in a palace with combinations of two-black and five-yellow (stars of illness, injuries, and accidents) in the Earth Base and Facing stars.
- Likewise, combinations of two-three and three-two (stars of disharmony) are undesirable.
- Combinations of nine-seven and two-seven promote fire, especially if there is a fireplace or woodstove in this room. The chance of fire hazard increases if the Mountain Star is nine-purple.
- The best Earth Base and Facing stars for this room are one-white, four-green, six-white, and eight-white—the stars of health, prosperity, and harmony.
- It is sufficient to have the stars of health, prosperity, and harmony as either the Earth Base or Facing Star, provided that the other stars in the palace are not combinations of two-black and five-yellow.

Let's look at the family rooms in the floor plans shown in figures 7.1, 7.2, and 7.3. In figure 7.1, we see that the family room is located in a very unfavorable area. The combination five-five-nine forebodes severe and fatal illness, and frequent use of this room enhances this malevolent effect. The combination one-nine-five is also negative. The one-white of the Earth Base cannot neutralize the five-yellow of the Mountain Star, because the malevolent star is enhanced by the Facing Star nine-purple. I recommend that the occupants use the living room as a family room and frequent the family room itself as little as possible.

The family room in figure 7.2 is occupied by the combination two-eight-six. The Facing Star eight-white completely neutralizes the negative impact of two-black (in the Earth Base), leaving a small positive effect carried by the Mountain Star six-white. This is a viable area for a family room.

In figure 7.3, the combination four-eight-three is found in the family room. The unconditional interaction of four-eight brings health, prosperity, and success, making this an excellent location for the family room.

STUDY / HOME OFFICE

If this room is situated in a palace occupied by the stars of prosperity and success, students will excel in school, and any business venture planned and conducted in this room will thrive. These are the points to remember when you are evaluating the feng-shui of a study:

- When the room is used primarily by students, the best combinations are six-eight, four-six, one-four, one-six, and eight-six. These are all stars of academic excellence.
- Do not use a room with the combination seven-six or six-seven as a study, because these combinations suggest that the student's academic career will be a constant struggle.
- The presence of five-yellow and/or two-black in either the Earth Base or the Facing Star or both forebodes misdeeds and behavioral problems in school.
- Combinations of two-three and three-two also are not desirable for a study, because they contribute to stiff competition and peer pressure in school.

These are the points to remember when you are evaluating the feng-shui of a home office:

- The best combination for a home office is one-four. It means that ingenious business ideas will be generated, leading to promotion or increase in wealth.
- The combination two-eight is excellent for a home office if the room is situated in the northwest corner occupied by the directions hsü, ch'ien, or hai.

- The combination three-seven will encourage good ideas, but you will not get the credit for them.
- Do not place the office in a room with the combination seven-six or six-seven, because they portend business failures leading to the loss of income and job.
- Do not put the office in a room with the combination three-two or two-three, because stiff competition in business ventures and slim chances of promotion will ensue.
- Do not position the office in a room with two-black or five-yellow in the Earth Base and/or Facing Star, since they presage disasters in business ventures and bankruptcy. Moreover, these business failures will lead to illness, injury, and death in the family.
- Do not situate the office in a room with the combination seven-nine, because it fosters political intrigues.

In general, combinations of one-white, four-green, six-white, and eight-white in the Earth Base and Facing Star are desirable for both study and home office. The presence of even one of these stars in the Facing Star position is viable, provided that the other stars in the palaces are not two-black and five-yellow.

Let's examine the rooms designated as study / home office in figures 7.1, 7.2, and 7.3. In figure 7.1, the study / home office is located in an extremely auspicious area. The combination four-six-eight encourages prosperity, health, and success.

In figure 7.2, the study / home office is found in an inauspicious area. The one-white of the Earth Base is unable to counter the joint effects of five-yellow (Mountain Star) and nine-purple (Facing Star). The result of the interaction is a negative effect associated with illness. I suggest that this area be used as a storage room or a guest room, provided that guests do not stay for more than six months. The occupants can do homework or home accounting in the master bedroom or family room, where the effects from the stars are positive.

The study / home office in figure 7.3 also is placed in an unfavorable area. Seven-red, a neutral Facing Star, cannot neutralize the malevolent stars five-yellow and two-black. The result of the interaction is a negative effect associated with illness. I suggest that the study or home office be moved to the room with the combination four-eight-three, if that room is available. Otherwise, the home office should be moved into the master bedroom, where there is a small benevolent effect carried by the Mountain Star four-green. Alternatively, a study area can be set up in the family room, where the combination of the stars is auspicious.

LIVING ROOM

The importance of the living room depends on the frequency of its use. If it is used to entertain guests with business connections or if it is used often as a sitting room, it becomes important. If not, you can give this room low priority in planning the allocation of space in the house.

These are the points to remember in evaluating the feng-shui of the living room if it is used frequently by the occupants or to entertain guests with business connections:

- The best stars for this room are Earth Base / Facing Star combinations of one-white, four-green, six-white, and eight-white, since these are the stars of health, prosperity, and good fortune. It does not matter which number is the Earth Base and which is the Facing Star.
- The worst stars are Earth Base / Facing Star combinations of two-black and five-yellow, because these are the stars of illness and death. Again, it does not mat-

ter which number is the Earth Base and which is the Facing Star.
- The combinations two-three and three-two are not desirable, because they encourage quarrels and disharmony.
- The combinations six-seven and seven-six are not auspicious, especially if the living room is used to entertain guests with business connections, because these stars forebode robbery.
- The combination seven-three is not advantageous if the room is used to entertain guests with business connections, because it promotes business treachery.
- The combinations nine-seven and two-seven are not desirable regardless of the living room's use, because these combinations are associated with fire hazard and injury by fire.
- If the living room has no auspicious star combinations, the next best choice is to situate the room in an area with neutral stars.

Now look at the floor plans shown in figures 7.1, 7.2, and 7.3. The house in figure 7.1 has favorable stars in all the areas of the living room, making this room an excellent place to entertain guests. Since the family room is located in such a troublesome area (see earlier discussion of the family room), this large room can be partitioned to accommodate both living room and family room.

The living room pictured in figure 7.2 also has auspicious stars (nine-one-four and four-six-eight) that make it an excellent room for entertaining guests. The living room depicted in figure 7.3 has several problems. First, it is triangular in shape and therefore collects malevolent energy in the corners. Second, it is occupied by the combination two-one-five. Here, the one-white of the Facing Star barely can neutralize the combined negative effects of the stars two-black and five-yellow. Given this condition, I suggest that guests be entertained in the dining room, where there is a small positive effect carried by the Mountain Star four-green.

DINING ROOM

If the dining room is used frequently, it is important to have stars of health in that area. If not, it can occupy an area with neutral stars. These are the points to remember when you are evaluating the feng-shui of a dining room:

- The best stars are the stars of health and prosperity—combinations of one-white, four-green, six-white, and eight-white, regardless of which number is the Earth Base and which is the Facing Star. The exception is the inauspicious combination eight-four, which can affect the health of children in the household.
- The worst stars are the stars of illness—combinations of two-black and five-yellow, regardless of which number is the Earth Base and which is the Facing Star.
- The combinations two-three and three-two contribute to quarrels during dinner. For this reason, they are also undesirable stars for the dining area.

In figure 7.1, we find that the dining room is located in an area with viable feng-shui. The Facing Star eight-white completely neutralizes the two-black in the Earth Base, leaving a small positive effect carried by the Mountain Star six-white.

The dining room depicted in figure 7.2 is not very desirable. The additive interaction of one-nine-five leaves a negative effect associated with illness. This is not a good space for the dining area if the room is used frequently.

Finally, the dining room shown in figure 7.3 has viable feng-shui. The additive interaction of three-nine-four leaves a small positive effect carried by the Mountain Star four-green.

BATHROOMS, UTILITY ROOMS, STORAGE ROOMS, AND UNFINISHED ATTICS AND BASEMENTS

Bathrooms, utility rooms, storage rooms, and unfinished attics and basements are not frequented. It is best to have such stars as nine-purple, five-yellow, and two-black in these rooms. Even a combination of two-seven or nine-seven, the stars of fire hazard, are acceptable in the bathroom and utility room, because these rooms usually have sinks and running water. Storage rooms and closets are dormant space. They are best occupied by adverse stars, such as Earth Base / Facing Star combinations of two-black and five-yellow. Unfinished attics and basements (and crawl spaces in these areas) are analogous to closets and are treated as dormant space. Finished basements are considered part of the house. In basements, however, positive energy is diminished, and negative energy is enhanced (see box 7.1).

Now that you have an idea of how the Nine Palaces of the geomantic chart affect the usage of space in a house, do exercise 7.1. You may want to rank your priorities in the usage of space before you evaluate the Nine Palace stars of each room. For example, for one household, the priority ranking might be bedrooms, kitchen, family room, study, bath, and utility room. For a household in which occupants do not like to cook, the priorities might be bedrooms, family room, study, kitchen, bath, and utility room.

BOX 7.1

THE BASEMENT

The flow of energy in the basement is not as good as the flow of energy in the upper levels of a building, because expansive energy from the outside cannot enter a basement directly. Moreover, any negative energy that may accumulate in the basement cannot be routed out effectively. In the basement, therefore, the benevolent effects of the stars of the Nine Palaces are diminished, and the malevolent effects are enhanced. For this reason, we give basements a negative modifier when we are evaluating the feng-shui of a house.

We identify an area of the house as a basement when it is sunk into the ground *and* does not have good exposure to the outside. Ceiling windows and small windows in the areas of the basement that are slightly above ground level are insufficient to let expansive energy enter. The exception is the walkout basement in houses built on a slope. Because walkout basements have full-size windows facing the downward side of the slope, they are not considered true basements. If the walkout basement is partitioned so that the rear sections do not have windows, those sections are treated as true basements (figure B7.1).

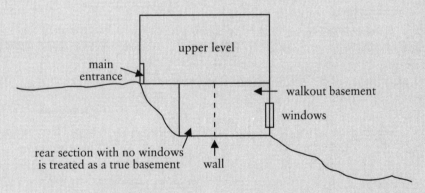

Figure B7.1 The true basement versus the walkout basement.

Given the overall negative effect of basements, we should not place bedrooms, the home office, or the study there. Ideally, the basement should be a storage space, for example, a utility room, storeroom, darkroom, or even library. If you are short on space, it is acceptable to put the family or recreational room in the basement. The exception to this rule is the walkout basement with full-size windows.

EXERCISES

EXERCISE 7.1

Evaluate the usage of space in the floor plans in figure 7.4 using the methods you have learned so far. No. 1 is a partially worked example. The geomantic chart is generated for you in No. 2. You need not evaluate the bedrooms in the exercise.

1.

Kitchen—8/4/9

The combination 8/4 forebodes unhealthy children. If there are children in the house, this kitchen has undesirable feng-shui. The nine-purple in the Mountain Star increases the threat, but if there are no children in the household, the problem does not apply.

Family room—6/6/2

The combination 6/6 is very auspicious. It is associated with health, prosperity, and good fortune. Although two-black is a malevolent star, it has very little effect, because it is only the Mountain Star. Moreover, the extremely auspicious unconditional interaction 6/6 wipes out the negative potential, with plenty of benevolent energy left over.

(Continue with the analysis.)

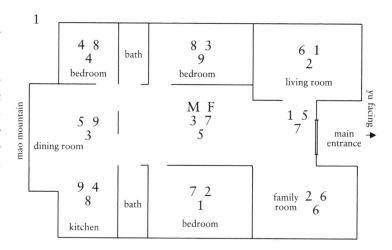

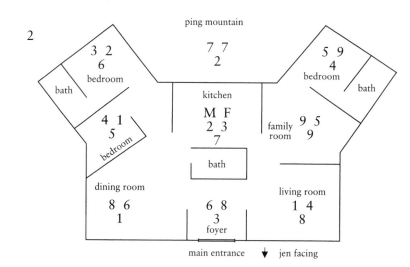

Figure 7.4 Evaluating the usage of space in two sample houses.

ANSWERS

EXERCISE 7.1

See figure 7.4.

1.

Living room—2/1/6

One-white is used up to neutralize two-black, leaving a small benevolent effect carried by six-white. This is a very suitable area for a living room.

Dining room—3/9/5

The dining room is a problem area. Nine-purple magnifies the negative quality of the Mountain Star five-yellow. Since five-yellow is associated with illness, this is not a good spot for a dining room if the space is used frequently. If it is used infrequently, the threat is negligible.

Foyer and entrance—7/5/1

The additive interactions of the three stars yield a moderate negative effect after one-white is used to counter five-yellow. Because it is the entryway, frequent traffic accentuates the negative potential. Since five-yellow is associated with illness, its presence in the entrance means that illness will affect everyone in the household.

Hallway—5/7/3

The additive interactions of the three stars yield a modest negative effect carried by five-yellow, the star of illness. Again, because this is the hallway, frequent traffic will amplify the problem.

2.

Kitchen—7/3/2

The combination 7/3 suggests gains in business that lead to robbery. Since the kitchen is used often in most households, this is a very undesirable area for a kitchen.

Family room—9/5/9

This family room is a disaster area. First, all three stars are malevolent. Second, the combination 9/5 promotes severe illness. Enhanced by nine-purple in the Mountain Star, the severe illness may become terminal. This is an extremely dangerous area to situate a family room.

Living room—8/4/1

The combination 8/4 forebodes unhealthy children. If there are children in the household, this is not a good area for them to frequent. If there are no children in the household, the effect is absent, and the area becomes a viable space.

Dining room—1/6/8

The combination 1/6 is associated with health, prosperity, and good fortune. This is an extremely auspicious spot and should be used frequently.

Foyer and entrance—3/8/6

The additive interactions of the three stars yield a sizable benevolent effect carried by the stars eight-white and six-white. The positive impact is enhanced by traffic through the entrance, which makes the entryway very auspicious.

The palace with 2/7/7 is outside the house and does not enter into the analysis.

8

Matching Occupants to a House

Once you have worked out the geomantic chart and interpreted its meaning for the entire house and for each room, the next step is to match the occupants to the house and bedrooms. To do this, we need to identify the guardian star of each occupant.

In feng-shui philosophy, each person is said to be born under the guardianship of a star of the Nine Palaces and its element. When our guardian star and its element are nourished, we will enjoy good health and good fortune. When our guardian star and its element are weakened, we will be plagued by illness and misfortune. It follows that the conditions that benefit our guardian star and element also will benefit us, and conditions that are destructive to our guardian star and element also will be destructive to us.

DETERMINING THE GUARDIAN STARS OF INDIVIDUALS

The year of birth determines which star of the Nine Palaces and its element act as our guardian. Figures 8.1, 8.2, and 8.3 provide us with this information. Persons born between 1864 and 1923 should consult figure 8.1, persons born between 1924 and 1983 should consult figure 8.2, and persons born between 1984 and 2043 should consult figure 8.3. Those persons born in January or February will need to find out whether their birth dates fall in the Chinese year before or after the Western year (refer to figure 4.2).

Let's work through a few examples. To determine the guardian element for a female born in June 1958, we look at figure 8.2 and locate the year 1958 in the column for females. We find that the guardian star is nine-purple and the element is fire. To pinpoint the guardian star for a male born on January 21, 1921, we first need to find out whether this birth date occurs before or after the Chinese New Year. Looking at figure 4.2, we find that January 21 fell before the Chinese New Year in 1921 (which was on February 2). Therefore, we treat this birth date as if it fell in the previous year, 1920. To figure out the guardian star and element for a male born in 1920, we refer to figure 8.1, and we find that

UPPER ERA
1864 through 1923

STAR	ELEMENT	MALE	FEMALE
one-white	water	1864, 1873, 1882, 1891, 1900, 1909, 1918	1869, 1878, 1887, 1896, 1905, 1914, 1923
nine-purple	fire	1865, 1874, 1883, 1892, 1901, 1910, 1919	1868, 1877, 1886, 1895, 1904, 1913, 1922
eight-white	earth	1866, 1875, 1884, 1893, 1902, 1911, 1920	1867, 1876, 1885, 1894, 1903, 1912, 1921
seven-red	metal	1867, 1876, 1885, 1894, 1903, 1912, 1921	1866, 1875, 1884, 1893, 1902, 1911, 1920
six-white	metal	1868, 1877, 1886, 1895, 1904, 1913, 1922	1865, 1874, 1883, 1892, 1901, 1910, 1919
five-yellow	earth	1869, 1878, 1887, 1896, 1905, 1914, 1923	1864, 1873, 1882, 1891, 1900, 1909, 1918
four-green	wood	1870, 1879, 1888, 1897, 1906, 1915	1872, 1881, 1890, 1899, 1908, 1917
three-jade	wood	1871, 1880, 1889, 1898, 1907, 1916	1871, 1880, 1889, 1898, 1907, 1916
two-black	earth	1872, 1881, 1890, 1899, 1908, 1917	1870, 1879, 1888, 1897, 1906, 1915

Figure 8.1 Guardian stars and elements for males and females born in the Upper Era.

the star is eight-white and the element is earth.

What is the guardian star and element for a female born on February 19, 1991? Again, we need to consult figure 4.2, because the birth date is in February. In this case, February 19 fell after the Chinese New Year (which was February 15). In this case, we treat the birth year as 1991 and refer to figure 8.3. Looking down the column of dates for females, we find that the guardian star is six-white and the element is metal.

To familiarize yourself with working out the guardian star and element of a person, do exercise 8.1.

When there is more than one star to an element, the strength of the elements is different for each star. Look at any table of the guardian stars and elements (figures 8.1, 8.2, or 8.3). You will notice that there are nine stars and five elements. The element earth is associated with three palace stars—two-black, five-yellow, and eight-white. The element wood is associated with two palace

MIDDLE ERA
1924 through 1983

STAR	ELEMENT	MALE	FEMALE
one-white	water	1927, 1936, 1945, 1954, 1963, 1972, 1981	1932, 1941, 1950, 1959, 1968, 1977
nine-purple	fire	1928, 1937, 1946, 1955, 1964, 1973, 1982	1931, 1940, 1949, 1958, 1967, 1976
eight-white	earth	1929, 1938, 1947, 1956, 1965, 1974, 1983	1930, 1939, 1948, 1957, 1966, 1975
seven-red	metal	1930, 1939, 1948, 1957, 1966, 1975	1929, 1938, 1947, 1956, 1965, 1974, 1983
six-white	metal	1931, 1940, 1949, 1958, 1967, 1976	1928, 1937, 1946, 1955, 1964, 1973, 1982
five-yellow	earth	1932, 1941, 1950, 1959, 1968, 1977	1927, 1936, 1945, 1954, 1963, 1972, 1981
four-green	wood	1924, 1933, 1942, 1951, 1960, 1969, 1978	1926, 1935, 1944, 1953, 1962, 1971, 1980
three-jade	wood	1925, 1934, 1943, 1952, 1961, 1970, 1979	1925, 1934, 1943, 1952, 1961, 1970, 1979
two-black	earth	1926, 1935, 1944, 1953, 1962, 1971, 1980	1924, 1933, 1942, 1951, 1960, 1969, 1978

Figure 8.2 Guardian stars and elements for males and females born in the Middle Era.

stars—three-jade and four-green. The element metal is associated with two palace stars—six-white and seven-red. Fire and water each have one palace star—nine-purple and one-white, respectively. In their order of strength, earth in five-yellow is strongest, followed by two-black, and then eight-white. Wood in three-jade is stronger than wood in four-green, and metal in seven-red is stronger than metal in six-white. Among the stars of the Nine Palaces, there are also differences in strength. Five-yellow, two-black, and nine-purple are the strongest guardian stars. Three-jade, four-green, and seven-red are the next strongest. The weakest guardian stars are six-white, eight-white, and one-white. Strong guardian stars are less susceptible to harm caused by their antagonist stars, whereas weaker guardian stars are more vulnerable. For example, the earth of five-yellow will not

LOWER ERA
1984 through 2043

STAR	ELEMENT	MALE	FEMALE
one-white	water	1990, 1999, 2008, 2017, 2026, 2035	1986, 1995, 2004, 2013, 2022, 2031, 2040
nine-purple	fire	1991, 2000, 2009, 2018, 2027, 2036	1985, 1994, 2003, 2012, 2021, 2030, 2039
eight-white	earth	1992, 2001, 2010, 2019, 2028, 2037	1984, 1993, 2002, 2011, 2020, 2029, 2038
seven-red	metal	1984, 1993, 2002, 2011, 2020, 2029, 2038	1992, 2001, 2010, 2019, 2028, 2037
six-white	metal	1985, 1994, 2003, 2012, 2021, 2030, 2039	1991, 2000, 2009, 2018, 2027, 2036
five-yellow	earth	1986, 1995, 2004, 2013, 2022, 2031, 2040	1990, 1999, 2008, 2017, 2026, 2035
four-green	wood	1987, 1996, 2005, 2014, 2023, 2032, 2041	1989, 1998, 2007, 2016, 2025, 2034, 2043
three-jade	wood	1988, 1997, 2006, 2015, 2024, 2033, 2042	1988, 1997, 2006, 2015, 2024, 2033, 2042
two-black	earth	1989, 1998, 2007, 2016, 2025, 2034, 2043	1987, 1996, 2005, 2014, 2023, 2032, 2041

Figure 8.3 Guardian stars and elements for males and females born in the Lower Era.

be harmed by its antagonist, wood, as much as the earth of eight-white.

The strength of the stars and elements has nothing to do with the character or personality of the person. A person with a weak guardian element does not necessarily have a weak personality. Guardian stars and elements in feng-shui function differently than birth stars in astrology. In feng-shui, a weaker guardian star and element mean that the per-

son needs extra protection from destructive energy, because his or her guardian star cannot act very well as protector.

The interactions of the five elements (metal, wood, water, fire, and earth) form the basis of matching the occupants to a house and to the bedrooms. In learning how to match individuals to a dwelling, you need to be familiar with the relationships of the five elements in their nourishing and destructive cycles. These

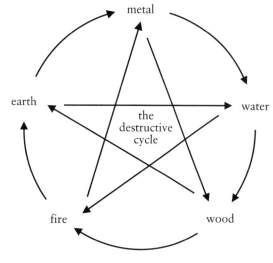

the creative/nourishing cycle

Figure 8.4 The creative (nourishing) cycle and the destructive cycle of the five elements. For the nourishing relationships, follow the arrows of the circle. For the destructive relationships, follow the arrows of the star.

relationships are shown in figure 8.4. Study this figure carefully, because you will need to understand the relationships of the elements when you match occupants to a house and install countermeasures and enhancers. (See chapters 10 and 11 for discussions of countermeasures and enhancers.)

The effects of each element on nourishing, destroying, weakening by creating or nourishing, and weakening by destroying are shown in figure 8.5. You should study these relationships carefully. Eventually, you want to be able to use this information without referring to the table. In the meantime, you can photocopy figure 8.5 so that you can have it in front of you as you read the discussions in this chapter. Once you have identified the guardian star and element of each occupant and you are clear about the interactions of the five elements, you are ready to match the occupants to a house.

	METAL	WOOD	WATER	FIRE	EARTH
Metal	NE	WD	WN	D	N
Wood	D	NE	N	WN	WD
Water	N	WN	NE	WD	D
Fire	WD	N	D	NE	WN
Earth	WN	D	WD	N	NE

Figure 8.5 Relationships of the five elements. N, nourishing; D, destructive; WN, weakened by nourishing; WD, weakened by destroying; NE, no effect. Looking at the first row as an example, metal has no effect on metal, metal is weakened when it is used to destroy wood, metal is weakened when it is used to nourish water, metal is destroyed by fire, and metal is nourished by earth.

MATCHING HEADS OF HOUSEHOLD TO THE EARTH BASE OF THE FRONT ENTRANCE

wu facing

front door

4 1	8 6	6 8
6	2	4
bedroom	living room	bedroom

M F

5 9	3 2	1 4
5	7	9
bathroom and storeroom	living room	bedroom

9 5	7 7	2 3
1	3	8
outside	dining room	kitchen

tzu mountain

male head of family: one-white water
female head of family: five-yellow earth
male child: seven-red metal
grandmother: nine-purple fire

Figure 8.6 Geomantic chart of example discussed in the text. The guardian stars and elements of the occupants of the house also are shown.

First we will examine how the elements of the heads of household interact with the Earth Base of the palace where the front door is located. This interaction tells us how effective the head(s) of the household will be in providing support for the occupants.

Let's work through an example. Suppose that in a family both the husband and wife provide equal support. Figure 8.6 shows the geomantic chart for the family's house and the occupants' guardian stars. The front door is situated in the square where two-black is the Earth Base. In this example, the guardian element of the wife is earth (five-yellow). The relationship between her element and the element of the Earth Base at the door is neutral. Although her career may not have obstacles, it will not be very prosperous. The husband, however, will meet with obstacles in employment, because his guardian element, one-white water, is blocked (or destroyed) by earth. (Refer to figure 8.4 for the relationships of the five elements.)

Now do exercise 8.2 and determine how effective the head(s) of household are in supporting the family.

MATCHING OCCUPANTS TO THE BEDROOMS

Second, we find out which bedroom is the best for each occupant of the house. Some-times the best match may not be obvious at first, especially when there are many occupants. There are several important points to remember when matching occupants to bedrooms:

- Rooms with very inauspicious stars, such as Earth Base and Facing Star combinations of two-black and five-yellow and the stars of fire hazards (two-seven and nine-seven), should not be used as bedrooms at all.
- The bedroom should not be located in an area with the combination seven-nine, because this interaction presages severe illness. (Note that this unconditional interaction applies only to bedrooms. In all other rooms, it is to be treated as an additive interaction.)
- It is preferable for bedrooms to be rooms with either neutral or auspicious Facing stars.
- A bedroom with two-black as the Earth Base is suitable only for persons with two-black or five-yellow as their guardian star, and a bedroom with five-yellow as the Earth Base is suitable only for persons with five-yellow as their guardian star.
- A room with the combination six-nine should not be assigned to the eldest in the household, since the stars forebode illness for the eldest person.
- Rooms with the combinations two-three and three-two should not be assigned as bedrooms, because these combinations contribute to quarrels.

Example 1

When we match an individual to a bedroom, we examine the relationship between the person's guardian star and element and the Earth Base of the bedroom. To illustrate the process of fitting individuals to bedrooms, let's consider an example. Look at the geomantic chart and plan for the usage of space shown in figure 8.6. There are three bedrooms, with six-white, four-green, and nine-purple as Earth Base stars. The guardian elements and stars for the family occupying the house are one-white water (husband), five-yellow earth (wife), seven-red metal (male child), and nine-fire purple (grandmother).

Let's first consider which bedroom is best for the husband and wife. The bedroom with four-green wood in the Earth Base is not good for the wife, because wood destroys earth (refer to figure 8.5). It also is not good for the husband, because his guardian element, water, is weakened to create or nourish wood. The bedroom with six-white metal in the Earth Base is good for the husband, because water is nourished by metal. In this case, however, the wife's element (earth) will be weakened when it is used to nourish the metal of six-white in the Earth Base. Last, the bedroom with nine-purple fire in the Earth Base will be good for the wife, because fire nourishes her guardian element, earth. On the other hand, it is extremely bad for the husband, because his guardian element (water) will be weakened when it is used to destroy fire.

In our example, each bedroom has its problems, but which one has the least problem for the couple? Based on our analysis, the room with six-white metal in the Earth Base has the least harmful potential. Recall from the previous discussion that as a guardian star, five-yellow earth is stronger than one-white water. Thus, if the couple uses the room with six-white metal in the Earth Base as the bedroom, the woman's guardian element will be weakened only slightly, while the man will benefit tremendously. If they use the room with nine-purple fire in the Earth Base, the woman will benefit from it, but the man's guardian element, water, will be harmed severely. Since it is easier and safer to bolster the strength of a stronger star and element with countermeasures, the room with six-white metal in the Earth Base should be the couple's bedroom. When countermeasures are put in place (see chapter 10), the bedroom should become safe and usable.

Next, we will consider which bedroom is the best for the child, whose guardian star / element is seven-red metal. The room with nine-purple fire in the Earth Base clearly is not suitable, because fire destroys metal. The room with six-white metal in the Earth Base is neutral, because both six-white (the Earth Base) and seven-red (the child's guardian star) are associated with metal. The room with four-green wood in the Earth Base appears to be untenable, because metal is weakened when it destroys wood. Given this situation, I suggest that the child stay in the room with the parents if he is young. If he is old enough to have his own room, he should be put in the room with four-green wood in the Earth Base. Countermeasures (see chapter 10) should be set up to strengthen the child's guardian star / element (seven-red metal) or weaken the Earth Base Star's element (wood). Since four-green is only moderate in strength (see earlier discussion), it can be offset easily by the placement of countermeasures.

Finally, let's consider which bedroom is best for the grandmother. In our example, the guardian star / element of the grandmother is nine-purple fire. The room with six-white metal as the Earth Base is not appropriate, because fire is weakened when it destroys metal. The room with four-green wood as the Earth Base is excellent, because wood nourishes the grandmother's guardian element, fire. The room with nine-purple fire in the Earth Base is neutral toward her. Since this room is harmful for everybody else and neutral to her, this is the most suitable room.

Let's look at one more example of matching occupants to the house and the bedrooms.

Example 2

We have a house built in the seventh cycle with kuei as the mountain direction and ting as the facing direction. The occupants are a single mother with three teenage children. Their guardian stars and elements are two-black earth (the mother), three-jade wood (female teenager born in 1988), six-white metal (male teenager born in 1985), and eight-white earth (female teenager born in 1984). Our tasks are to evaluate the interaction between the guardian star / element of the head of household (two-black earth) and the Earth Base at the front door and to find suitable bedrooms for all four occupants.

Figure 8.7 shows the Nine Palaces superimposed onto the floor plan of the upper level of the house, where the bedrooms are located. The front door, in the lower level, is situated in the square with the combination two-six-eight. First, examining the relationship between the guardian star / element of the head of household and the Earth Base at the front door, we find that they are compatible. Both stars are two-black, which means that the career of the mother will be neither enhanced nor hampered by the Earth Base Star.

Second, looking at the floor plan of the upper level of the house, we find that there are four potential bedrooms, one large and three smaller ones. The room with the combination five-nine-five should not be used as a bedroom, because of the presence of the stars of illness. We would want to use this room for

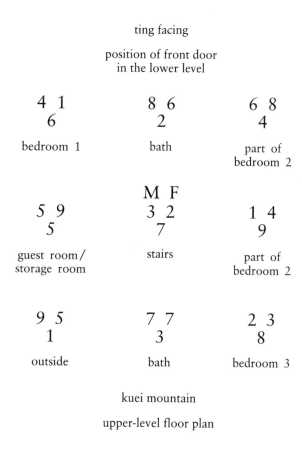

ting facing

position of front door
in the lower level

4 1	8 6	6 8
6	2	4
bedroom 1	bath	part of bedroom 2

M F

5 9	3 2	1 4
5	7	9
guest room / storage room	stairs	part of bedroom 2

9 5	7 7	2 3
1	3	8
outside	bath	bedroom 3

kuei mountain

upper-level floor plan

female head of family: two-black earth
female child: three-jade wood
male child: six-white metal
female child: eight-white earth

Figure 8.7 Geomantic chart of example 2 discussed in the text. The guardian stars and elements of the occupants of the house also are shown.

storage or as a guest bedroom. (Persons who do not use a room for at least six months are not affected by the Nine Palace stars of the room.) This leaves us three bedrooms to consider—the large one (bedroom 2) with the combinations four-eight-six and nine-four-one, and the two smaller ones (bedrooms 1 and 3) with the combinations six-one-four and eight-three-two, respectively.

Before we begin to match the occupants to their bedrooms, let's rank the occupants' guardian stars in terms of their strengths. Usually we try to find a suitable bedroom for the occupant with the weakest guardian star first, because he or she needs the most protection. In our example, ranking the guardian stars from weakest to strongest, we get eight-white earth, six-white metal, three-jade wood, and two-black earth.

First, we will try to find a suitable bedroom for the female occupant whose guardian star / element is eight-white earth. The room with eight-white earth in the Earth Base is compatible with this individual's guardian star / element and is therefore a viable choice. The room with six-white metal in the Earth Base will weaken the energy of eight-white, because its earth energy is used to create or nourish metal. In the large bedroom, the section with nine-purple fire in the Earth Base will nourish the guardian star / element eight-white earth. The other half of the room, with four-green wood in the Earth Base, is not suitable for her, because wood destroys earth. Given this analysis, we have three choices. The first is to give this occupant the bedroom with eight-white earth in the Earth Base. This room will neither help nor harm her. The second possibility is to divide the large bedroom into two rooms and make the room with nine-purple fire in the Earth Base the bedroom for this girl. The third choice is to have the two female children share the large room. This alternative will depend on how the rest of the family members are matched to the bedrooms.

Second, we will consider the male teenager with the guardian star / element six-white metal. The room with eight-white earth in the Earth Base is best for him, because earth nourishes metal. The room with six-white metal in the Earth Base is compatible with his guardian star / element and is therefore a viable choice. The large room has Earth Base stars that destroy or weaken his guardian star / element. (The fire of nine-purple destroys six-white metal, and six-white metal is weakened when it is used to destroy the wood in four-green.)

The guardian star / element of the third occupant, a teenage girl, is three-jade wood, which is compatible with the section of the large bedroom where four-green wood is the Earth Base. Looking at the Earth Base stars of the other rooms, we find that her guardian star / element will be weakened when it is used to nourish the fire of nine-purple and destroy the earth of eight-white. Furthermore, it will be destroyed by the metal of six-white. Thus, the only suitable room for this occupant is the section of the room with four-green wood in the Earth Base. Given this analysis, there are two alternatives. The first is to partition the large room and assign the room with four-green wood in the Earth Base to the teenage daughter whose guardian star / element is three-jade. The second choice is to have the two teenage daughters share this large room. We can put the bed for the daughter whose guardian / star element is three-jade wood in the section with four-green wood in the Earth Base and put the bed for the other daughter, whose guardian star / element is eight-white earth, in the section where nine-purple fire is the Earth Base.

The mother's guardian star / element is two-black earth, which is compatible with the room with eight-white earth in the Earth Base. Looking at the other rooms, we find that her guardian star / element will be weakened in the room with six-white metal in the Earth Base and destroyed in the section of the large room where four-green wood is the Earth Base. She will be nourished, however, in the part of the large room where nine-purple fire is the Earth Base.

Given this analysis, here is the conclusion. If they are willing, the two female teenagers should share the large room. The one with three-jade wood as her guardian star / element will have the section of the room with four-green wood in the Earth Base, and the one with eight-white earth as her guardian star / element will have the section with nine-purple fire in the Earth Base. If they are not willing to share a room, then I suggest the large room be partitioned. The male teenager, whose guardian star / element is six-white metal, will have the room with six-white metal in the Earth Base. Finally, the mother, whose guardian star / element is two-black earth, will have the bedroom with eight-white earth in the Earth Base.

Throughout the two examples, you will notice that the effects of the Earth Base guardian stars on all the occupants of the house are considered before a decision is made. It is rare that all the occupants can be put in bedrooms with an Earth Base Star that nourishes their elements. Very often you will need to juggle the possibilities before you can arrive at a satisfactory decision. The process of matching occupants to bedrooms is not easy. You will need considerable practice before you become competent. Now do exercise 8.3 and familiarize yourself with the principles of the interactions of the five elements in matching people to appropriate bedrooms.

EXERCISES

EXERCISE 8.1

Identify the guardian stars and elements of people with the following birth dates. Remember that for a person born in January or February, you need to check whether the date falls before or after the Chinese New Year. No. 1 is a worked example.

1. Female born on August 23, 1928
  The guardian star / element is six-white metal.

2. Male born on January 31, 1967
3. Male born on March 1, 1998
4. Female born on December 26, 1934
5. Female born on February 12, 1916

EXERCISE 8.2

Evaluate the interaction between the guardian star and element of the head of household and the Earth Base located at the front door. No. 1 is a worked example.

1. Earth Base of six-white and female born on November 1, 1956
  The guardian star / element is seven-red metal, and it is compatible with the Earth Base six-white metal. The effect of the interaction is neutral.

2. Three-jade and male born on February 19, 1946
3. One-white and male born on June 3, 1923
4. Five-yellow and female born on December 22, 1924
5. Eight-white and female born on January 3, 1961

EXERCISE 8.3

Match these occupants to bedrooms and give reasons for your choice. No. 1 is a worked example.

1. The occupants are one couple—a male born on July 7, 1953, and a female born on April 11, 1961—and their female child, born on March 4, 1991. The Earth Base stars of potential bedrooms are six-white, three-jade, and eight-white. Guardian star / elements for the couple are these: two-black earth for the male and three-jade wood for the female. The female child has six-white metal for her guardian star and element.

Room 1: Earth Base six-white metal
  This room is harmful to the guardian star / element two-black earth, because earth en-

ergy is dissipated to create metal. It also is harmful to three-jade wood, because metal destroys wood. It is compatible with the guardian star / element six-white metal, because they are identical. This room is viable for the individual whose guardian star / element is six-white metal.

Room 2: Earth Base three-jade wood

This room is damaging to the guardian star / element two-black earth, because wood destroys earth. It is compatible with three-jade wood, because they belong to the same element (wood). It is harmful to six-white metal, because metal energy is drained to destroy wood. This room is unsuitable for all three occupants.

Room 3: Earth Base eight-white earth

This room is compatible with the guardian star two-black, because they both belong to the element earth. It is harmful to three-jade wood, because wood energy is drained to destroy earth. It nourishes six-white metal, because earth creates metal. This is an excellent room for the individual whose guardian star / element is six-white earth.

In the final match, the couple should have the bedroom with three-jade as the Earth Base, because two-black earth is a stronger guardian than three-jade wood. It is easier to use countermeasures to protect two-black earth against the Earth Base three-jade wood than it is to protect three-jade wood against the Earth Base two-black earth. The child, of course, should occupy the room with eight-white earth as the Earth Base.

2. The occupants are one couple—a female born on November 1, 1965, and a male born on January 7, 1960. The Earth Base stars of the potential bedrooms are nine-purple, seven-red, and six-white.

3. The occupants are one mother and two children—a female born on July 9, 1952; a female born on August 19, 1987; and a male born on March 31, 1982. The Earth Base stars of the potential bedrooms are one-white, four-green, seven-red, and eight-white.

ANSWERS

EXERCISE 8.1

2. Seven-red metal (corrected for 1966)
3. Two-black earth
4. Three-jade wood
5. Three-jade wood

EXERCISE 8.2

2. Nine-purple fire is nourishing.
3. Five-yellow earth is harmful.
4. Two-black earth is compatible.
5. Three-jade wood is harmful.

EXERCISE 8.3

2. The guardian star / element for the female is seven-red metal and for the male is five-yellow earth (corrected for 1959).

Room 1: Earth Base nine-purple fire

This room is not suitable for the female, since fire destroys metal. It will nourish the male, because fire nourishes earth. Since seven-red metal is a guardian of moderate strength, it is not advisable to put the couple in this room.

Room 2: Earth Base seven-red metal

This room is suitable for the female, since her guardian star / element is the same as the Earth Base. The seven-red metal will dissipate the energy of five-yellow earth, because earth nourishes metal. For this reason, this room is not appropriate for the male.

Room 3: Earth Base six-white metal

The analysis is similar to that for room 2. Given this situation, we should put the couple in the room with six-white metal as the Earth Base. Since five-yellow earth is a very strong guardian star, it will be easier to protect the individual with this guardian than the person with the weaker guardian seven-red metal. The protection measures also will be more effective against six-white metal, which is weaker than seven-red metal.

3. The guardian stars / elements are these: three-jade wood (mother), two-black earth (male child), and nine-purple fire (female child).

Room 1: Earth Base one-white water

This room will nourish the guardian star / element three-jade wood, since water creates wood. It is harmful to two-black earth, because earth energy is drained to block water. It is also detrimental to nine-purple fire, because water destroys fire. This room is best for the individual whose guardian star / element is three-jade wood.

Room 2: Earth Base four-green wood

This room is compatible with the guardian star / element three-jade wood (both elements are wood). It is harmful to two-black earth, because wood destroys earth. It is nourishing to nine-purple fire, because wood creates fire. This room is viable for the individual whose guardian star / element is three-jade wood, but it is excellent for the individual whose guardian star / element is nine-purple fire.

Room 3: Earth Base seven-red metal

This room is harmful to the guardian star / element three-jade wood, because wood energy is destroyed by metal. It also is detrimental to two-black earth, because earth energy is dissipated to create metal. And it is harmful to nine-purple fire, because fire energy is drained to destroy metal. This room is unsuitable for all three occupants.

Room 4: Earth Base eight-white earth

This room is damaging to the guardian star / element three-jade wood, because wood energy is drained to destroy earth. It is compatible with two-black earth, because both elements are earth. It is harmful to nine-purple fire, because fire energy is dissipated to create earth. This room is appropriate for the individual whose guardian star / element is two-black earth.

The final match of appropriate bedrooms for each person is Earth Base one-white water with guardian star / element three-jade wood, Earth Base four-green wood with nine-purple fire, and Earth Base eight-white earth with two-black earth.

9

Placement of Furniture

The last thing we do in analyzing the feng-shui of a house is to consider the placement of furniture, appliances, and interior features, such as fireplaces.

SUPERIMPOSING THE GEOMANTIC CHART ONTO EACH ROOM

Before we can work on the placement of furniture and appliances, we need to superimpose the geomantic chart onto the microcosm of each room. When superimposing the stars of the Nine Palaces onto a room, we interpret the meanings of the Earth Base, the Facing Star, the Mountain Star, and their combinations in the same way as when we superimposed the Nine Palaces onto the macrocosm of the building. The only difference is that there is no Facing Palace and thus no conditional interaction. Applying the interactions of the numbers of the Nine Palaces to a room tells us how to place furniture and plan usage of space in that room.

Figure 9.1 shows an example of the geomantic chart for the house fitted to an individual room. Note that the chart is oriented in the same way as it is for the macrocosm of the house. Before we begin to evaluate the meanings of the stars of the Nine Palaces in each room, we need to have an idea of the frequency of activity in each room.

The bedrooms are the most important rooms in the house. Considering that most people sleep for at least six hours a day, the bedroom turns out to be the room with the highest level of use. Next in importance is the kitchen, which is associated with health and livelihood. Depending on the occupants, the family room, study / home office, or the living room may be next in order of significance. Finally, the bathroom, utility room, and storage rooms usually have the lowest frequency of usage. Let's look at the ways in which we can use the information of the stars of the Nine Palaces to place furniture and appliances.

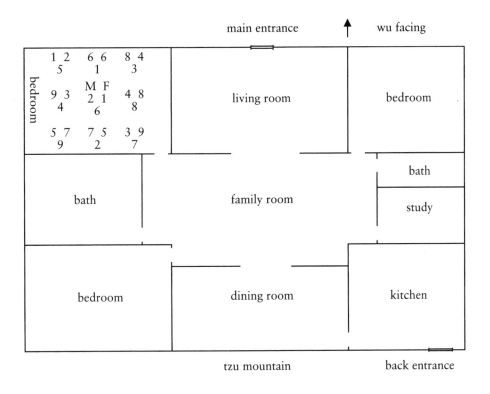

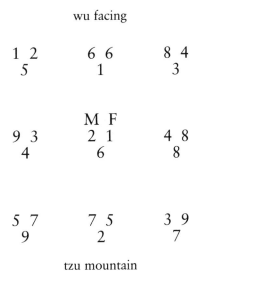

Figure 9.1 Superimposing the Nine Palaces onto a room in a house.

Bedrooms

These are the points to remember when you are arranging furniture in the bedroom:

- The bed should be in an area with stars of health and good fortune. Earth Base / Facing Star combinations of one-white, four-green, six-white, and eight-white are ideal. It does not matter which number is the Facing Star and which is the Earth Base. If it is not possible to position the bed in such a location, you should put it in a spot where one of these auspicious stars is the Facing Star. The exception is the combination eight-four, which is associated with childhood illness. If children are not occupying that room, the interaction is not applicable.
- Never place the bed in areas where there are stars of illness. Earth Base / Facing Star combinations of five-yellow and two-black are the worst, and it does not matter which number is the Earth Base and which is the Facing Star. In fact, you should not put the bed in an area where either two-black or five-yellow is the Facing Star or the Earth Base.
- Additional furniture, such as desks, should be placed in areas where there are stars of good health and fortune (Earth Base / Facing Star combinations of one-white, four-green, six-white, and eight-white).
- Mirrors should not face the bed, windows, or doors.
- Make sure that there are no exposed beams or ceiling edges above the bed. Ceiling edges are transitions between ceilings of different heights. Some houses have internal balconies that look down into the living room or family room, for instance. This design creates a difference in ceiling height in the room below the balcony. Rooms also may have a recessed ceiling in one area, which creates ceiling edges. A ceiling edge acts like a guillotine poised over the people who sit underneath.

Figure 9.2 shows an example of how furniture is placed in a bedroom. In the bedroom showing the superimposed Nine Palaces (bedroom 1), the unconditional interactions are these:

- Five-two: This combination forebodes serious illness, making it a bad spot for a bed.
- One-six: This is an extremely auspicious combination, signifying good health and prosperity. This is an excellent position for a bed or a desk.
- Six-one: This is another excellent area, associated with good health and prosperity.
- Eight-eight: This area is also excellent. It promotes good health and prosperity and is therefore a good location for a bed or desk.
- Seven-nine: This combination occupies the doorway to the bedroom. It foreshadows political intrigues and problems with the government. You should never do your taxes in an area with this combination!
- Two-five: This combination portends serious illness. The bed or desk should not be placed here.
- Nine-seven: This combination presages fire caused by human activity. The occupant needs to be very careful with objects that may cause fire, such as matches, electrical outlets, and the like.

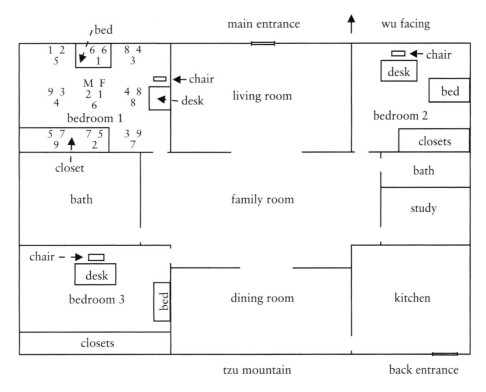

Figure 9.2 Placing furniture in bedrooms.

The additive interactions in the bedroom are these:

- Three-four-eight: Three-jade is neutral, but four-green and eight-white are auspicious stars, both carrying benevolent energy. The net effect makes this a good spot for a bed or desk.
- Four-three-nine: Four-green is auspicious, but as the Earth Base it has only a modest level of influence. The Facing Star, three-jade, is neutral. Because there are no inauspicious unconditional interactions or malevolent stars here, the nine-purple has no effect. This is a viable spot for a table or a dresser.

Kitchen

These are the points to remember when you are arranging appliances and furniture in the kitchen:

- Appliances such as the cooking stove, microwave oven, toaster, and so on, should not be placed in areas where nine-purple fire is the Facing Star or the Earth Base. Otherwise, there will be injuries associated with fire. If the stove cannot be moved easily to avoid the nine-purple, countermeasures will have to be installed (see chapter 10).
- The kitchen table should not be posi-

tioned in areas with combinations of two-three or three-two. These combinations foster disharmony at dinner.

- The eating area should be located where there are stars of good health and good fortune—combinations of one-white, four-green, six-white, and eight-white in the Earth Base and Facing Star. (The exception is the combination eight-four, which is associated with illness in children.) If this is not possible, you should situate the table in an area where one of these auspicious stars is the Facing Star.
- Do not place the kitchen table or chairs and sofas under exposed beams or ceiling edges.

Figure 9.3 depicts an example of the placement of appliances and furniture in the kitchen.

The Family Room / Recreation Room

The most important pieces of furniture in the family room are the ones that are used frequently. These can include couches, television, video and stereo systems, recreation equipment (such as video game machines and computers), pianos, playpens, and exercise equipment.

These are the points to remember when

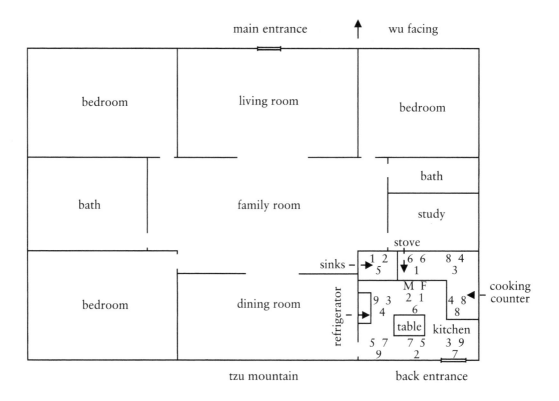

Figure 9.3 Placing furniture and appliances in the kitchen.

you are arranging furniture in the family room:

- In general, frequently used furniture and objects should not be placed in areas where there are two-black and five-yellow combinations in the Facing Star and Earth Base.
- Specifically, objects that are shared among the occupants should not be situated in areas where there are stars of disharmony—combinations of two-three and three-two.
- The ideal spots for frequently used furniture and objects are areas where one of the auspicious stars (one-white, four-green, six-white, and eight-white) is the Facing Star.
- If the fireplace is located in an area where nine-purple is either the Facing Star or the Earth Base, countermeasures will have to be installed to neutralize the fire hazard (see chapter 10).
- Do not place chairs or sofas under exposed beams or ceiling edges.

Figure 9.4 shows an example of the placement of furniture in the family room.

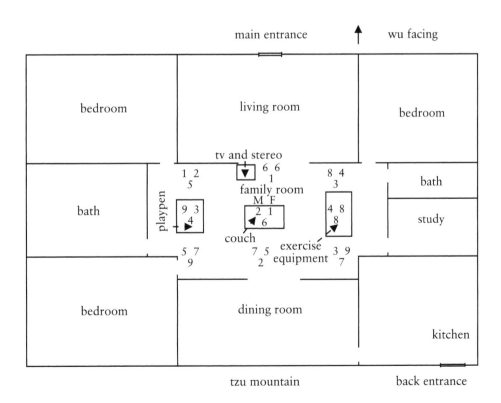

Figure 9.4 Placing furniture in the family room.

The Study / Home Office

Desks and computer workstations should be situated in areas where the stars of prosperity and academic success are located. These are the points to remember when you are arranging desks and computer workstations:

- The ideal spots are areas in the room with the Earth Base / Facing Star combinations of one-four, four-one, six-eight, and four-six. It does not matter which number is the Earth Base and which is the Facing Star.
- Areas with combinations of one, four, six, and eight, except for the combination eight-four, also are desirable, because they are stars of good fortune.
- The worst spots are areas that have Earth Base / Facing Star combinations of two-black and five-yellow. It does not matter which number is the Earth Base and which is the Facing Star.
- Spots with combinations of seven-six and six-seven are undesirable, because they forebode loss of fortune.
- Spots with combinations of two-three and three-two also are undesirable, because they contribute to competition and quarrels.
- Work areas should not be located where there are combinations that promote fire—two-seven and nine-seven.
- Do not put a desk or workstation in an area with the combination seven-nine, because these stars augur problems involving government matters.
- The facing directions of the desk and workstation are important. Ideally, these items should face an area that is occupied by auspicious stars. If this is also

the doorway to the room, the auspicious effects are enhanced.
- Do not place desks, computer workstations, and chairs under exposed beams or ceiling edges.

Figure 9.5 shows an example of the placement of desks and computer workstations in the study or home office.

Living Room

If the living room is used frequently by the occupants or to entertain guests with business connections, the furniture should be placed in areas occupied by auspicious stars. If it is used infrequently, the furniture can be situated in areas with neutral stars. Regardless of the frequency of usage, furniture should not be positioned in areas where there are inauspicious stars.

These are the points to remember when arranging furniture in the living room:

- If the room is used frequently, chairs and sofas should be placed in spots occupied by auspicious stars—Earth Base / Facing Star combinations of one, four, six, and eight. It does not matter which number is the Earth Base and which is the Facing Star. The exception is the combination eight-four.
- Even if the living room is not used often, the sitting furniture should not be positioned in spots occupied by inauspicious stars—combinations of two-three, three-two, six-seven, or seven-six.
- Do not place furniture in areas with Earth Base / Facing Star combinations of two-black and five-yellow.
- Ideally, the fireplace should not occupy an area with combinations of two-seven

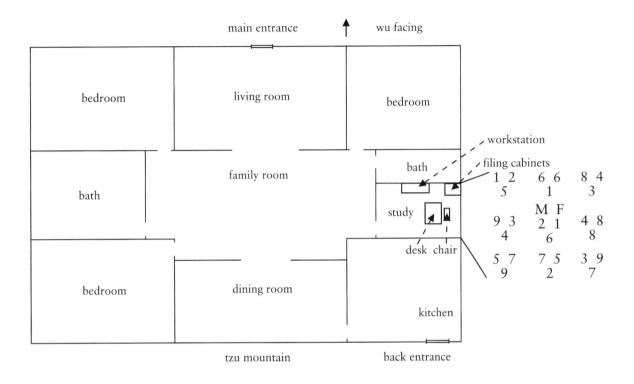

Figure 9.5 Placing furniture in the study and home office.

and nine-seven—the stars of fire hazard. Because it is difficult to move a fireplace once it is built, countermeasures will have to be installed if the fireplace is located in an area with a risk of fire. (See chapter 10 for methods of neutralizing fire hazards.)

- Do not place chairs or sofas under exposed beams or ceiling edges.

Figure 9.6 shows an example of the placement of furniture in the living room.

Dining Room

If the dining room is used regularly by the occupants of the house, the dining table and chairs should be placed in areas with auspicious stars. If it is used infrequently, the furniture can be situated in areas with neutral stars. Regardless of the frequency of use, the dining table should not be placed in an area occupied by inauspicious stars.

These are the points to remember when you are arranging furniture in the dining room:

- The best spots are areas occupied by Earth Base / Facing Star combinations of one, four, six, and eight. It does not matter which number is the Earth Base and which is the Facing Star. The exception is the combination eight-four.
- The worst spots are areas occupied by

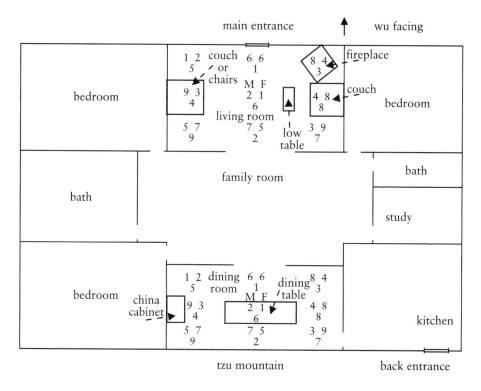

Figure 9.6 Placing furniture in the living room and dining room.

the combinations two-three, three-two, six-seven, and seven-six. Even if the dining room is used infrequently, the dining table should not be placed in these areas.

- Do not position the dining table and chairs in areas occupied by Earth Base / Facing Star combinations of two-black and five-yellow.
- If there is a fireplace, and if it is in an area occupied by two-seven or nine-seven, countermeasures will have to be installed (see chapter 10).
- Do not situate the dining table and the chairs under exposed beams or ceiling edges.

See figure 9.6 for an example of the best

placement of dining room furniture.

Now that you have an idea of how furniture should be positioned according to the arrangement of the stars of the Nine Palaces within a room, do exercise 9.1.

This concludes the introduction to the basics of feng-shui.

After you have understood the materials and completed the exercises in part one, you are ready to work on the special topics in part two. Part two assumes that you have mastered the materials in part one. If you are unsure about any aspects of the basics of feng-shui, this is the time to go back and review them.

EXERCISES

EXERCISE 9.1

Generate the geomantic charts for the floor plans shown in figure 9.7. First, evaluate the positions of the appliances and furniture in the kitchens. Then work out the placement of furniture (beds, tables, desks, computer workstations, couches, and home entertainment equipment) in the bedrooms, family room, study, living room, and dining room in each example. The facing direction and the cycle in which each house was built are given in the floor plan. No. 1 is a partially worked example.

1.

Kitchen
- *The cooking stove is located in an area occupied by the combination 2/2/6. The 2/2 combination is associated with illness. This is not a good area to place a cooking stove.*
- *The sink is in a neutral location.*
- *The breakfast table is situated in an area with beneficial effects carried by four-green in the Facing Star and eight-white in the Mountain Star. Nine-purple is neutral, because it is not in the presence of malevolent stars. This is a good place for the breakfast table.*

Now evaluate the placement of the counter and the refrigerator.

Complete the project by superimposing the geomantic chart onto the other rooms and positioning furniture. Note that sometimes you will need to consider the makeup of the room as well as the palace stars when you place furniture. For example, the hallway or the entranceway into a room may have beneficial stars, but it would be inappropriate to place a dining table there.

2. and 3.

For examples 2 and 3, generate the geomantic charts and evaluate the placement of kitchen appliances and furniture. Superimpose the charts onto the rooms and position furniture in the other rooms. Since no specific room is designated as a study, place desks in the bedrooms.

1

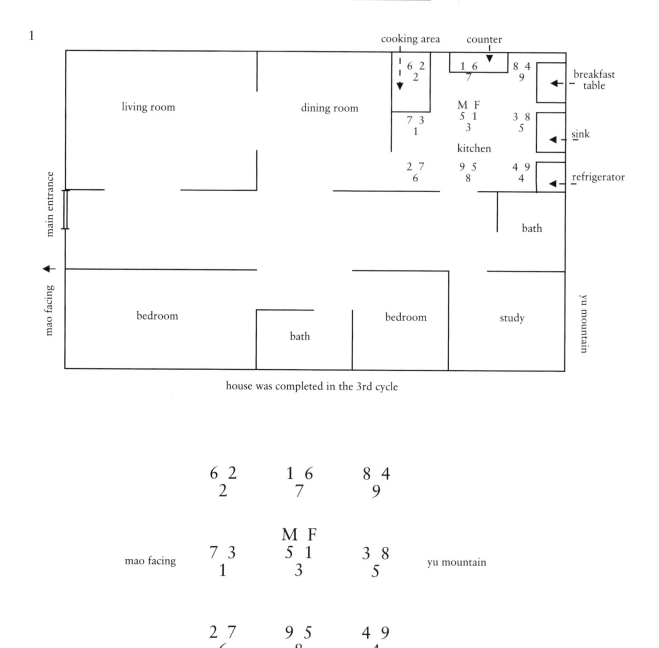

Figure 9.7 Evaluating the placement of appliances in the kitchen and the placement of furniture in three sample houses (continued on next page).

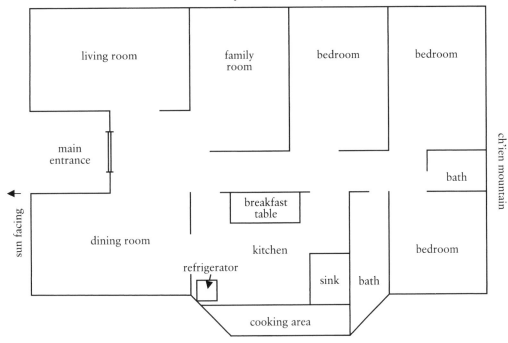

2

house was completed in the 6th cycle

living room

family room

bedroom

bedroom

ch'ien mountain

main entrance

bath

sun facing

dining room

breakfast table

kitchen

bath

bedroom

refrigerator

sink

bath

cooking area

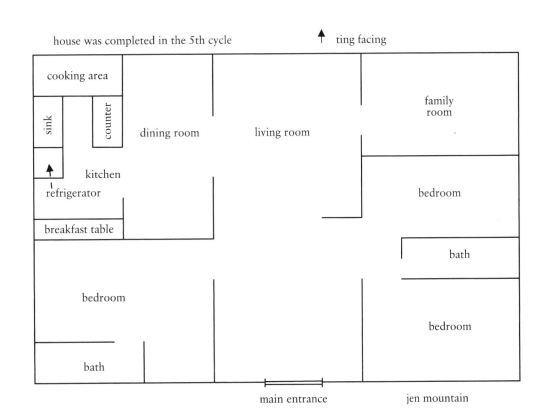

3

house was completed in the 5th cycle

ting facing

cooking area

family room

sink

counter

dining room

living room

kitchen

bedroom

refrigerator

breakfast table

bath

bedroom

bedroom

bath

main entrance

jen mountain

ANSWERS

EXERCISE 9.1

1.

Kitchen
- The counter is located at a spot that forebodes robbery—7/6. It should not be used frequently.
- The refrigerator is placed in a beneficial spot. The additive interaction yields a sizable benevolent effect carried by four-green in the Earth Base and in the Mountain Star. Nine-purple is neutral, because it is not in the presence of two-black or five-yellow.

Bedrooms
- Beds should be placed in the spots occupied by 4/9/4, 9/4/8, or 1/3/7.

Study
- Desks should be situated in the spot occupied by 4/9/4 and face 9/4/8 or in 9/4/8 and face 4/9/4.

Living room
- Couches, chairs, and home entertainment equipment should be placed in spots occupied by 9/4/8, 4/9/4, and 1/3/7.

Dining room
- The dining table should be positioned lengthwise occupying the squares 1/3/7, 3/1/5, and 5/8/3.

2.

Reoriented chart

```
        3  9      1  2      5  7
          1          3          8


                     M  F
sun      8  4      7  5      6  6    ch'ien
facing     5          6          7        mountain


        Facing
        Palace


        9  3      4  8      2  1
          4          9          2
```

Kitchen
- The cooking area is located in an area occupied by 9/8/4 and 4/3/9. Although 9/8 is associated with fame, we need to be careful about the presence of nine-purple, especially when nine-purple is found in the cooking area. This is a viable area for the stove if countermeasures are introduced to lessen the threat of fire.
- The sink is positioned in an area associated with robbery and violence. Frequent use of this place will increase the threat.
- The breakfast table is situated in an area with the stars of disharmony—3/2. This is not a good place for the breakfast table.
- The refrigerator is located in a spot with a modest beneficial effect, carried by

four-green in the Earth Base. Nine-purple is not a problem here, because it is not in the presence of two-black and five-yellow and it is not located in the cooking area.

Bedrooms
- Beds should be placed in the spots occupied by the combinations 1/9/3, 4/3/9, or 9/8/4. The desk should be placed in the spot occupied by 9/8/4 (the stars of fame), and it should face 4/3/9 or 1/9/3.

Living room
- Couches, chairs, and home entertainment equipment should be placed in areas occupied by the combinations 1/9/3, 5/4/8, 4/3/9, or 8/7/5. The spot occupied by the auspicious combination 9/8 is the entranceway. Furniture cannot be placed there, but frequent use of that area will enhance the benevolent effects of this combination.

Dining room
- The dining table should be situated toward one side of the room, in the squares occupied by the combinations 1/9/3, 5/4/8, and 4/3/9. It is also possible to position a shorter dining table in the squares 9/8/4 and 4/3/9.

Family room
- Furniture and home entertainment systems should be placed in the areas with the combination 1/9/3, 5/4/8, 4/3/9, or 8/7/5. The spot with the auspicious combination 9/8 is the entranceway. Furniture cannot be placed there. Frequent use of the area, however, will enhance the benevolent effects of this combination of stars.

3.
Geomantic chart

ting facing

2 1	6 5	4 3
4	9	2
	Facing	
	Palace	

M F

3 2	1 9	8 7
3	5	7

7 6	5 4	9 8
8	1	6

kuei mountain

Kitchen
- The cooking area is located in an area occupied by 4/1/2, 9/5/6, and 2/3/4. Since the location of the stove is constrained by the sink and counter on both ends, the stove occupies an area with a combination that fosters illness—9/5. This is a bad area for cooking food.
- The right side of the cooking area is occupied by the combination 2/3, the stars of disharmony, making this a bad area for preparing food. Unfortunately, the area with the auspicious combination 4/1 is tucked away in the corner and therefore cannot be utilized fully.
- The sink is located in an area with the combination 3/2, the stars of disharmony. These stars forebode quarrels over dishwashing and cleaning.

- The breakfast table is positioned in an area with auspicious stars. The combination 6/8 means success in business, the combination 8/6 indicates success in artistic pursuits, and the combination 1/4 presages success in academic pursuits. This is a good area to work on the household finances or even to do homework.
- The counter is located at a spot where there is a small benevolent effect carried by the Mountain Star eight-white.
- The refrigerator is found in a spot with the combination 3/2, the stars of disharmony. This promotes quarrels over food and the use of the refrigerator.

Bedrooms

- Beds should be placed in the spots occupied by 8/6/7, 1/4/5, 4/1/2, or 6/8/9, as should desks.

Living room

- Couches, chairs, and home entertainment equipment should be placed in areas occupied by the combinations 4/1/2, 8/6/7, 1/4/5, and 6/8/9. Furniture also can be put in the square with the combination 7/7/8, where there is a small benevolent effect.

Dining room

- The dining table should be positioned toward one side of the room, in the squares occupied by the combinations 8/6/7, 1/4/5, and 6/8/9. It is also possible to put a shorter dining table in the squares 6/8/9 and 7/7/8.

Family room

- Furniture and home entertainment systems should be placed in the squares with the combinations 8/6/7, 1/4/5, 6/8/9, 4/1/2, and 7/7/8.

PART TWO

SPECIAL
TOPICS

In part two, you will learn how to install countermeasures and enhancers and how to incorporate the principles of feng-shui into remodeling and renovations. Since these techniques are applied after the external and internal environments and the stars of the Nine Palaces have been evaluated, you will need to be familiar with the materials covered in part one before you attempt to study the chapters in this section.

10

Installing Countermeasures

Countermeasures deal with adverse conditions and are designed to help us avoid, dissolve, weaken, or remove destructive energy. Ideal feng-shui conditions are rare; most of the time we have to live with what we can get or what we have. Countermeasures can be used to work with the external and internal environments, the stars of the Nine Palaces, and the guardian elements of the occupants. We will cover each of these topics in turn.

COUNTERMEASURES FOR THE EXTERNAL ENVIRONMENT

Protection Measures

Protection is a very important factor in the feng-shui of a place. If there is no existing protection, you will have to create your own. For protection at the back, a row of trees can be an effective Black Tortoise. If planting trees is not feasible, a fence or a wall with vines or ivy can serve the purpose. Bushes, preferably evergreen, will make an effective Green Dragon, and a white stone wall can be a viable White Tiger. If you need protection in front, you can build a low red-brick wall or a low redwood fence to serve as the Red Raven.

Types of Countermeasures Against Harmful Structures

Recall from chapter 1 that harsh and sharp objects; precarious, falling, or colliding objects; and reflective objects all carry destructive energy. If any of these objects are in the immediate vicinity of a building, countermeasures should be set up to neutralize them. The destructive energy imparted by harmful structures and objects can be countered by strategic placement of artifacts that will reflect, absorb, deflect, bounce, block, or destroy (figures 10.1 and 10.2).

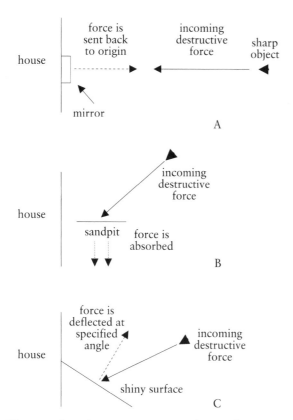

Figure 10.1 Countermeasures that reflect (A), absorb (B), and deflect (C).

REFLECTORS

Reflectors send the destructive effect back to the harmful object, thus preventing it from entering the house. Mirrors, a large piece of foil or shiny aluminum surface, and a basin or pool of water all can be used as reflectors. When you position a reflector, make sure that the structure or object you want to ward off is imaged on it. While you can reflect small objects with a small mirror, you may need a large mirror to reflect a large structure.

ABSORBERS

Absorbers are designed to absorb or "eat up" the destructive power of a structure or object and prevent it from spreading. It is like

pushing a needle into a pincushion or cushioning the impact of a rock with a bed of cotton wool. A sandpit or a pile of cedar chips can work well as an absorber. For the absorber to be effective, it must be placed in the angle at which the sharp structure is pointing. Therefore, the absorber type of countermeasure typically is used when the harmful object is higher than the house. For example, a sandpit can be positioned in the backyard of a house to counter the effect of an antenna that is pointing down from a hilltop.

DEFLECTORS

Deflectors are designed to redirect the path of destructive energy away from a building. A system of reflective surfaces, such as mirrors, can be used as a deflector if their angles are adjusted so that the reflection is directed at another place rather than the source of incoming destructive energy. Deflectors are tricky to set up. Novice feng-shui practitioners should not use this countermeasure, because an error in the placement of deflectors can send destructive energy to a neighboring house and harm the occupants.

BOUNCERS

Bouncers are designed to bounce the effect of a harmful structure away from the building. Because there is no way of controlling the direction toward which the incoming destructive force will be bounced, this countermeasure should be used only if there are no neighboring buildings that can be harmed. Effective bouncers include coils of springs, a baseball bat, or boxing gloves mounted on the ends of sticks—or pictures of these objects.

BLOCKERS

Blockers are designed to stop an incoming destructive effect and prevent it from entering

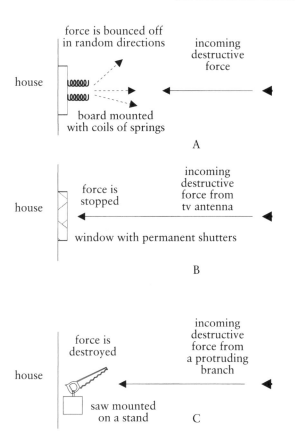

force is bounced off
in random directions   incoming
                              destructive
                              force

house

board mounted
with coils of springs

A

force is   incoming
stopped   destructive
house   force from
                tv antenna

window with permanent shutters

B

                incoming
force is   destructive
destroyed   force from
                a protruding
house   branch

saw mounted
on a stand   C

Figure 10.2 Countermeasures that bounce (A), block (B), and destroy (C).

a building. They work like a closed door; in fact, boarded-up windows or windows with permanent shutters are the most common kind of blocker.

DESTRUCTORS

Destructors are designed to destroy the incoming harmful energy, and this type of countermeasure must be an object that can overcome the source of the destructive energy. Typically, the countermeasure itself is an object of destruction. Moreover, for the countermeasure to work properly, it must be stronger than the structure it is designed to destroy. For example, if the harmful object is a protruding branch, you might use a saw (figure 10.2). If it is a sculpture with pointed arrows, you might use a gun or a cannon (figure 10.3). If it is a set of power lines, bury scissors or knives in the ground underneath the power lines with the blades directed toward the lines.

How to Use Countermeasures Against Harmful Objects

Harsh, sharp, and threatening structures and objects—rocky escarpments, knife-edge rock slabs, buildings with irregular and razor-like edges, tree branches, antennas, sculpture that resembles weaponry or other implements of destruction, power transformers, and similar harmful objects or their images—are best countered by such countermeasures as reflectors, deflectors, absorbers, blockers, and destructors. Bouncers are too dangerous to use against these types of structures.

Precarious, falling, and colliding objects—large boulders overlooking the house, slopes with loose rocks, and driveways and roads pointing at the house—are best countered by reflectors, deflectors, bouncers, blockers, and absorbers. Remember, bouncers should be used only where there are no neighboring buildings. The most effective countermeasure against driveways and roads is a mirror. (See box 10.1 for setting up countermeasures against harmful road patterns.)

Reflecting objects—satellite dishes, solar panels, shiny surfaces of cars, reflections off windows or pools—are best countered by deflectors and blockers. Do not use bouncers and destructors, since your countermeasure will be reflected back to you. Absorbers simply do not work against reflecting objects.

Now that you are familiar with the different types of countermeasures used to neutralize harmful effects in the external

Figure 10.3 A miniature cannon used as a countermeasure. A one-foot ruler is shown for scale.

environment, try exercise 10.1. Designing countermeasures is an art. Creativity and experience both play a large part in creating an effective and elegant countermeasure against harmful structures and situations. You can refine this skill by finding objects that carry destructive energy and then trying to design ways to neutralize them.

COUNTERMEASURES FOR THE INTERNAL ENVIRONMENT

These are the interior structures that need to be neutralized by countermeasures:

- If structures and objects that are associated with fire, such as fireplaces, woodstoves, and cooking stoves, are located in an area where nine-purple is the Earth Base and/or the Facing Star, the fire hazard can be serious. The countermeasure for fire is water. The physical presence of water, as in a fountain, water tank, humidifier, or images of waterfalls and waves, is an appropriate option. Pictures of stagnant or still water will not work. The artifact used as countermeasure should be placed as close as possible to the object that carries the fire element. Thus, you can hang a picture of a waterfall above the fireplace or position a fish tank nearby. If there is a sink near the

BOX 10.1

COUNTERMEASURES AGAINST HARMFUL ROADS

Some harmful road patterns require strong countermeasures. Figure B10.1 shows suggested countermeasures for four especially dangerous road patterns. The pa-k'ua mirror is a powerful object designed to ward off disasters (figure 10.12a in the text). The mirror in the center is used to reflect incoming destructive forces, and the eight trigrams (pa-k'ua) surrounding the mirror help gather and focus cosmic energy to strengthen the reflective power of the mirror. Each trigram is made up of a combination of solid and broken lines representing types of cosmic energy. Starting at the top and moving clockwise, the eight types of cosmic energy represented by the trigrams are sky, lake, water, thunder, earth, mountain, fire, and wind. Note that in the pa-k'ua, the bottom line of the trigram is the one closest to the mirror.

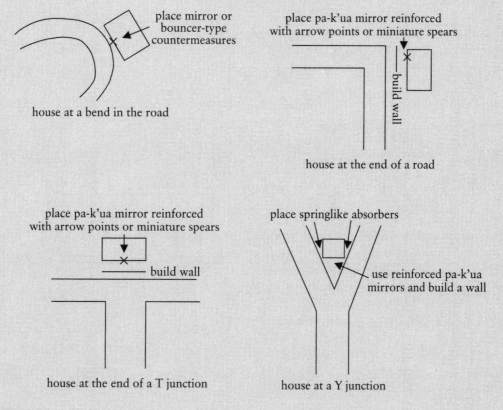

Figure B10.1 *Reinforcing the pa-k'ua mirror with accessories against dangerous road patterns.*

cooking stove, the threat of fire is neutralized. If the stove is situated in an area where nine-purple is the Earth Base and/or the Facing Star, however, the presence of water needs to be strengthened by placing a bowl of water or a picture of moving water in that area.

- Uneven ceilings are neutralized by remodeling into a flat or domed shape. Slanting ceilings and ceilings with discontinuities in height can be leveled and made uniform by installing a false ceiling. An apex in a ceiling can be nullified by putting in a flat ceiling.
- Beams are neutralized by covering them or by creating the visual impression that they are not there. A beam can be hidden by cloth or climbing plants.
- You should shorten the chains of lamps and fans that hang low from the ceiling. Also, do not suspend lamps or fans over the bed.
- Wood paneling with harsh, knotty patterns should be covered, replaced, or removed.
- Large windows and doors should be partially covered by blinds or curtains.
- Spiral staircases should be removed and replaced by conventional stairways.
- Narrow stairways should be widened.
- Stairways that face entrances create a situation where beneficial energy can flow out easily. To counter this problem, place a waterfall-type fountain beside the doorway. Water flowing in a waterfall-type fountain is unidirectional, compared with typical fountains, where water gushes up and flows outward in all directions. In general, water from fountains should not flow toward the door or windows. Water symbolizes wealth, which can escape from the house if the water flows in the direction of an exit. Since the water flow is unidirectional (figure 10.4a–d), such a fountain serves to direct beneficial energy into the house and offset the flow of energy from the stairway to the outside.
- Doorways that expose the kitchen to the front entrance area should be blocked by a permanently closed door.

The countermeasures described here are not difficult to implement, since they involve only the placement of objects and minor remodeling. If the floor plan itself is untenable or if there are significant interior design problems, however, major renovations may be needed. The subject of renovations is discussed in detail in chapter 12.

Figure 10.4a A small indoor waterfall-type fountain.

Figure 10.4b A large indoor waterfall-type fountain.

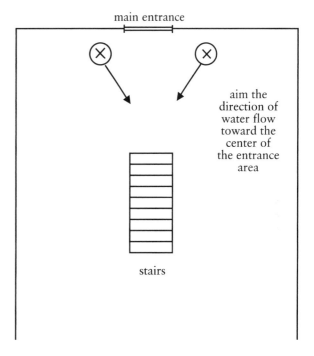

main entrance

aim the direction of water flow toward the center of the entrance area

stairs

⊗   indoor fountain

Figure 10.4c Placement of indoor waterfall-type fountain to counter stairs that face the front door.

Figure 10.4d The indoor waterfall-type fountain in figure 10.4b is used to route energy back into the house. Notice its position relative to the door.

COUNTERMEASURES FOR THE STARS AND ELEMENTS OF THE NINE PALACES

There are two ways to counter the harmful effects of malevolent stars in the Nine Palaces: avoidance and intervention.

Avoidance

Avoidance is a passive type of countermeasure. It is based on the principle that an effect on a location is heightened if there is movement in the area and is lessened if there is no activity. The best way to deal with malevolent stars, therefore, is to avoid them by not frequenting the space they occupy. Thus, rooms with combinations of five-yellow, two-black, or nine-purple or where there is a threat of fire (two-seven or nine-seven) should be used as storerooms.

A destructive effect also is minimized if you do not put moving objects in that place. Such objects include fans, clocks, videocassette/ DVD players, televisions, stereo equipment, and computers. Finally, the destructive effect of a malevolent star can be minimized if you do not work, play, or sit there.

Intervention

Intervention is an active type of countermeasure, because it annuls the action of the malevolent stars by neutralizing the element associated with them. The principle behind intervention lies in the interactions among the five elements—metal, wood, water, fire, and earth. Setting up countermeasures against malevolent stars in the Nine Palaces involves manipulating the elements in their creative and destructive cycles (figure 10.5). You already have encountered these relationships in

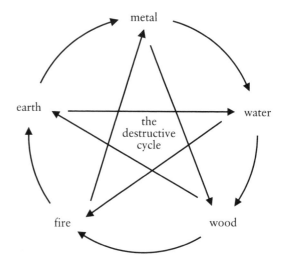

the creative / nourishing cycle

Figure 10.5 The creative (nourishing) cycle and the destructive cycle of the five elements. For the nourishing relationships, follow the arrows of the circle. For the destructive relationships, follow the arrows of the star.

chapter 8, where you learned how to match occupants to bedrooms. You should spend some time now memorizing the relationships of the five elements in their creative and destructive cycles, because it will help you learn the materials covered in the rest of this chapter.

Based on the creative and destructive interactions of the elements, we can construct a matrix of relationships among the five elements. This matrix is shown in figure 10.6. Study figure 10.6 carefully. You will notice that the energy of an element can be destroyed by its antagonist, can be dissipated by nourishing another element, or can be used up or drained when it destroys another element.

	METAL	WOOD	WATER	FIRE	EARTH
Metal	NE	WD	WN	D	N
Wood	D	NE	N	WN	WD
Water	N	WN	NE	WD	D
Fire	WD	N	D	NE	WN
Earth	WN	D	WD	N	NE

Figure 10.6 Relationships of the five elements. N, nourishing; D, destructive; WN, weakened by nourishing; WD, weakened by destroying; NE, no effect. Looking at the first row as an example, metal has no effect on metal, metal is weakened when it is used to destroy wood, metal is weakened when it is used to nourish water, metal is destroyed by fire, and metal is nourished by earth.

These are the three ways of countering the malevolent stars of the Nine Palaces. Each star of the Nine Palaces is associated with an element (figure 10.7); if the element associated with that star is neutralized, it has no effect. Notice that some stars are stronger than others. These differences in strength affect how you set up countermeasures.

PALACE STAR	ELEMENT	STRENGTH
one-white	water	weak
two-black	earth	strong
three-jade	wood	intermediate
four-green	wood	intermediate
five-yellow	earth	strong
six-white	metal	weak
seven-red	metal	intermediate
eight-white	earth	weak
nine-purple	fire	strong

Figure 10.7 The stars of the Nine Palaces, their related elements, and their levels of strength.

MANIPULATING THE FIVE ELEMENTS IN DESIGNING COUNTERMEASURES

1. The method of destruction is based on countering force with force. The most effective way of removing the power of an element is to use its antagonist to destroy it. This method is risky, because if the antagonist is not strong enough, it can be destroyed along with the element or the individual it is designed to protect. When you use this method, you will need to make sure that the antagonist element is bolstered. Destruction is most effective against a strong element like fire.

2. The method of dissipation is based on weakening the energy of an element by using it to nourish another element. This is the safest way of countering an element, because it does not use force against force. It tames the destructive forces by directing them toward a creative or nourishing activity. This method is most effective against the elements water, earth, wood, and metal.

ELEMENT	DESTROYED BY	DISSIPATED BY	DRAINED BY
metal	fire	water	wood
wood	metal	fire	earth
water	earth	wood	fire
fire	water	earth	metal
earth	wood	metal	water

Figure 10.8 The methods of destroying, dissipating, and draining an element.

3. The method of draining an element is based on using the element in question to counter another, so that its energy is used up in the process. This is not as safe as channeling the element's energy toward nourishing another element, but it is safer than destroying it. Rather than fighting force with force, we provide a condition where the element's energy can be vented at another element, thereby weakening it. This method is not very effective against fire, but it is effective against water, earth, wood, and metal.

Figure 10.8 shows how the three methods work.

COUNTERING SPECIFIC COMBINATIONS OF THE STARS OF THE NINE PALACES

Some of the most challenging interactions between specific stars of the Nine Palaces have been worked out by feng-shui practitioners. Study these ready-made solutions and learn the logic behind their design.

- To counter the effect of combinations of five-yellow and two-black, the stars of illness, use a chiming clock or a set of metal wind chimes. These two items belong to the element metal. Their presence, sound, and movement will draw energy away from the earth elements in five-yellow and two-black, thus weakening their strength. Water is also a good countermeasure in this context, because it can drain the earth element in both two-black and five-yellow. To be safe, use both metal and water as countermeasures against the combinations two-black and five-yellow.

- To offset the effect of a combination of two-seven or nine-seven, the stars of fire and burning, place artifacts of water in the area of these stars. A fountain, a fish tank, or even a bowl of water can serve the purpose. Alternatively, images of water, like pictures of a waterfall or waves on a beach, also will work.

- To balance the effect of combinations of two-black and three-jade, the stars of disharmony, use a strong light. A standing lamp or a spotlight mounted on the wall will suit the purpose. The strong light is a manifestation of the element fire, and the fire will draw energy from the wood of three-jade, thus weakening it.

- To negate the effect of combinations of seven-red and six-white, the stars of robbery and treachery, place six moving objects in a bowl of water in the area where the combination is located. Water dissipates the energy of metal (both six-white and seven-red are metal), because metal nourishes water. Since movement increases the strength of energy, using objects that move in the water will enhance the strength of water to counter metal. The moving objects can be fish swimming in a tank. You also can use mechanical fish, available in novelty stores and Asian gift shops. The mechanical or live fish should be dark in color. Do not use red or orange fish, because fire manifests in the color red. These colors in the water will weaken its effect.

- If the combinations five-yellow and two-black are accompanied by nine-purple, place water artifacts in addition to the chiming clocks. Water counters the fire of nine-purple, while the metal of the chiming clocks will draw energy from the earth elements of five-yellow and two-black.

COUNTERING THE EFFECTS OF MALEVOLENT STARS OF THE NINE PALACES

Recall that each star of the Nine Palaces is associated with an element (refer to figure 10.7). To neutralize the general effects of malevolent stars, we use the five elements to offset each other. There are two ways of doing this. The first technique uses the stars of the Nine Palaces and their associated elements to counter each other; the second uses artifacts to counter the malevolent palace stars.

Using the Stars of the Nine Palaces as Natural Countermeasures

Sometimes the stars of the Nine Palaces in the geomantic chart can neutralize each other. For example, an Earth Base Star of nine-pur-ple fire can be neutralized by the presence of one-white water in the Facing Star. Thus, the stars themselves (and their elements) can destroy, dissipate, and drain other elements, as described earlier. We use the stars of the Nine Palaces as natural countermeasures when there are no conditional and unconditional interactions between the Earth Base and the Facing Star. The general method (or the zero-sum method) is used in the palaces where nine-purple is absent, and the specific method is used in palaces where nine-purple is present.

THE GENERAL METHOD (OR THE ZERO-SUM METHOD)

In the general method, we look at the additive interactions of the stars in each palace and find out whether the beneficial effects can neutralize the negative effects. I call this the zero-sum method because we weigh all the auspicious stars against the inauspicious ones and look at the net result.

You encountered the first part of this method when you learned to evaluate the additive effects of the stars within a palace in chapter 6. (If you need a review, refer to pages 121–122.) In general, the effect of the Facing Star is strongest, followed by the Earth Base, and finally the Mountain Star. The malevolent effect of a Mountain Star usually can be balanced out by either the Facing Star (with residual positive energy) or the Earth Base. The destructive effect of an Earth Base Star can be annulled by the Facing Star alone. The malevolent effect of a Facing Star can be neutralized by a combination of the Earth Base and Mountain Star.

Let's try several examples to familiarize you with this method. Remember, in the following examples, the first number is the Earth Base, the second number is the Facing Star, and the third number is the Mountain Star.

Six-two-two. The auspicious star six-white in the Earth Base is not sufficient to neutralize the presence of two-black in the Facing Star and the Mountain Star. We have residual destructive influences that need to be countered by artifacts.

Five-seven-three. The destructive effect of five-yellow in the Earth Base cannot be offset by the neutral star seven-red in the Facing Star. The neutral Mountain Star three-jade does not contribute as a natural countermeasure. There is a residual destructive influence in the Earth Base that needs to be countered by artifacts.

Eight-three-two. The auspicious star eight-white in the Earth Base is sufficient to neutralize the destructive power of two-black in the Mountain Star. Three-jade, the neutral Facing Star, does not contribute. In this case, there are no remaining destructive effects. Therefore, no countermeasure artifacts are necessary.

Two-six-eight. The auspicious six-white as the Facing Star counteracts the destructive two-black in the Earth Base. The auspicious Mountain Star eight-white is not used in the process; therefore we have a leftover beneficial effect. Again, no countermeasure artifacts are necessary.

THE SPECIFIC METHOD

The specific method is used when you are dealing with nine-purple and when fire is present in a room—for example, in the kitchen or in rooms where there is a fireplace or woodstove. In the specific method, we look at the element of each star in the palace and see how each interacts with the others.

The best way to describe this method is to work through a few examples. If you have not memorized the cycles of creation and destruc-

tion and the list of the stars and their elements (figures 10.5, 10.6, and 10.7), do so now. Otherwise, you will have a difficult time following this discussion. If you have problems memorizing, keep copies of these figures in front of you when you are following the examples.

One-five-nine (in any room). Here, the adverse stars are five-yellow and nine-purple. The one-white water of the Earth Base is used to counter the fire of nine-purple in the Mountain Star, but there are other factors to consider. First, the presence of five-yellow earth in the Facing Star weakens the effect of water, because earth blocks or destroys water (in the destructive cycle of the five elements). Second, five-yellow itself is a strong star. Moreover, as the Facing Star, its strength is magnified. The situation is worsened when five-yellow is in the presence of nine-purple. Five-yellow in the Facing Star is not opposed, and the water element in the Earth Base one-white also is severely weakened. Third, because Earth Base stars have intermediate strength, the water element of one-white is only moderately strong. When all these factors are taken into account, we find that the water of one-white is barely able to nullify the fire of nine-purple. In this case, countermeasure artifacts are needed to neutralize five-yellow and bolster the water of one-white. (See next section on how to place artifacts to counter the malevolent stars of the Nine Palaces.)

Nine-one-eight (in the kitchen or in a bedroom). In this example, the water of one-white in the Facing Star is used to counter naturally the fire of nine-purple in the Earth Base. We won't know the effectiveness of the water element in one-white, however, until we have looked at other factors in the palace. First, eight-white in the Mountain Star is associated with the element earth. Although earth blocks and therefore weakens water, its impact is minimal. The reasons are that the earth of eight-white is weak and it is only a Mountain Star. Third, as a Facing Star, the water of one-white is very strong. It is unlikely that the earth of eight-white will diminish the power of water. When all these factors are taken into account, we find that the strength of one-white water is sufficient to neutralize the nine-purple fire of the Earth Base.

Nine-four-one (in the kitchen or in a bedroom). In this situation, it is clear that the water of one-white in the Mountain Star is insufficient to neutralize the fire of nine-purple in the Earth Base. We still need to work out the interactions among the three stars in the palace, because this information is needed to design countermeasures. First, the Facing Star four-green belongs to the element wood. Wood nourishes fire (in the creation cycle of the five elements). This means that the presence of wood in the palace will strengthen the fire of nine-purple. Second, water nourishes wood. The water energy of one-white will be weakened when it is used up to nourish the wood of four-green. Third, while the wood of four-green is of intermediate strength, its strength is enhanced because it is the Facing Star. Taken together, we have the situation of a very strong wood element that amplifies the strength of fire and weakens the effect of water. The effect of one-white water of the Mountain Star in nullifying the nine-purple fire of the Earth Base is minimal. Given this circumstance, we will need to place countermeasure artifacts in this square to neutralize the fire of nine-purple.

By now, you will realize that to evaluate the interactions of stars in the Nine Palaces and to work out the necessary countermeasures, you need to be extremely familiar with the relationships of the five elements and their associated stars. For this reason, you should make an effort to memorize the creative and destructive relationships of the five elements.

Placing Artifacts to Counter the Malevolent Stars of the Nine Palaces

When you discover that the elements of the Nine Palace stars cannot neutralize the malevolent stars naturally, you will need to position artifacts to counter the destructive effects. The artifacts are carriers of the energy of the elements; when designed and placed properly, they will help neutralize the influences of the unfavorable stars and their elements.

The design and placement of countermeasure artifacts are based on the principles of the interaction of the five elements. Applying the methods of destruction, dissipation, and draining, we can place artifacts to neutralize the effects of malevolent stars. The following is a set of general guidelines on how to use the five elements to counter each other when designing and positioning countermeasure artifacts. By now, you should have memorized figures 10.5 and 10.6. If not, you should have these figures in front of you as you follow the discussions.

FIRE

Fire is destroyed by water, dissipated when it is used to nourish earth, and drained when it destroys metal. Fire is a very strong element, best countered by a strong antagonist, such as water. To offset the threat of fire from nine-purple, place artifacts that are carriers of the element water in that location, including pictures of moving water, objects of the colors blue and green, and, of course, water itself.

You also can counter fire by having it nourish earth, thus dispersing its power. Artifacts that carry earth energy include ceramics, dirt, and stone and can take the form of sculptures. Because of fire's strength, it will not be dissipated easily through nourishing another element. Putting in place a metal object for the fire to consume will dissipate the strength of fire further, giving us a better chance of neutralizing its destructive effect. I recommend using water against fire, along with either metal or earth as a supplement.

The placement of countermeasure artifacts will not work if there are objects in the same location that strengthen the fire element. Make sure you do not put red objects in the vicinity of nine-purple. The color red is an enhancer; if red is placed in an area of fire, it will increase the strength of the fire element there. Avoid red-colored drapes, curtains, blinds, couch covers, bed covers, wall hangings, cushions, carpets or rugs, vases, and so on. Do not put plants in the area of nine-purple. Wood nourishes fire, and the presence of plants will strengthen the fire element in that area.

EARTH

Earth is destroyed by wood, dissipated when it is used to nourish metal, and drained when it destroys water. You can use metal to reduce the strength of earth. Place a clock or a metal wind chime in the areas where you want to neutralize the effect of earth. If the chimes are blown by wind or if the clock has a swinging pendulum, the strength is enhanced.

You also can counter earth with its antagonist, wood. Plants, especially small trees, are good carriers of wood energy. Carved wood objects also will work. Living plants are preferred, because growth is a form of movement and movement enhances the strength of the artifact.

Yet another way to counter earth is to drain

its strength by giving it an object to destroy. Earth blocks water. Thus, the presence of water can be used to drain the energy of earth. A bowl of water or a picture with water images will serve the purpose. I find that flowers in a glass vase filled with water are the optimal choice. As growing plants, flowers are carriers of wood energy. Glass, which has a visual resemblance to ice, is a carrier of water energy. And, of course, there is the physical presence of water in the vase.

WOOD

Wood is destroyed by metal, dissipated when it is used to nourish fire, and drained when it destroys earth. To counter the destructive effect of wood, you can use its antagonist, metal. Such metal objects as sculptures, tools, pewter, and clocks with a swinging metal pendulum are good choices.

You also can use artifacts representing fire to disperse the energy of wood, because wood nourishes fire. Strong lights are carriers of fire, so it is feasible to use a lamp or a ceiling light to counter wood. In fact, a ceiling light with a moving fan acts as a good countermeasure, since the movement of the fan will enhance the strength of the light. Do not use objects incorporating fire itself, such as candles, oil lamps, a woodstove, or a fireplace. The fire element carried in these objects is too strong and may introduce a fire hazard.

METAL

Metal is destroyed by fire, dissipated when it is used to nourish water, and drained when it destroys wood. To counter the threat of metal, you can use its antagonist, fire, in the form of strong lights, for example. You can weaken the effects of metal by arranging objects or images of water; the strength of metal will diminish when it nourishes water. Again, pictures of water images or the physical presence of water will serve the purpose. You may put in place wooden objects to drain the energy of metal. Here, metal will expend energy to destroy wood. Plants or wooden sculpture are viable objects for this use.

WATER

Water is destroyed by earth, dissipated when it is used to nourish wood, and drained when it destroys fire. To counter the threat of water, you can use its antagonist, earth. Earthen objects, such as ceramics, stone, and slate, are appropriate countermeasures. If you wish to dissipate water, situate wooden objects and plants in the area of water to nourish the wood. Finally, you can place objects that are carriers of fire in the area of water, to drain its energy in the effort to destroy fire.

Applying the Principles for the Use of the Stars of the Nine Palaces

These are the principles and guidelines for designing and implementing countermeasure artifacts to neutralize the malevolent Nine Palace stars and their elements. Notice that some artifacts are objects that have the physical properties of an element, such as a bronze sculpture (metal) or a plant (wood); some are visual images of the element, such as a picture of a waterfall (water); some are objects that convey the feel of an element, such as a strong light (fire); and some are colors associated with the element, such as blue (water). All of these types of artifacts will work if they are used properly.

Figure 10.9 lists the elements and examples of objects and colors associated with each element. Notice in the list that the color red is not used as a countermeasure. It is an enhancer. When it is placed in an area with aus-

picious stars, the beneficial effects of those stars will be amplified. On the other hand, when it is placed in an area with malevolent stars, the destructive effects will be strengthened. Never place red-colored objects in areas where there are combinations of two-black and five-yellow and Earth Base / Facing Star combinations that forebode fire—two-seven and nine-seven. I also recommend that you do not place red-colored objects in areas where nine-purple is present.

In the foregoing discussion, I have not mentioned crystals or prisms. While these objects are used widely in the practice of New Age–type feng-shui, they have never been a part of traditional Chinese feng-shui. No traditional Chinese practitioner uses them. In a discussion among practitioners in Hong Kong, the comments were that a crystal could be considered either a rock (and therefore a

ELEMENT	COLOR	OBJECTS
metal	silver, gold	bronze, iron, brass objects and sculpture, aluminum foil
wood	green	plants, wooden objects and sculpture
water	blue	images of waterfalls or waves, glassware, water in container
fire	orange	strong light
earth	earth tones	ceramic objects and sculpture, slate, stone, sand

Figure 10.9 The five elements, their related colors, and examples of their associated objects.

carrier of earth energy) or glass, because of its appearance (and therefore a carrier of water energy). When an object's energy is ambiguous, its behavior and effect become unpredictable, making it unsuitable as a countermeasure.

Working Through an Example

Now that you have learned how to design and place countermeasure artifacts based on the principles of the interactions among the five elements, we will address the question of how these measures are applied to deal with malevolent stars in a geomantic chart. Figure 10.10 shows a geomantic chart. We will study each of the squares of the Nine Palaces, analyze the interactions of the stars, and design the necessary countermeasures to neutralize the effects carried by the malevolent stars.

You should place countermeasures in the spot where the problem manifests in the macrocosm of the house and the microcosm of the room. For example, if you wish to neutralize the combination two-three in a northwest room of the house, you would position a strong light in the northwest corner of that room. Assessing each square of the Nine Palaces in turn, we come to the following analysis.

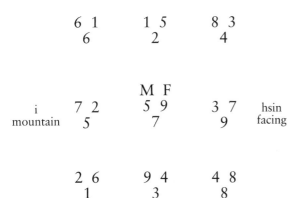

Figure 10.10 The geomantic chart of the example discussed in the text.

SIX-ONE-SIX

All the stars are auspicious. Therefore, there is no need for countermeasures, but it may be beneficial to place enhancers here to bolster the effects of the auspicious stars (see chapter 11).

TWO-FIVE-ONE

The interaction of two-five forebodes illness. We would use a metal chiming clock and a bowl of water to counter this combination. This countermeasure breaks up the combination two-five, thereby neutralizing the threat. Once we take care of two-five, the residual auspicious effect of one-white, albeit small, can be felt.

FOUR-THREE-EIGHT

Two auspicious stars (four-green and eight-white) and one neutral star (three-wood) together make this an auspicious spot. There is no need to place countermeasures here.

FIVE-TWO-SEVEN

This area has problems. The interaction of five-two presages illness. Seven-red, the neutral Mountain Star, cannot counter the destructive effects of the other two stars. We need to use a chiming clock with a swinging metal pendulum to dissipate the energy of five-yellow. We also need to put a bowl of water in the area, because water can drain the energy of earth. I recommend placing two sets of countermeasures here, because five-yellow and two-black are both strong stars. Do not put any red-colored objects here, since they will exacerbate the problems of the five-two combination.

SEVEN-NINE-FIVE

The combination seven-nine-five portends terminal illness. This is an extremely dangerous spot and should be left dormant. Since all three stars can be weakened by water, we should place a small waterfall-type fountain here.

NINE-SEVEN-THREE

The combination nine-seven forebodes fire caused by human activity. Again, a bowl of water, a waterfall-type fountain, and/or a picture with images of flowing water should be positioned here.

ONE-SIX-TWO

The combination of one-white and six-white means success, health, and prosperity, but the effect is lessened because of the presence of two-black in the Mountain Star. Although the Mountain Star does not exert much influence, we still need to use a small countermeasure to neutralize it, so that it will not weaken the auspicious effect of the one-six combination. If we place a metal-type countermeasure here, the two-black will be weakened, thereby allowing the full effect of the combination one-six to be felt.

THREE-FOUR-NINE

Assuming that this is neither a bedroom with a fireplace nor a kitchen, this is a fairly good spot. The benevolent energy is carried by the Facing Star four-green. Three-jade, being a neutral star, does not contribute to the additive interaction. In the presence of nonmalevolent stars, nine-purple is not a threat. There is no need for countermeasures here.

EIGHT-EIGHT-FOUR

This an extremely auspicious square. All three stars are associated with health, success, and prosperity. Enhancers should be placed to bolster the auspicious stars. (See chapter 11 for details on how to place enhancers.)

From the foregoing analysis, you will notice that it is not enough to determine which element can counter the element of a malevolent star. The proper countermeasure element is one that can neutralize the undesirable effects but does not harm the auspicious stars.

Now do exercise 10.2.

USING COUNTERMEASURES TO PROTECT THE GUARDIAN ELEMENTS OF THE OCCUPANTS

In chapter 8, you learned that each person is born under the guardianship of a star of the Nine Palaces and its elements. Some individuals are more suited to certain rooms, because their guardian elements are nourished by the Earth Base Star of the room. What happens when none of Earth Base stars of the bedrooms are compatible with the occupants? In this case, you will need to place countermeasures to strengthen the guardian star and element of the occupant and/or to neutralize the influence of the Earth Base Star.

Remember, rooms with very inauspicious stars, such as Earth Base and Facing Star combinations of two-black and five-yellow, seven-nine, and the stars of fire hazards (two-seven and nine-seven) should not be used as bedrooms at all. No countermeasure will be strong enough to protect the occupants in these bedrooms. A room with five-yellow as the Earth Base is suitable only for a person whose guardian star / element is five-yellow, and a bedroom with two-black as the Earth Base is suitable only for persons with two-black or five-yellow as guardian stars.

The principles behind using countermeasures to make a bedroom suitable for an occupant are the same as those used to neutralize the effects of malevolent stars. As in earlier discussions, our methods here are based on the interactions of the five elements.

Strengthening the Guardian Star and Element of the Occupant

You can strengthen the guardian star / element of an individual with artifacts that nourish that guardian star / element. You need to be careful that the artifact does not enhance the antagonistic Earth Base in the bedroom. Let's look at some examples to see how this is done. Remember, you need to be concerned only with the Earth Base of the bedroom when you are attempting to protect and strengthen the guardian star / element of the occupant of that room.

EXAMPLE 1

The Nine Palace stars for the bedroom are eight-six-six, and the guardian star / element of the occupant is nine-purple fire. Since fire creates or nourishes earth, the guardian element will be weakened when it interacts with the Earth Base eight-white earth. The element that can strengthen nine-purple fire is wood, which turns out to be a good choice, because wood also destroys earth. Placing wood artifacts in the bedroom will simultaneously strengthen the guardian element (fire) of the occupant as well as neutralize the eight-white earth.

EXAMPLE 2

The Nine Palace stars of the bedroom are nine-four-one, and the guardian star / element of the occupant is seven-red metal. Since metal is destroyed by fire, the guardian element will be harmed when it interacts with the Earth Base nine-purple fire. The element that can strengthen metal is earth. Since earth dissipates fire (because fire is understood to nourish or create earth) and simultaneously bolsters metal, using earth artifacts to strengthen the guardian element metal is an ideal solution.

EXAMPLE 3

The Nine Palace stars of the bedroom are four-four-four, and the guardian star / element of the occupant is one-white water. The energy of water, the guardian element, is dissipated when it is used to nourish wood, the element of the Earth Base. The element that strengthens water is metal. Since metal also can destroy wood, using metal artifacts to strengthen the guardian element water is ideal.

Countering the Antagonistic Earth Base

You also can protect an occupant by neutralizing the antagonistic Earth Base. You need to be careful that the countermeasure element does not weaken the guardian star / element of the occupant. Let's look at examples of how this is done.

EXAMPLE 1

The Nine Palace stars for the bedroom are eight-six-eight, and the guardian star / element of the occupant is four-green wood. Since wood destroys earth, the guardian star is weakened when it interacts with the Earth Base eight-white earth. We therefore need to put in place an artifact that will counter earth. The three elements that can counter the earth element are metal (which dissipates earth, because earth is used to nourish metal), water (which drains earth, because earth is used to destroy water), and wood (which destroys earth). In this situation, metal is not a good countermeasure, since the presence of metal also will weaken four-green wood, the guardian star / element of the occupant. Wood is viable, because it is compatible with the guardian element of the occupant. Water is best, because it counters earth as well as strengthens wood. Placing water artifacts in the bedroom will simultaneously neutralize the earth of the Earth Base and strengthen the guardian star / element (four-green wood) of the occupant.

EXAMPLE 2

The Nine Palace stars for the bedroom are one-seven-seven, and the guardian star / element of the occupant is six-white metal. Since metal nourishes water, the guardian star is weakened when it interacts with the Earth Base one-white water. The three elements that can counter water are fire (by draining), wood (by dissipating), and earth (by destroying). Fire is not a good choice as a countermeasure, because it will harm the guardian star / element six-white metal. Wood also is not suitable, because the guardian element (metal) will be weakened when it is used to destroy wood. The element earth is the best option, because earth not only destroys water but also nourishes metal. We should place earth artifacts in the bedroom to make it suitable for the occupant.

Now do exercise 10.3.

After you have studied the examples given earlier, you will notice that the element that strengthens an individual element against an antagonistic Earth Base also will neutralize the element of the Earth Base and that the second method may turn out to be superfluous. There are some situations, however, where you may need to try all the possible countermeasures that can neutralize the element of the Earth Base. This is why you need to be familiar with both methods of using countermeasures to protect the guardian element of the occupant.

Consider this situation. Suppose that a bedroom has the palace stars three-nine-three and the occupant's guardian star / element is two-black earth. The element fire appears to be the countermeasure of choice, because it strength-

ens the guardian element earth and dissipates the three-jade wood of the Earth Base. Now suppose that the room has a fireplace. This makes the situation more complex. If we use fire as a countermeasure, there will be too much fire in the room. The Facing Star, which has a strong influence, already carries the fire element. If we add more fire by using a fire-type countermeasure, we will create a dangerous fire hazard. We cannot use a fire element as a countermeasure in this situation.

How do we solve this problem? Here is a solution. The two elements (other than fire) that can counter the Earth Base star three-jade wood are metal and earth. Metal is not viable, because it dissipates the occupant's guardian star / element two-black earth. The other possible countermeasure element, earth, is compatible with two-black earth and therefore has no effect on it. Moreover, it can destroy earth. Given this analysis, we should select earth-type countermeasures to neutralize the three-jade wood of the Earth Base.

SPECIAL COUNTERMEASURE OBJECTS

In the foregoing discussions on countermeasures, we have used ordinary objects as artifacts. In feng-shui, there are specially designed objects that are more effective than ordinary ones in warding off destructive influences. Care should be taken in arranging these objects. If placed incorrectly, they can cause harm to the occupants. Here are examples of such objects and the ways in which they can be used as countermeasures.

Door Guardians

Figure 10.11a and b shows the images of two door guardians. When positioned on both sides of the door (figure 10.11c), these guardians will ward off any destructive forces that enter through the front door. These

Figure 10.11a Door guardian. The pa-k'ua mirror at the top, above the guardian, adds strength to this artifact (*above, left*).

Figure 10.11b Door guardian with pa-k'ua mirror as reinforcement (*above, right*).

Figure 10.11c Placement of the two door guardians and the pa-k'ua mirrors on each side of a front door (*right*).

images can be used against destructive forces of a driveway pointing at your house and/or incoming traffic from a road leading straight to your house. Most door guardians are images painted or glued onto wooden plaques. Some are pictures that require framing before you can hang them. You can purchase these types of door guardians from large Asian grocery stores or gift stores in most North American cities. In Hong Kong and other Asian cities, you can obtain them at Buddhist and Taoist temple supply stores.

Figure 10.12b The pa-k'ua mirror can be hung underneath the eaves.

Pa-k'ua Mirrors

Another power object is the *pa-k'ua* mirror (figure 10.12a and b). This is a plaque with a mirror in the center surrounded by the trigrams of the pa-k'ua. The pa-k'ua mirror is generally used to ward off pointing objects, falling objects, objects of destruction (such as a sculpture of a warrior holding a spear), and traffic and driveways directed at your house. The pa-k'ua mirror can be obtained at Asian grocery stores and gift stores in most North American cities. In Hong Kong and other Asian cities with a large Chinese community, you can find them at Buddhist and Taoist temple supply stores.

Figure 10.12a A pa-k'ua mirror. Most of these mirrors come with a hook, indicating the top orientation. Should you get one without a hook, be sure when you position it that the segment with the three solid lines is oriented at the top.

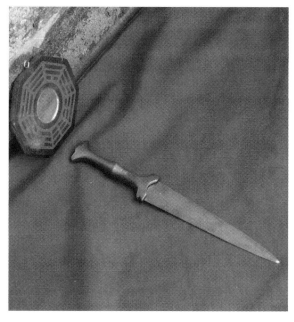

Figure 10.13a A pa-k'ua mirror strengthened by arrowheads.

Figure 10.13b A pa-k'ua mirror strengthened by a dagger.

Miniature Weapons

These miniatures of spears, swords, arrows, tridents, and shields are used to counter objects of destruction, incoming traffic, and driveways pointed at your house. They also are used to increase the strength of pa-k'ua mirrors. Figure 10.13a and b shows the enhancement of a pa-k'ua mirror by an arrow point or a dagger. In especially dangerous situations, for example, when a house is located at a T junction, we may need to add a shield to the arsenal of countermeasures to offset the onrush of destructive energy from the traffic and the road. In Hong Kong and other large Asian cities, miniature swords, spears, arrows, and tridents (about five inches in length) are manufactured specifically for this purpose. In North America and Europe, you may have to make your own miniature weapon. I find that arrowheads work very well, and you can purchase them from hunting supply stores. Other types of miniature weapons, such as cannons (figure 10.3), guns, swords, knives, and spears (figure 10.14a–c) can be purchased at martial arts supply stores, cutlery stores, and specialty knife stores.

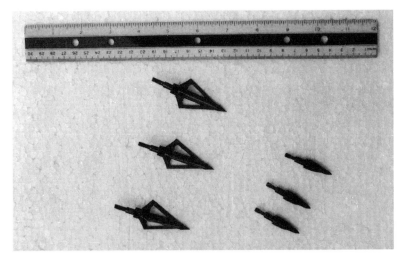

Figure 10.14a–c Miniature weapons.

Figure 10.14a Arrow points. A one-foot ruler is shown for scale.

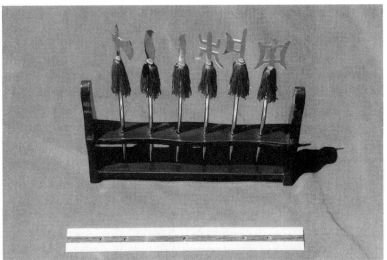

Figure 10.14b Miniature traditional Chinese weapons in a stand. A one-foot ruler is shown for scale.

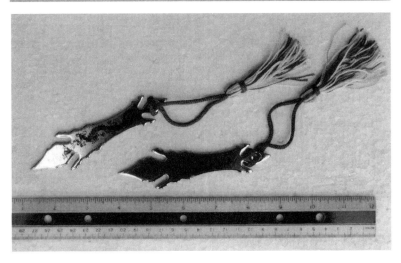

Figure 10.14c Darts. A one-foot ruler is shown for scale.

Talismans

Talismans are words of power woven into a special script. The script calls on the guardians of the cosmos to help ward off destructive forces. Figure 10.15 shows a talisman that is designed to protect the occupants of a house from harm. Placement of the talisman at the front entrance serves the same function as the pa-k'ua mirror and the door guardians. The talisman must be handwritten in red ink on yellow paper by an adept in the art. Do not attempt to copy the talisman reprinted in this book yourself. It will not work and may draw anger from the guardian deities if it is improperly written or placed. If you wish to use this method, you should seek the services of someone who practices talismanic Taoism. In Hong Kong and other Asian cities with a large Chinese population, you can obtain talismans from almost any temple. In North America and Britain, you may need to inquire in the Chinatowns to locate someone who can write talismans. Never place the special countermeasure objects casually. They are not art or novelty objects. Incorrect placement (such as positioning objects upside down) will harm the occupants of the house.

This concludes your introduction to the use of countermeasures for adverse conditions. The art of designing and placing countermeasures against negative energy is one of the most difficult skills in feng-shui. To excel in it requires experience, intuition, creativity, and a deep understanding of the relationships of the five elements and the Nine Palaces. Remember, countermeasures can only turn bad feng-shui into neutral feng-shui. They cannot convert negative feng-shui into positive feng-shui. Good feng-shui is carried by auspicious stars in the Nine Palaces, and if you discover that there are no positive stars in the house, you should probably find another place to live.

Figure 10.15 A talisman of protection.

EXERCISES

EXERCISE 10.1

Place countermeasures to neutralize the threats in the external environments depicted in figure 10.16. No. 1 is a worked example.

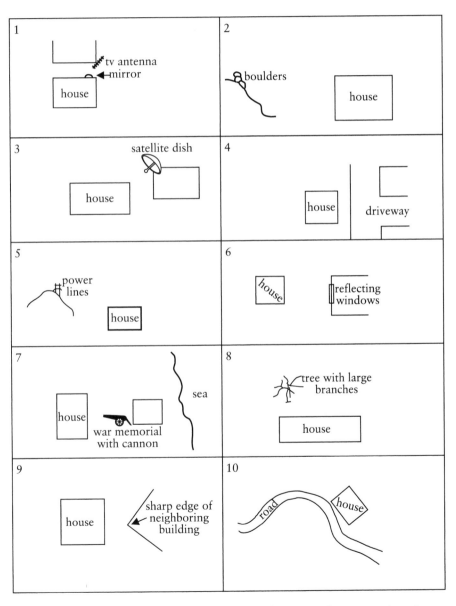

Figure 10.16 Designing countermeasures against threats in the external environment.

EXERCISE 10.2

Evaluate the following sets of Nine Palace stars and specify whether the stars themselves can act as natural countermeasures. Use the zero-sum method or the specific method of dealing with nine-purple where appropriate. Recommend the type of countermeasure (metal, wood, water, fire, and/or earth) to be used, if necessary, and give reasons for your choices. No. 1 is a worked example.

1. 2/4/7

The four-green of the Facing Star neutralizes the threat of two-black in the Earth Base. No extra countermeasure artifacts are necessary.

2. 4/2/9
3. 1/5/6
4. 4/9/2

EXERCISE 10.3

What countermeasures and objects are needed to strengthen the guardian star / element of the individuals in the following bedrooms? State reasons for your choice. No. 1 is a worked example.

GUARDIAN STAR / ELEMENT	PALACE STARS OF THE BEDROOM
1. one-white water	*3/9/6*

The countermeasure element metal should be used. Metal destroys the wood of three-jade and drains the fire energy of nine-purple. It also nourishes the guardian star / element one-white water.

2. three-jade wood	7/4/2
3. two-black earth	1/2/7
4. nine-purple fire	6/6/9

ANSWERS

EXERCISE 10.1

See figure 10.17.

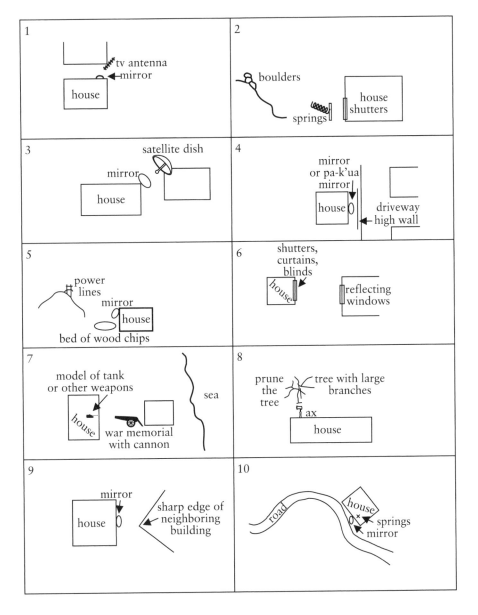

Figure 10.17 Answers to exercise 10.1.

EXERCISE 10.2

2. 4/2/9

The Earth Base four-green is insufficient to counter the Facing Star two-black, especially when two-black is enhanced by nine-purple. Water is the best countermeasure. It enhances the four-green, drains the energy of two-black, and destroys the fire of nine-purple.

3. 1/5/6

The Earth Base one-white and Mountain Star six-white are used jointly to counter the Facing Star five-yellow. No extra countermeasures are needed.

4. 4/9/2

The threat of two-black in the Mountain Star is heightened by nine-purple. A water-type countermeasure should be used. Water drains the energy of earth, destroys fire, and enhances the Earth Base four-green.

EXERCISE 10.3

2.

The countermeasure element water should be used. Water dissipates the metal energy of the Earth Base seven-red and nourishes the guardian star / element three-jade wood.

3.

The countermeasure fire should be used, since nine-purple is absent. Fire drains the water energy of the Earth Base one-white and nourishes the guardian star / element two-black earth.

4.

The countermeasure wood should be used. Wood drains the metal energy of the Earth Base six-white and nourishes the guardian star / element nine-purple fire.

11

Installing Enhancers

While countermeasures are used to neutralize undesirable effects, enhancers are designed to foster desirable effects. Enhancers facilitate the movement of benevolent energy and promote the beneficial effects of the auspicious stars of the Nine Palaces.

WHEN AND WHERE TO USE ENHANCERS

The following is a set of guidelines concerning when and where to use enhancers.

Generally, we should place enhancers in the following locations:

- Areas where all three stars (Earth Base, Facing Star, and Mountain Star) are auspicious
- Areas where the Earth Base and Facing Star combination is auspicious and the Mountain Star is neutral

Specifically, we should place enhancers in these places:

- Entranceways that are occupied by extremely auspicious stars, such as Earth Base / Facing Star combinations of one-white, four-green, six-white, and eight-white (with the exception of the combination eight-four)
- Entrances, corridors, stairways, and hallways that are occupied by auspicious Nine Palace stars
- Rooms where all three stars of the palace are auspicious
- Areas where the Facing Star needs to be strengthened to counter the malevolent effects of the other stars

TYPES OF ENHANCERS

The placement of enhancers is not as complicated as the placement of countermeasures.

There are four different types of enhancers—movement, special enhancer objects, colors, and the nourishing interactions of the five elements.

Movement

Movement in an area increases the effect of the Nine Palace stars of that area. If the stars are auspicious, introducing movement will enhance their positive qualities. Movement can be introduced into a space by frequent use, by adding a moving object, and by the interactions of occupants with a moving object.

Most of us spend at least six hours a day sleeping. For this reason, it is a good idea to turn a room with favorable stars into a bedroom (provided that the occupant's guardian element is not harmed by the room's Earth Base element). The next best utilization of this space is to make it a family room, a recreation room, or a home office, depending on the frequency of use.

Another way to enhance an auspicious space is to put a moving object there. Fans, moving sculptures, clocks with swinging pendulums, fish tanks with pumps, clockwork novelty objects, televisions, and stereo equipment are all objects that have moving components. Some of these objects, such as ceiling fans, small moving sculptures, and novelty items, are ideal for enhancing hallways that are occupied by propitious Nine Palace stars.

Finally, we can enhance a space occupied by auspicious stars by interacting with a moving object located in that area. Playing a musical instrument, playing a video game, using a computer, and working out on exercise equipment are all ways of enhancing an auspicious space through use and movement.

Figure 11.1 shows a geomantic chart and floor plan of a house and the way in which movement can be used to promote the benevolent effects of the auspicious stars.

Special Enhancer Objects

Special objects (other than the ones with moving components mentioned earlier) can enhance an auspicious area.

Mirrors are typically used to increase the flow of energy in constricted places. They are especially suited to directing and facilitating the flow of benevolent energy down winding and narrow stairways that lead into basements (figure 11.2). When placing mirrors, however, you need to make sure that they do not face windows and doors, or the benevolent energy will be directed out of the house.

Bright lights also can be used as enhancers. They are best installed in areas where all three stars—the Earth Base, Facing Star, and Mountain Star—are auspicious. If only one or two of the stars are auspicious, the enhancer may end up amplifying the effect of the inauspicious ones as well.

Colors

The color red is an enhancer. The brighter and more saturated the red, the greater will be the effect. Orange will work, but it is not as effective as red. Pink will not work. Red can be used *only* when all three stars of the palace are auspicious. Again, if only one or two of the stars are auspicious, the color red may heighten the effect of the inauspicious ones as well. Never put red-colored objects in areas where nine-purple is present, because red enhances the fire element of nine-purple, thus reinforcing the threat of fire. As an enhancer, red can be the color of couch covers, cushions, area rugs, bed covers, curtains, wall hangings, and objects.

Figure 11.3 shows a geomantic chart and floor plan of a house and the use of the color red as an enhancer. Make sure that you do not

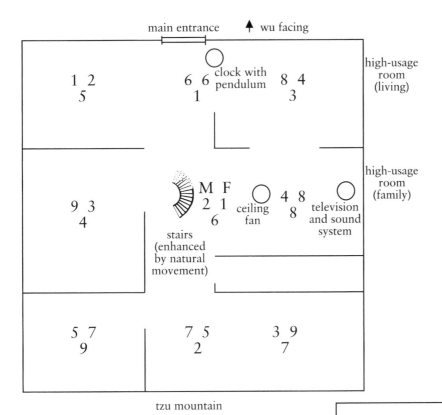

Figure 11.1 Using movement as an enhancer (*above*).

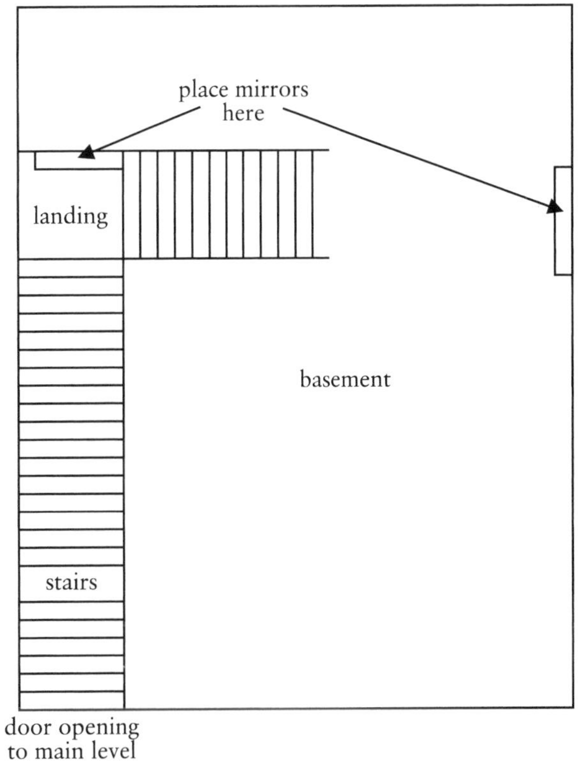

Figure 11.2 Enhancing the basement with mirrors (*right*).

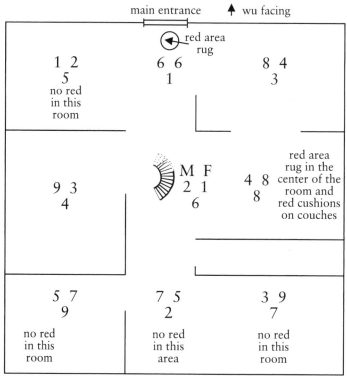

main entrance   ▲ wu facing

red area
rug

1 2
5
no red
in this
room

6 6
1

8 4
3

9 3
4

M F
2 1
6

4 8
8

red area
rug in the
center of the
room and
red cushions
on couches

5 7
9
no red
in this
room

7 5
2
no red
in this
area

3 9
7
no red
in this
room

tzu mountain

Figure 11.3 Using the color red as an enhancer.

place enhancer objects in troublesome areas in the microcosm of the room. For example, when enhancing a room that is situated in the one-six-six area of the macrocosm of the house, make sure that you do not place a red-colored carpet in the areas of the microcosm where there is five-yellow, two-black, or nine-purple.

Creative Interaction of the Five Elements

Here we use the creative or nourishing cycle of the five elements to enhance the benevolent stars of the Nine Palaces. This method can be used only to enhance the Facing Star.

There are two circumstances in which an element can be used to enhance the Facing Star. The first situation is when the strength of the Facing Star is insufficient to counter the malevolent stars in the palace. In this situation, we increase the strength of the Facing Star with enhancers, so that its benevolent effects will outweigh the destructive effects. For example, in the combination five-four-five, we need to bolster the Facing Star four-green against the five-yellow stars (which are extremely strong malevolent) in the Earth Base and Mountain Star. Although the Facing Star is the strongest of the three, we have to make sure that it is powerful enough to ward off the destructive effects of the five-yellow stars. To be safe, we would place water in the area. Water nourishes wood and increases the strength of four-green. Moreover, the enhancer gives us a bonus, because it also can drain the earth energy of the two five-yellow stars (earth blocks water).

The second situation is when we do not want to exhaust the benevolent effect of the Facing Star to counter the malevolent stars. For example, in the combination two-six-seven, the six-white of the Facing Star is sufficient to counter the malevolent two-black of the Earth Base. (The seven-red of the Mountain Star is neutral.) If we want six-white to have beneficial energy left over after it has been used to counter two-black, we can introduce an earthen object in the area to nourish

six-white metal. Look at figure 11.4 to gain an idea of the installation of enhancers in a house.

You should now be ready to do Exercise 11.1.

The placement of countermeasures and enhancers is probably the most complicated aspect of feng-shui. To be competent in these skills requires creativity, a good sense of logic, and a thorough understanding of the relationships of the five elements and the stars of the Nine Palaces. Remember, incorrect placement of countermeasure and enhancer artifacts can harm the occupants of a house. Do not attempt to install them until you have mastered the materials in chapters 10 and 11.

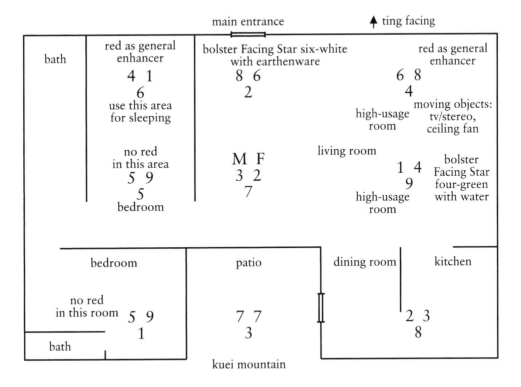

Figure 11.4 Example of how to place enhancers in a house.

EXERCISES

EXERCISE 11.1

Generate geomantic charts for the houses shown in figure 11.5 using the information on the facing direction and the cycle in which the house was built. Then superimpose the charts onto the floor plans and place enhancers in the appropriate locations. No. 1 is a worked example.

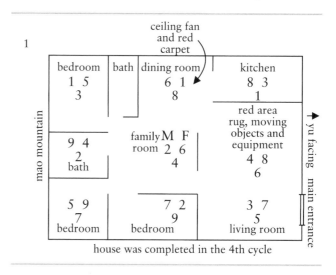

Figure 11.5 Generating the geomantic charts and placing enhancers in three sample houses.

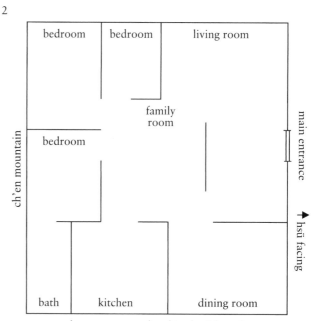

3

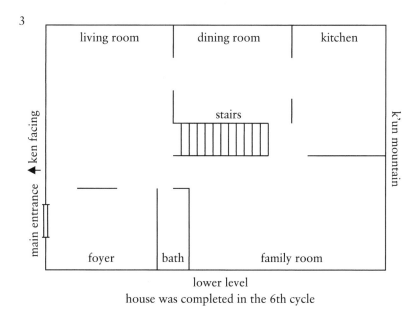

lower level
house was completed in the 6th cycle

upper level

ANSWERS

EXERCISE 11.1

Refer to figure 11.6 for answers to exercise 11.1. Despite the presence of auspicious stars in the Earth Base and the Facing Star, red generally is not used as an enhancer in the kitchen, because the fire element is already strong. Aggravation of the element will increase the risk of fire hazard. In No. 3, no enhancers can be used, because there is no single square with three auspicious stars.

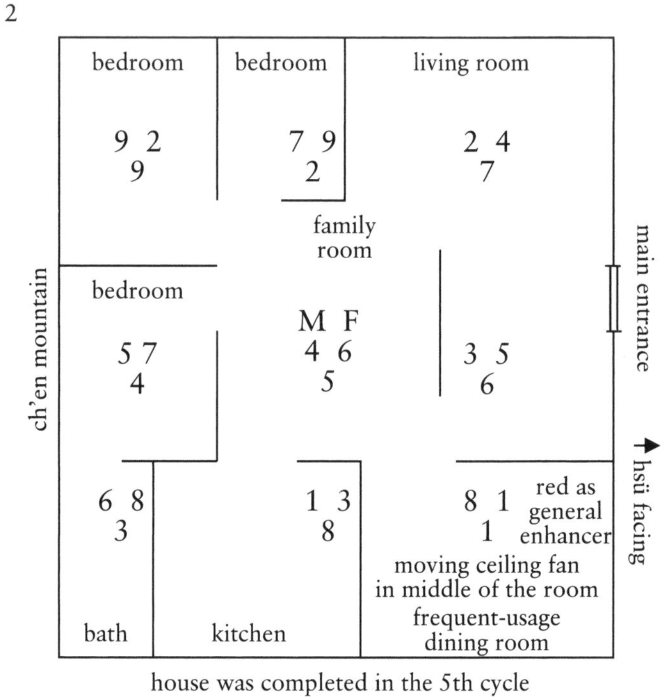

Figure 11.6 Answers to exercise 11.1.

2

bedroom	bedroom	living room
9 2	7 9	2 4
9	2	7

family room

bedroom	M F	
5 7	4 6	3 5
4	5	6

main entrance

ch'en mountain

hsü facing

6 8	1 3	8 1 red as general enhancer
3	8	1

moving ceiling fan in middle of the room

frequent-usage dining room

| bath | kitchen | |

house was completed in the 5th cycle

3

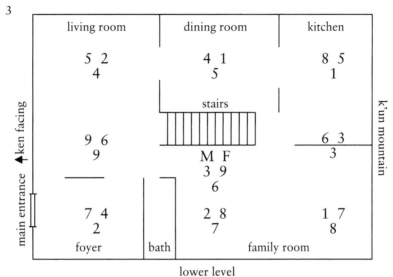

living room | dining room | kitchen

5 2
4

4 1
5

8 5
1

ken facing

main entrance

k'un mountain

stairs

9 6
9

6 3
3

M F
3 9
6

7 4
2

2 8
7

1 7
8

foyer | bath | family room

lower level

house was completed in the 6th cycle

no enhancers

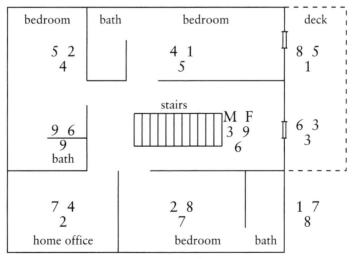

bedroom | bath | bedroom | deck

5 2
4

4 1
5

8 5
1

stairs

9 6
9
bath

M F
3 9
6

6 3
3

7 4
2

2 8
7

1 7
8

home office | bedroom | bath

upper level

12

Renovations

In this chapter, we will look at when and how to implement renovations. First, we need to concern ourselves with the details of renovations in cases where more than one-third of the floor plan of a building has been changed in remodeling. Extensive remodeling alters the energy of a space: it is as if a new building has been erected. The geomantic chart for the renovated building is based on the year the renovations were finished rather than the year the building was completed initially. For example, the geomantic chart for a 1929 building that was remodeled extensively in 1975 is calculated based on the sixth cycle instead of the fourth cycle diagram in the appendix.

Second, renovations can be used as countermeasures. If a house has an unfavorable geomantic chart, it is possible to alter the facing direction, the Earth Base, and the fit of the Nine Palace stars onto the floor plan, thereby giving the renovated building a more favorable geomantic chart. We shall address each of these types of possible renovations in this chapter.

HOW TO DEAL WITH EXISTING RENOVATIONS

It is a good practice to ask about renovations when you purchase or rent a space. If more than one-third of the floor plan has been altered in remodeling, the geomantic chart should be based on the cycle in which the renovations were completed. If the renovations were carried out in a cycle different from the one in which the building was completed initially, the Earth Base as well as the Facing and Mountain stars will be different from those of the original house. If the renovations were done in the same cycle as the one in which the building was completed but the facing direction has been altered by the remodeling, then the building will have new facing and mountain directions even though the Earth Base number will be the same. To illustrate these situations, let's look at several examples.

Example 1

Figure 12.1 shows the floor plans of a house built in 1918, the new floor plan that was the result of remodeling done in 1985, and their respective geomantic charts. Comparing the two floor plans, it is obvious that more than one-third of the original floor plan has been changed in the 1985 renovation. For this reason, in the renovated house, the Earth Base stars of the Nine Palaces will be based on the seventh cycle. Because of the change in the Earth Base, the Facing and Mountain stars are altered as well, though the facing direction is still wu.

Example 2

Figure 12.2 shows the floor plans of a house built in 1932, the new floor plan that was the result of remodeling done in 1987, and their respective geomantic charts. Comparing the old and the new floor plans, we find that here, too, more than one-third of the original floor plan has been altered. The Earth Base stars of the new geomantic chart will be from the seventh cycle. Now let's see if the renovations also changed the facing direction of the house. In this example, the house is situated on flat land with no distinctive geographic features defining the front and back of the building. Before the renovation, the side of the house with the most open views—wu—was the facing direction. After the renovations, the layout of the windows has changed. These changes have redefined a new

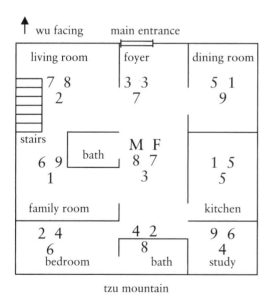
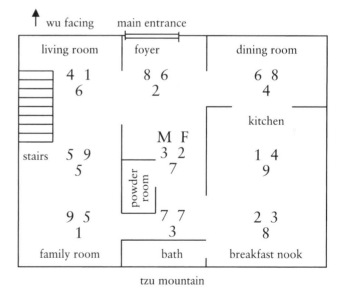

Figure 12.1 The original and the remodeled floor plans and their respective geomantic charts (example 1 in text).

facing direction for the house. It now faces keng (refer to figure 12.2), the side with the main entrance and the picture window. In this example, the remodeling gave us a new Earth Base Star (based on the cycle the renovations were completed) and new Facing and Mountain stars (based on the new facing and mountain directions).

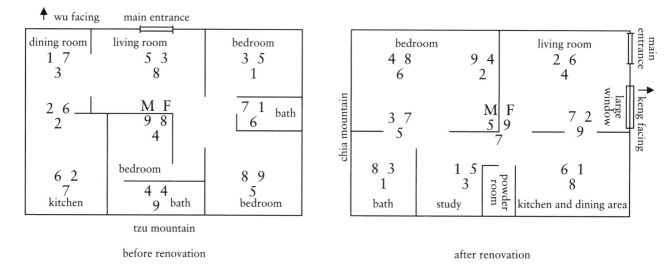

Figure 12.2 The original and the remodeled floor plans and their respective geomantic charts (example 2 in text).

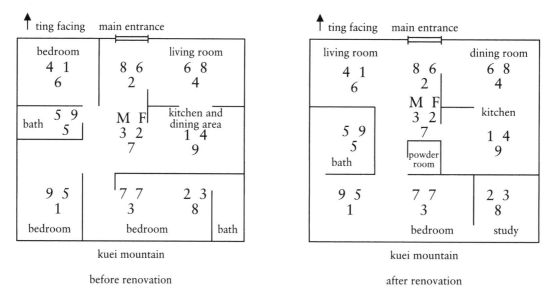

Figure 12.3 The original and the remodeled floor plans and their respective geomantic charts (example 3 in text).

Example 3

What about a house that was built in 1985 and renovated extensively in 1998? In this case, the house was built and renovated in the same (seventh) cycle. If the renovations did not result in a change of facing direction, the geomantic chart will be the same as that of the original house. The new chart, of course, will be superimposed onto the current (new) floor plan instead of the old floor plan (figure 12.3). If the renovations resulted in a change in the facing direction, however, the new geomantic chart will reflect that change, because we then would take the compass readings based on the current facing direction of the house (figure 12.4).

Now do exercise 12.1.

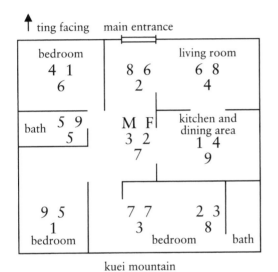

before renovation

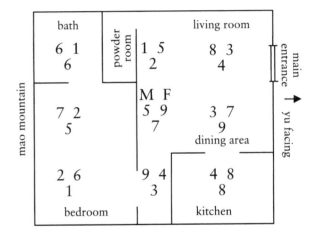

after renovation

Figure 12.4 The original and the remodeled floor plans and their respective geomantic charts (example 3 in text) showing change in facing direction.

USING RENOVATIONS AS COUNTERMEASURES

Renovations can be used as countermeasures to neutralize problems associated with the layout of the Nine Palaces in the floor plan of a building. We will look at two kinds of countermeasure remodeling—small-scale renovations that do not change the stars of the Nine Palaces and large-scale renovations that result in a new geomantic chart.

Using Small-Scale Renovations to Recover Desirable Areas and Avoid Troublesome Areas

Small-scale renovations are renovations that alter less than one-third of the original floor plan. Repositioning walls, adding and removing sections of living space, and changing positions of entrances can help us incorporate areas occupied by benevolent stars into the living space, avoid areas occupied by malevolent stars, and move problem-causing features (such as large fireplaces) to less hazardous areas. Although some of these alterations are not trivial from a structural perspective, they are still considered small-scale renovations when they do not alter more than one-third of the existing floor plan. As

you will see, when it is done skillfully, small-scale remodeling can make untenable floor plans viable. Let's look at several examples.

EXAMPLE 1

Look at figure 12.5, which shows the way in which an undesirable situation in the living room can be rescued by stretching the geomantic chart and putting in some artifacts. In panel A of figure 12.5, you can see that the combination nine-purple in the Earth Base and seven-red in the Facing Star forebodes fire. This fire hazard is heightened because the fireplace is located in the position occupied by the fire-hazard stars in the microcosm of the living room. Panel B shows a possible solution to the problem. In the remodeling, an atrium, or enclosed indoor garden, is added to the liv-

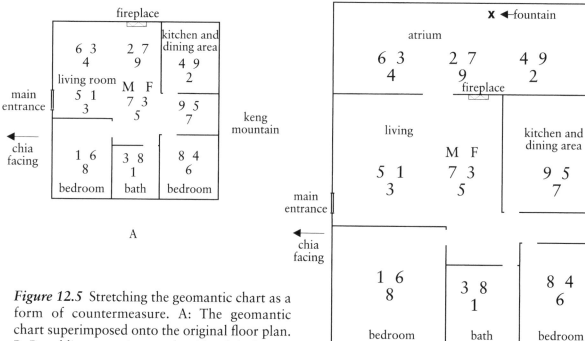

Figure 12.5 Stretching the geomantic chart as a form of countermeasure. A: The geomantic chart superimposed onto the original floor plan. B: By adding an atrium to the side of the house, the geomantic chart is stretched in the new floor plan.

ing room side of the house, thus stretching the geomantic chart when it is superimposed onto the new floor plan. The fireplace is now situated in the square with the five-three-seven combination. In the new plan, a fountain is installed to neutralize the threat of fire in the nine-seven location.

EXAMPLE 2

Now consider the renovations shown in figure 12.6. Here, instead of adding a new section and stretching the geomantic chart, the renovations are designed to exclude an inauspicious area from the house by making it lie outside the building. After remodeling, the unfavorable area of seven-nine-five is a patio outside the house.

EXAMPLE 3

When auspicious stars lie outside the house, the areas can be recovered by making them part of the living space (figure 12.7). In the original floor plan, the area with the auspicious combination one-six-six was outside the house. By making that area a part of the house and repositioning the front door, we have improved the feng-shui of the house and the entrance dramatically. After remodeling, the auspicious combination of one-six-six is located at the front entrance. Moreover, the area's positive feng-shui will be enhanced by frequent use.

When remodeling is used to change the position of the Nine Palace stars in the rooms of a building, it is important that we alter less than one-third of the original floor plan. If the renovations are too extensive, we will end up with an entirely new geomantic chart derived from the cycle in which renovations took place.

Now do exercise 12.2.

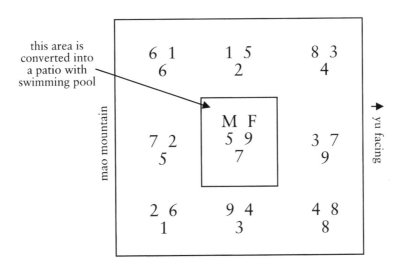

Figure 12.6 Using renovations to exclude an inauspicious palace from the house.

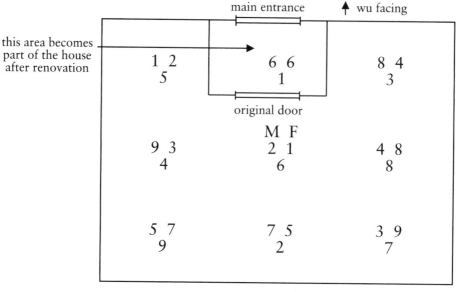

Figure 12.7 Using renovations to include an auspicious palace in the house.

Using Large-Scale Renovations to Obtain a New Geomantic Chart

A new geomantic chart is generated when more than one-third of the original floor plan is altered by remodeling and if the following points apply:

- The remodeling is completed in a cycle different from the one in which the house was built. In this case, all the stars of the Nine Palaces will change regardless of whether the renovations result in a change in the facing direction (figure 12.8, panel A).
- The remodeling is completed in the same cycle that the house was built originally, but the facing direction is changed by the renovations. In this case, the Earth Base will remain the same, but the Facing and Mountain stars will be different,

thus generating a different set of interactions between the Earth Base stars and the Facing Star (figure 12.8, panel B).

No new geomantic chart will be generated if the remodeling occurred in the cycle when the house was built and if there is no change in the facing direction. The old (original) geomantic chart is simply fitted onto the new floor plan.

Now that you understand how remodeling can give us new geomantic charts, you are ready to learn how to use renovations as countermeasures. In the practice of feng-shui, remodeling is not done haphazardly. If you plan to remodel, you need to find out whether the feng-shui of the building will improve as a result of the remodeling. More important, you don't want the feng-shui to get worse as the result of renovations. To illustrate these points, let's look at a hypothetical situation.

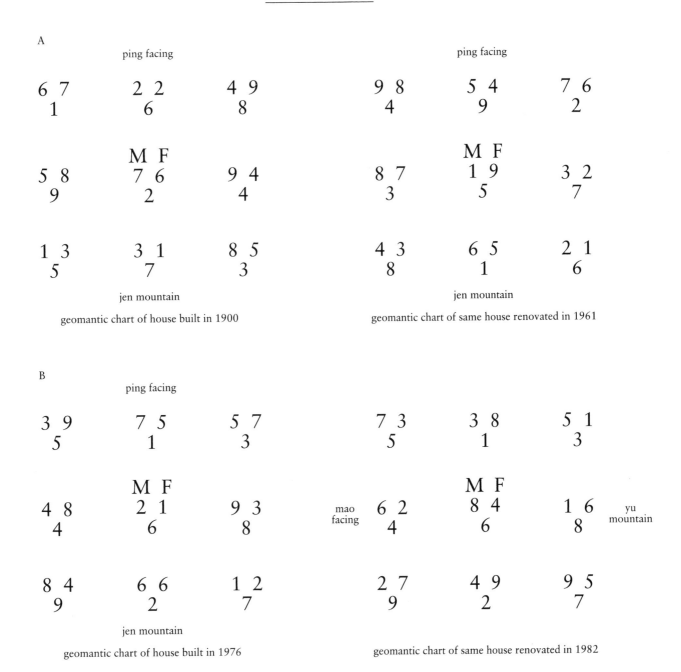

A

ping facing

6 7 1	2 2 6	4 9 8
5 8 9	M F 7 6 2	9 4 4
1 3 5	3 1 7	8 5 3

jen mountain

geomantic chart of house built in 1900

ping facing

9 8 4	5 4 9	7 6 2
8 7 3	M F 1 9 5	3 2 7
4 3 8	6 5 1	2 1 6

jen mountain

geomantic chart of same house renovated in 1961

B

ping facing

3 9 5	7 5 1	5 7 3
4 8 4	M F 2 1 6	9 3 8
8 4 9	6 6 2	1 2 7

jen mountain

geomantic chart of house built in 1976

7 3 5	3 8 1	5 1 3
mao facing 6 2 4	M F 8 4 6	1 6 8 yu mountain
2 7 9	4 9 2	9 5 7

geomantic chart of same house renovated in 1982

Figure 12.8 Renovations that result in new geomantic charts. A: Although the facing direction (ping) is the same, the remodeled house has a new set of Nine Palaces, because the remodeling was completed in a cycle different from the one in which the house was built. B: Although the renovations were completed in the cycle in which the house was built, a new chart is generated, because the facing direction has been changed from ping to mao.

Consider the example of a house built in the fourth cycle and currently occupied by a person who has one-white water as his guardian star / element. The geomantic chart and floor plan of the original building are shown in figure 12.9. Alternate geomantic charts based on two proposed remodeling plans are shown in figures 12.10 and 12.11. Looking at the original floor plan and the geomantic chart, we notice that although the living room has auspicious stars, the two bedrooms do not. The auspicious combination of eight-one-six is wasted in the bathroom.

Let's now look at the alternate floor plans and the geomantic charts based on the two remodeling plans. In the first plan, depicted in figure 12.10, the facing direction and the front entrance are the same as in the original floor plan. Only the interior partitions have changed. Because the remodeling is projected to be completed in the seventh cycle, however, the renovations will generate a new geomantic chart based on the seventh cycle. Notice that owing to the change in the cycle, there are new sets of Earth Base, Facing, and Mountain stars. In the new floor plan, the front entrance is now located in a spot occupied by extremely auspicious stars—eight-eight-four. This is very desirable, because the auspiciousness of the benevolent stars will be enhanced by the traffic in and out the front entrance.

Ideally, the bedrooms should have auspicious stars. Notice that in this remodeling plan, the bedroom is now occupied by the auspicious combination six-one-six. The renovations have really turned the feng-shui of the bedroom around, making it an extremely desirable space. This bedroom is also very beneficial to its occupant, because his guardian star / element one-white water will

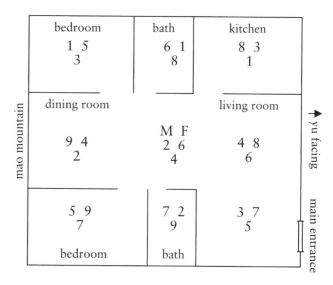

Figure 12.9 Original floor plan and geomantic chart.

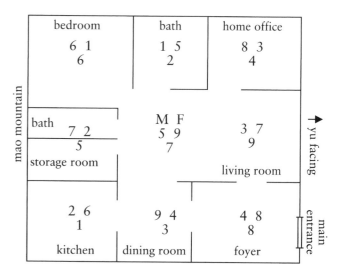

Figure 12.10 Proposed floor plan and geomantic chart for first remodeling plan.

be nourished by the Earth Base of the bed-room, which is six-white metal.

In planning the renovations, the next most important room to consider is the kitchen, because the kitchen is associated with health and livelihood. In the remodeling scheme, the kitchen is located in the lower left corner, the area with the combination one-six-two. The Earth Base / Facing Star interaction is very auspicious, since these are the stars of prosperity and health. The formal dining area is located next to the kitchen. This spot has decent feng-shui, because the Facing Star is four-green. The area formerly occupied by the kitchen is turned into a home office, because it has an auspicious Earth Base (four-green) and Mountain Star (eight-white). The bathrooms now take up the least desirable spots in the house—two-five-one and five-two-seven. Notice, too, that a section of the unfavorable area five-two-seven will be converted into a walk-in storage closet.

The only troublesome areas left in the house are the fire-hazard spot in the living room (nine-seven) and the seven-nine-five combination in the central square. The fire hazard and the inauspicious stars in the center can be neutralized in part by water-type countermeasures. Moreover, if we transform the large foyer into the living room and leave the present living area dormant, the auspicious combination eight-eight-four can be enhanced. With minimal usage and the placement of water-type countermeasures in the dormant living room, the fire hazard will be mitigated. We cannot completely neutralize the combination seven-nine-five in the center square, but if we put water-type countermeasures in the area, the problem will be diminished. In remodeling the house according to the first plan, the feng-shui of the house is improved greatly.

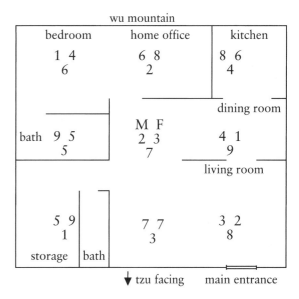

Figure 12.11 Proposed floor plan and geomantic chart for second remodeling plan.

Now let's look at the second plan, shown in figure 12.11. In this scheme, the facing direction is changed from yu to tzu. (Let's suppose that it is possible to change the facing direction from yu to tzu because the northern and western sides of the house both face open areas.) Here the entrance on the western side (yu) of the house is blocked. The bedroom in the upper left corner of the floor plan is enlarged so that one side of the bedroom is a home office. The most important point about this plan, however, is that the change in the facing direction has resulted in a Combination of Ten chart. I would choose the second remodeling plan, because it doesn't simply improve the feng-shui of the house—it perfects it.

Using renovation to improve the feng-shui of a building is one of the most challenging areas in the practice of the art. The following guidelines address when and how to use renovations as a countermeasure:

1. Examine the geomantic chart of the original floor plan closely to see whether the existing problems can be neutralized by small-scale renovations. There is no point to embarking on a large-scale renovation project if you don't need it.

2. If you decide that you need to remodel extensively, work out the new geomantic charts before you begin to design the floor plan. It will be easier to arrange the positions of the rooms if you have the Nine Palaces laid out in front of you.

3. Situate the important rooms first. Make sure that the bedrooms, the kitchen, and the frequently used rooms can be located in areas with auspicious stars and that the entrance is situated in an area where the Earth Base and/or Facing Star is not malevolent. Next, position the living room. Finally, situate the rooms with the lowest priority—the bathroom, utility room, and storage room.

4. Work out where you need to place countermeasure artifacts.

5. Compare all the proposed floor plans with the geomantic charts superimposed onto them.

6. Using a list of priorities, decide on which plan you want to implement. I suggest that you work out the list of priorities before you examine your plans. For example, for some people, cost is an important factor; for others, time and effort are key; and for still others, views and the aesthetics of the surrounding environment are essential.

There are no exercises on large-scale renovations, because subjective criteria play a large role. Study the section well. If you wish to practice on this topic, find ready-made floor plans in home-design books and devise your own renovation projects.

This concludes the coverage of special topics: countermeasures, enhancers, and renovations.

You now have learned the necessary basics of feng-shui to work on specific projects. At this point, you may want to go to the chapters in part three that address your specific feng-shui needs. Because part three is modular, you do not need to study the chapters in sequence or work on all of them. Make sure that you have a good grasp of all the information covered in parts one and two, however, before you proceed to work on the projects in part three.

EXERCISES

EXERCISE 12.1

Identify the houses in figure 12.12 where renovations resulted in new geomantic charts. Then generate the new geomantic charts and superimpose them onto the new floor plans. No. 1 is a worked example.

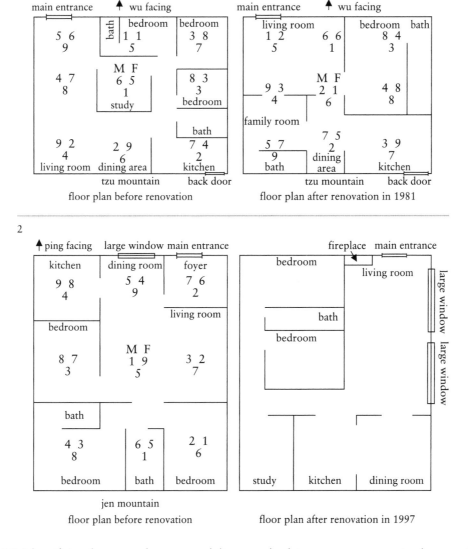

Figure 12.12 Identifying houses where remodeling resulted in a new geomantic chart and superimposing the chart on those houses (continued on next page).

3

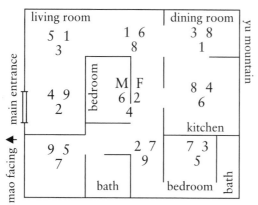

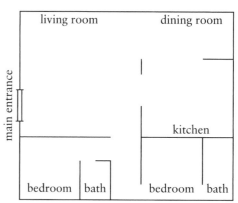

floor plan before renovation   floor plan after renovation in 1968

4

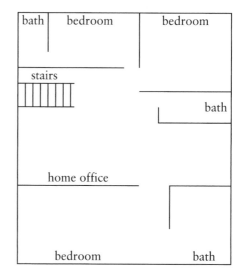

EXERCISE 12.2

Use small-scale renovations to improve the feng-shui of the houses shown in figure 12.13. Identify the problems in each house and then recommend the necessary changes. No. 1 is a worked example. The geomantic chart does not change.

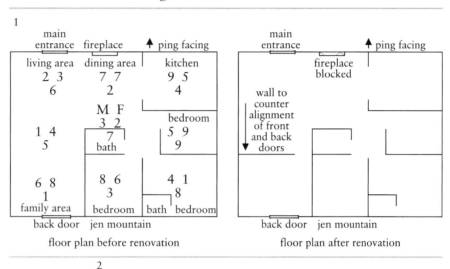

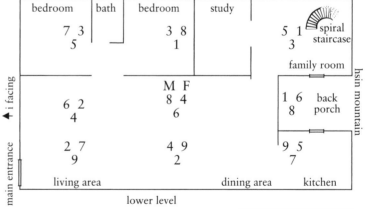

Figure 12.13 Using small-scale renovations to improve the feng-shui of two sample houses.

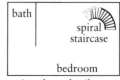

1.

- *A wall should be installed between the living room and family room so that the front and back doors are not aligned.*
- *The fireplace in the dining room should be blocked or removed because the fire-hazard combination two-seven is in both the macrocosm of the house and the microcosm of the room.*

ANSWERS

EXERCISE 12.1

Refer also to figure 12.14 for answers to exercise 12.1.

2.

The renovations altered at least one-third of the floor plan, resulting in a new facing direction and a new geomantic chart. The new facing direction is keng, because the front facing is rotated 90 degrees toward the side of the house with the most unobstructed view.

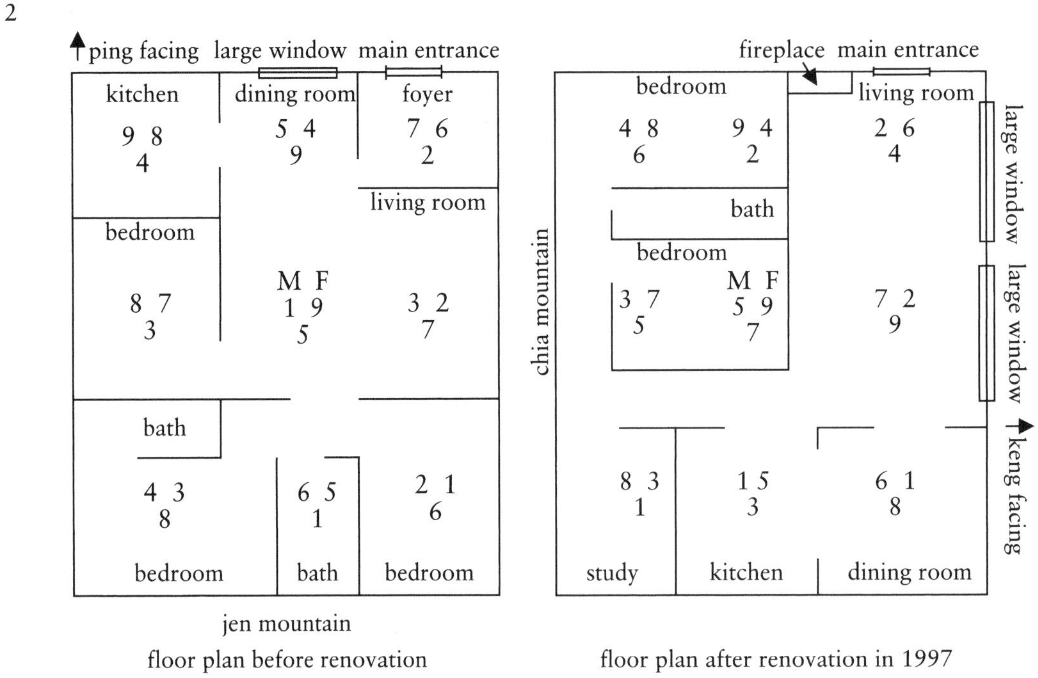

2

Figure 12.14 Answers to exercise 12.1 (continued on next page).

3.

Less than one-third of the floor plan was changed in the renovations. No new chart is generated. The old chart is superimposed onto the new floor plan.

4.

The addition of a level warrants a new geomantic chart, although the facing direction is the same. The new chart is superimposed onto both levels.

3

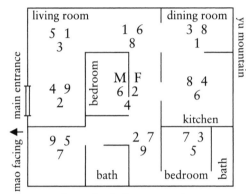

floor plan before renovation

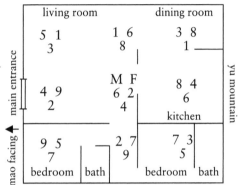

floor plan after renovation in 1968

4

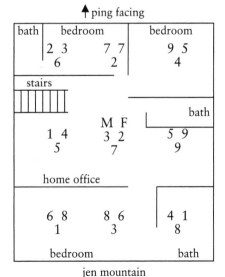

jen mountain

floor plan before renovation
new set of numbers are in brackets

jen mountain

upper level added in 1989
lower-level floor plan unchanged

EXERCISE 12.2

Refer also to figure 12.15 for answers to exercise 12.2.

2.

- The area with the auspicious combination eight-six-one should be recovered by making it a part of the house.

- The spiral staircases should be removed, and conventional stairways should be installed.

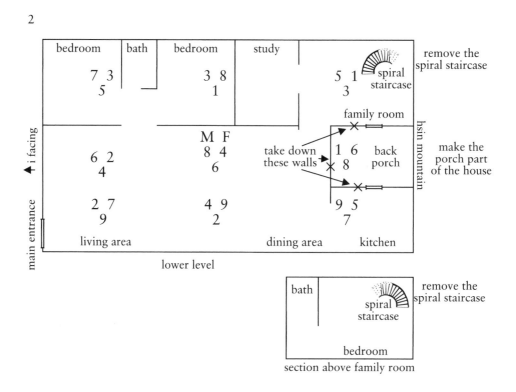

Figure 12.15 Answers to exercise 12.2.

SPECIFIC PROJECTS

Part three covers specific projects—building a new house, choosing an apartment, selecting and designing a business suite, and finding and designing a retail shop. You can work through the chapters sequentially or go to the chapter that fits your feng-shui needs.

13

Building a New House

In this chapter, you will learn how to apply the principles of feng-shui to building and designing a new house. The feng-shui involved in building a house is more complicated than that of evaluating an existing house. Because you are starting from scratch, however, you will have more flexibility in your choice of land, house orientation, and floor plan than when you are working with an existing house.

These are the steps we take in working out the feng-shui of a new house:

1. Choose a plot of land.

2. Find out which is the best general orientation of the house given the geographic features of the land.

3. Find out which is the best specific orientation (facing direction) of the house. This involves generating geomantic charts for all the directions in the selected general orientation and then choosing the chart (and thus the facing direction) that has the best combination of stars in the Nine Palaces.

4. Design the site plan and the floor plan, allocate the usage of space, and match the heads of household to the Earth Base at the front door and the occupants to the bedrooms for the selected geomantic chart.

5. Plan the placement of furniture, such as beds, desks, dining table, fireplaces, and appliances, according to the geomantic chart.

CHOOSING A PLOT OF LAND

The features in the external environment constitute the most important factor in the choice of a plot of land. Here I suggest a set of guidelines for selecting a building site.

Step 1: *Look for protection.*
Make sure that the plot of land is protected.

Land behind the house (the Black Tortoise) should be higher than the house itself, and land along the two sides (the Green Dragon and White Tiger) should form arms surrounding the house. Ideally, the Green Dragon formation should be higher than the White Tiger. Land to the front of the house (the Red

Raven) should not be too exposed. If the area is on flat land, you will need to see whether there are existing trees that can offer protection. If there are none, you must plan to plant trees and estimate when they will grow to become effective protectors.

If you are considering a plot in an urban area, you should look at the existing buildings surrounding the plot. Your new house should not be too close to tall buildings. Again, the plot of land (and the house) should be protected by a slightly taller building at the back, buildings along the two sides, and a lower building in front.

If you are considering a plot in a large suburban subdivision, you will need to identify the available building envelopes and determine whether the placement of a house on these pads is viable. Some large tracts of land have only small building envelopes, because sizable areas of the property fall on rocky outcrops, streams, lakes, or steep mountainsides.

Step 2: *Examine the surrounding features.* First, you should ascertain whether there are features (natural and constructed) that carry destructive energy in the vicinity of the plot of land. In an urban area, you should check whether there are buildings with sharp edges, reflective windows, satellite dishes, transmitting towers, power transmitters, and objects of destruction (including pictures on billboards). In rural regions, you should look for cliffs, sharp and rocky outcrops, rocks with grotesque shapes, steep and unstable slopes, bodies of stagnant water, white water or waterfalls dropping from great heights, dams with high walls, and power plants. A house should not be built in the vicinity of these destructive features.

Second, you should check for features that carry beneficial energy. In urban areas, they include dome-shaped buildings, fountains, parks, and greenery. In rural areas, look for round, smooth rock formations; trees; slow and smooth-running streams; clear, shallow lakes; and gentle slopes. These features all carry benevolent energy and will enhance the feng-shui of a house built nearby.

Third, you should determine the type of land use around the property. A house should not be built on ancient burial grounds, battlefields, concentration camp sites, or sites of massacres or near cemeteries, morgues, hospices, slaughterhouses, meatpacking plants, prisons, nuclear plants, garbage dumps, and any feature (natural or constructed) that is associated with death and decay.

Step 3: *Examine road and river patterns.* Roads and rivers are conduits of energy. If a plot of land is situated within a network of beneficial road and river patterns, energy from the land can be gathered and channeled to the house. If the plot lies within destructive road and river patterns, malevolent energy from the land can be amplified.

General Road and River Patterns

When examining road and river patterns, we first look at the layout of the road and river systems in the general area. In an urban environment, you should get a feel for the flow of the roads (straight or winding), the pattern of roads (grid, mazelike, or mixed), types of intersections (T junctions, Y junctions, scissorlike junctions, three-way, four-way, and so on), the gradient of the roads (steep or gentle), the size of the roads (one-lane, two-lane, eight-lane), the flow of traffic (large or small volume), and the locations of bridges, railroad and trolley tracks, vehicular tunnels, train tunnels, and elevated highways.

Here are the general rules for evaluating road patterns when choosing a building plot in an urban area:

- A plot along a winding street is better than one along a straight street.
- A plot in an area with mixed winding and straight streets is better than one within an area that has purely a grid-type or a mazelike road pattern.
- A plot on a one-lane or two-lane street is better than a plot on streets with four or more lanes.
- A plot on a street with a small flow of traffic is better than a plot on a street with a high volume of flow.
- Do not choose a plot near intersections. Intersections carry destructive and volatile energy and are harmful.
- Do not choose a plot along a steep road, because energy rushing down a steep slope becomes wild and destructive.
- Do not choose a plot near bridges, railroad and trolley tracks, tunnels, and elevated highways, because all these structures carry unpredictable and damaging energy.

Figure 13.1a shows an example of a desirable road pattern, and figure 13.1b shows an undesirable one. You may wish to refer to chapter 1 to review the types of road patterns and their effects on the feng-shui of a site.

Street patterns in rural areas are not as complicated as those in urban and suburban areas. There are generally two types of roads in rural areas—high-speed roads with high-volume traffic that connect towns and low-speed roads with low-volume traffic that serve a particular region. Make sure that your plot is not along a high-speed road. The plot of land also should not be situated near railroad tracks and bridges. Lots along steep, winding roads likewise are undesirable. Rivers function like roads, and principles that govern the feng-shui of roads apply to rivers. It is not advisable to build on a plot of land near fast-flowing streams or waterfalls dropping from great heights. You may wish to refer to chapter 1 for a review of the different types of beneficial and destructive road and river patterns.

Now that you are familiar with the principles of feng-shui that govern the choice of a plot of land, do exercise 13.1.

If you do not know how to read survey or contour maps, study the information presented in box 13.1. Before you go on to the next section, you should gain field experience by visiting plots of land that are on the real estate market. Look at urban plots, subdivisions in suburbs, and large tracts of land in rural areas. The more hands-on experience you have, the more competent you will be in choosing a suitable plot of land for building a new house.

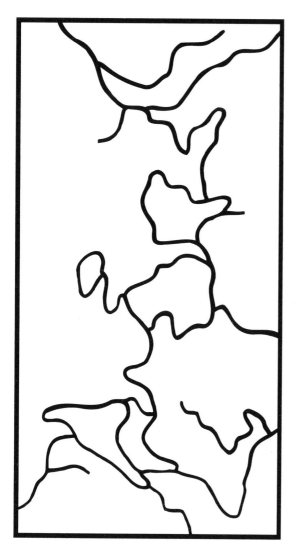

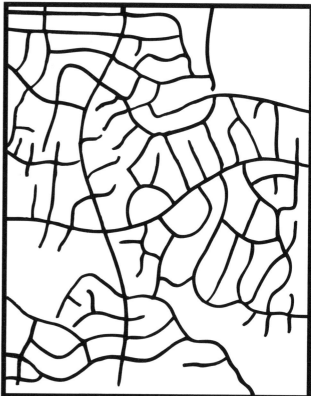

Figure 13.1a A desirable road pattern. The road winds gently without abrupt turns. There is a smooth flow and no sharp angles.

Figure 13.1b An undesirable road pattern. The roads are mazelike.

BOX 13.1

HOW TO READ SURVEY MAPS

Survey maps can tell us much about the terrain of the land, including information about elevations and geographic features. Knowing how to read survey maps can help you narrow down your choices of building plots before visiting them. The final decision on selecting a building site, however, should be made only after you have walked around each potential site.

Survey maps are sometimes called topographic maps or contour maps, because the information about elevation (or altitude) is depicted by contours. Contours are lines joining parts of the land that have equal elevations. The interval between contours will depend on the range of altitude in the area covered by the map. The contour interval may be small (ten feet) in an area with a small range of elevation (within one hundred feet) or large (one hundred feet) in an area with a large range of elevation (between one thousand and five thousand feet). A peak or high point typically is marked by a cross or an **X**, with its altitude (in feet or meters) printed next to it (figure B13.1a).

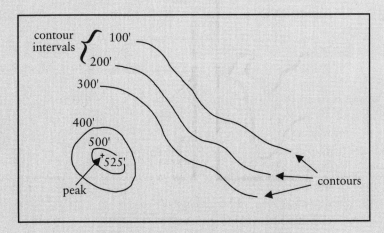

Figure B13.1a The contour map.

We can derive a general idea of the elevation of an area by looking at the proximity of the contour lines. The closer the contours are to each other, the steeper the slope. We also can evaluate the steepness of the terrain by taking a cross-sectional profile of the land across the contour lines. Figure B13.1b shows you how to do it.

step 1:
select an area for a cross-sectional profile

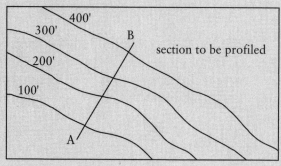

step 2:
put the edge of a sheet of paper against the selected
section and mark off the contours on the sheet (w, x, y, z)

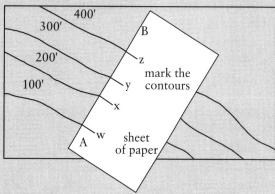

step 3:
transfer the marked contours onto graph paper
and join the marks (w, x, y, z)

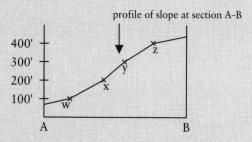

Figure B13.1b Translating contour information into a landform profile.

Figure B13.1c shows three profiles of landforms (A–A', B–B', C–C'). Notice that the area to the right, where the contours are widely spaced (A–A'), is fairly level. On the other hand, the area to the left, where the contours are narrowly spaced (C–C'), is rather steep. You can see that the area in the center contains a section of flat land with steep slopes behind it (B–B').

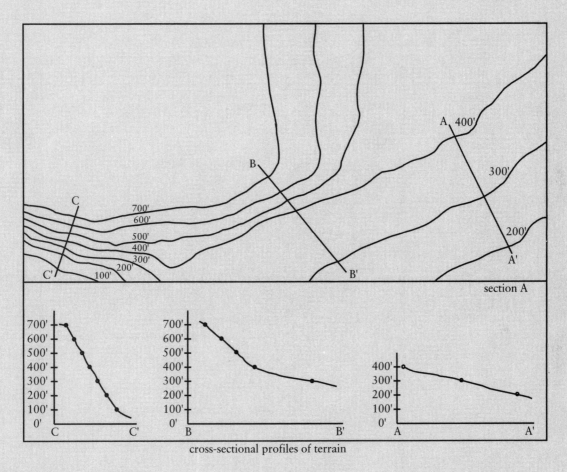

Figure B13.1c Examples of terrain profiles obtained from contour information.

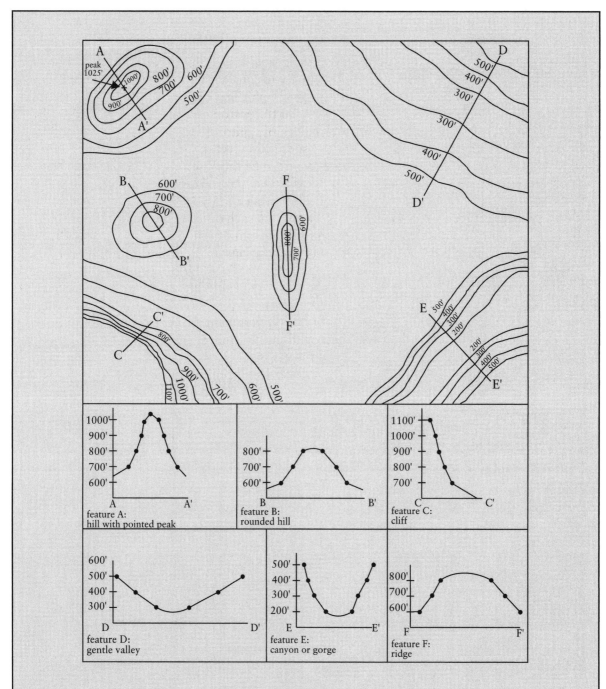

Figure B13.1d *Terrain features obtained from contour information.*

Contour maps also can tell us about geographic features. Since some landforms have desirable and others have undesirable feng-shui, it is useful to gain an idea of the types of landforms in a particular place before you consider visiting the building sites. In figure B13.1d, we can identify important geographic features on a contour map. For reference, the profile of each feature is shown at the bottom of the map.

First, hills are depicted by concentric circles of contours. Peaks are marked by a cross or an X, with the altitude of the peak specified in feet or meters (feature A in figure B13.1d). Conical or rounded hills are identified by the absence of an altitude point (feature B). Second, cliffs are depicted by very closely packed contours (feature C).

Third, valleys can be recognized by contours rising away from each other. In a valley with gentle slopes, the contours rising away from each other are widely spaced (feature D). In a gorge or canyon, these contours are narrowly spaced (feature E). Fourth, a ridge can be distinguished by contours whose elevations drop away on opposite sides (feature F).

Here's what you can do to familiarize yourself with identifying landforms in contour maps:

1. Get geographic survey maps issued by the government (in this country, United States Geological Survey maps) and property survey maps.
2. Work out selected profiles of terrain in the maps.
3. Check your accuracy in identifying landforms by visiting the area.

CHOOSING A GENERAL ORIENTATION FOR A HOUSE

Once you have selected a suitable plot of land for the new house, the next step is to orient the facing direction. Before we use the geomantic compass to work out the specific facing direction, we need to choose the general orientation of the building. Although there are twenty-four possible facing directions, some of them will be ruled out by constraints in the land or the surrounding features. For example, after the Black Tortoise has been identified to orient the back of the house, there may be only a few facing directions from which to choose. In urban lots, there are even more constraints, because the lot is bounded by a street in front and other buildings to the side.

In selecting the general orientation of a house, you first need to identify the protective features for the back of the house—hills, trees, and other buildings. These features determine the back facing of the property. If the plot is on flat land with no vegetation, you will need to select the direction for the back of the house and plan to plant trees or design landscape to act as the Black Tortoise.

If you cannot determine the back orientation of the plot, try to identify its front. Typically, the front of a house is the side that faces the downward slope. If there is no downward slope or if the direction of the downward slope is ambiguous, the side of the house that has the most open views is its front facing. As mentioned earlier, you should imagine the house as a chair and yourself sitting in this chair. Which direction is the back of the chair? Which direction would you face if you sat on the chair? The direction you face is the front of a house. By the time you have selected the front of the house, you will find that there are only a limited number of specific facing directions available.

Figure 13.2a–d shows examples of how landforms and surrounding buildings can place limits on the general orientation of a house. Notice that urban lots have the most constraints, followed by suburban lots and then rural lots in hilly areas. Rural lots on flat, open land have the fewest constraints, but they also have the least protection.

At this point you should do fieldwork. Visit several plots of land and practice choosing the general orientation of a new house. The first two steps in working out the feng-shui of a new house—choosing a plot and choosing the orientation—are the most time-consuming. This is not because the process is complicated: you simply need to evaluate many sites before you can narrow down your choices.

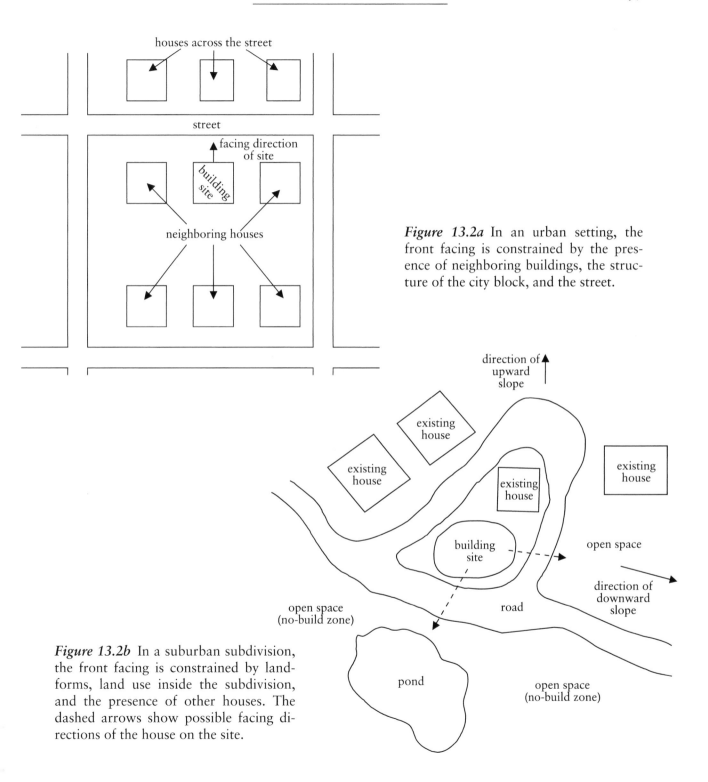

Figure 13.2a In an urban setting, the front facing is constrained by the presence of neighboring buildings, the structure of the city block, and the street.

Figure 13.2b In a suburban subdivision, the front facing is constrained by landforms, land use inside the subdivision, and the presence of other houses. The dashed arrows show possible facing directions of the house on the site.

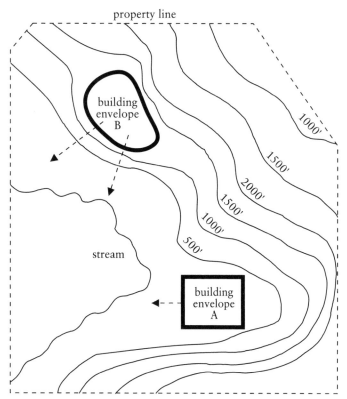

Figure 13.2c In a mountainous area, the building envelope and the facing direction of a house both are constrained by the landform. The dashed arrows show possible facing directions of houses on their respective sites. The altitude is cited above the appropriate contour line.

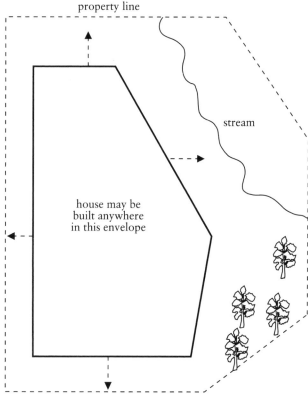

Figure 13.2d On flat land, the building envelope and the facing direction of a house are less constrained. The dashed arrows show possible facing directions of a house on a site.

CHOOSING A SPECIFIC
ORIENTATION FOR A HOUSE

After you have selected a general orientation for a new house, given the constraints of the surrounding environment, the next step is to choose a specific facing direction. The best way to illustrate the procedure is to look at an example.

Step 1: *Choose possible facing directions given constraints in the surrounding environment.*

Figure 13.3 shows a tract of land and a pad selected for the new house. Notice that in the example, given the surrounding landform, the house is restricted to a general easterly facing. Now we need to work out the geomantic charts for all the possible (easterly) facing directions of the house. To do this, we need to take compass readings for the possible facing directions. Let's say that we find three possi-

ble facing directions (figure 13.3)—chia, mao, and i (the three eastern-facing segments).

Step 2: *Generate geomantic charts for all the possible facing directions and choose one.*

The next step is to generate the geomantic charts for the three facing directions and find the best one. Since we plan to build our house before 2004, the geomantic chart of the new house will be based on the seventh cycle. Using the seventh cycle diagram (see the appendix), we generate the geomantic charts for the facing directions of chia, mao, and i (figure 13.4).

Looking at figure 13.4, we find that the geomantic charts for the facing directions mao and i are the same. We need to consider only two possibilities: chia and either mao or i.

Figure 13.3 Choosing a specific facing direction from the general front facing. The altitude is cited above the appropriate contour line.

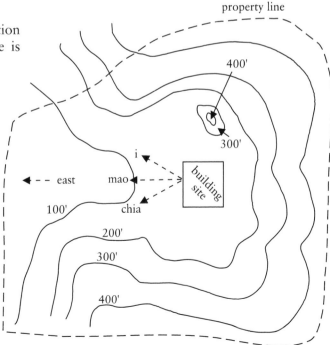

8 4 6	4 9 2	6 2 4
chia facing 7 3 5	M F 9 5 7	2 7 9 keng mountain
3 8 1	5 1 3	1 6 8

A

1 6 6	5 1 2	3 8 4
mao/i facing 2 7 5	M F 9 5 7	7 3 9 yu/ hsin mountain
6 2 1	4 9 3	8 4 8

B

Figure 13.4 Choosing a specific facing direction by selecting a geomantic chart. The mao and i facing charts are identical.

Comparing the two geomantic charts of the two choices, you will find that each chart has good and bad squares in the Nine Palaces. The Central Palaces are the same for all the charts, so the determining factors will lie in the rest of the squares. The chart with chia facing has three excellent squares—six-four-eight, eight-six-one, and one-eight-three. The chart with mao or i as the facing direction has two excellent squares—six-six-one and four-eight-three. In the chia-facing chart, however, there is the unfavorable square nine-seven-two. The nine-seven combination forebodes fire; coupled with two-black, it is likely that the fire will cause injuries. (For a review of the interactions among the stars of the Nine

Palaces, refer to chapter 6.) There are no big problems in the charts with the mao or i facing direction.

Which chart should we use for the new house? Most people will reject the chart with the chia facing because of the fire hazard of the nine-seven combination. It is possible to design a floor plan that will put the nine-seven combination square outside the house, though this will give the house an irregular shape.

My choice for the facing direction of the new house is either mao or i (they have the same chart), not chia. A house with a regular shape is more desirable than one with an irregular shape, because the flow of energy is smoother within in a symmetrical space.

Step 3: *Transfer the selected geomantic chart (and facing direction) onto the plot of land.*

After we have selected a facing direction for the house, we must transfer the information onto the land. We will need the geomantic compass, a ball of string, and nonmetal spikes. (Plastic tent pegs are excellent for this purpose.) Follow the instructions given here. You may wish to refer to figure 13.5 for clarification.

1. Line up the needle of the compass with the north-pointing arrow on the face of the compass and put it on the ground.

2. With the ring template in place on the compass (the marker on the tzu segment aligned with zero degree), read off the direction of the chosen facing direction. In our example, it is mao.

3. Hammer a peg into the ground and tie the string around it, leaving enough length on both ends. This spike will locate the center of the house.

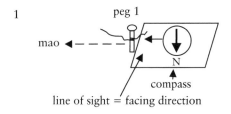

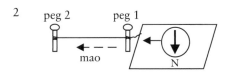

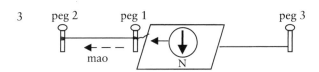

Figure 13.5 Transferring the facing direction onto the land. (See text explanation.) N, north.

4. Unroll the string and walk away from the first spike toward the facing direction of the house. Approximately ten feet away, with the string tied around a second peg, hammer the peg into the ground so that the two pegs are perfectly lined up.

5. Do the same thing for a third peg, which is to be placed behind the first one.

6. If necessary, adjust the positions of the pegs to align all three perfectly. You may need to place the compass at all three pegs to check the alignment. If you want more accurate measurements, you can set up more than three anchor positions.

7. The string connecting the three pegs specifies the facing direction of the house. To ensure that the builders know exactly what you want, you should work closely with the architect and the contractor. Once the foundation is poured, it will be difficult to make any changes.

To familiarize yourself with choosing a specific orientation (which implies selecting the best geomantic chart), do exercise 13.2.

DESIGNING A SITE PLAN AND A FLOOR PLAN

Once a building pad and the facing direction are chosen for a new house, the next step is to design the floor plan. At this point, you will need to work closely with your architect and builder. To expedite matters, you should have a basic idea of the usage of space based on the selected geomantic chart. Before you approach the architect, you should plan where you want to situate bedrooms, kitchen, living room, entranceway, and stairs.

Here are guidelines that will help you design the general floor plan of the house:

- It is preferable for the entrance road to the house to curve around and not to run straight toward the house.
- The garage should be detached from the house. If this is not possible because of the size of the property or covenant regulations, the garage should be off to the side (see chapter 2).
- The house should be as symmetrical as possible and not irregularly shaped.
- The main entrance should occupy a Nine Palace square that has benevolent stars. The Earth Base in the square where the main entrance is located should be beneficial or at least neutral to the heads of household. Remember, the front door does not necessarily have to be positioned in the facing direction of the house.
- The main entrance should be buffered from the rest of the house, including the upper levels.
- Stairs to the upper levels should be in areas that have benevolent or neutral stars. Never place stairs in areas with harmful combinations, such as five-five, two-five, or five-two.
- Choose locations for bedrooms first, because you need to make sure that the Earth Base stars of the bedrooms are benevolent or at least neutral to their occupants.
- After choosing spots for the bedrooms, you should position the kitchen.
- After locating the kitchen, you should situate the room with the most frequent use. Then you should situate the rest of the rooms according to frequency of use.
- You should fill the less desirable spaces in the Nine Palaces with bathrooms, walk-in closets, and utility rooms. These spaces are also good as buffer areas.
- Make sure that fireplaces, stoves, and electrical and mechanical equipment (such as the furnace and main electrical panel) are not located in areas with fire hazards (combinations of nine-seven and two-seven).

Let's go through an example to illustrate the procedure of designing a floor plan for a house. Suppose that in our example, the property is situated on ten acres of land in a hilly region. The projected house will have two levels, and there will be two occupants—a single father and a male child.

Positioning the Driveway

First, we plan the position of the driveway leading to the house. Looking at figure 13.6, we see that the road is constrained by the surrounding landforms. For practical reasons, most access roads and driveways follow the path of the smallest gradient. Recall that steep roads carry destructive energy.

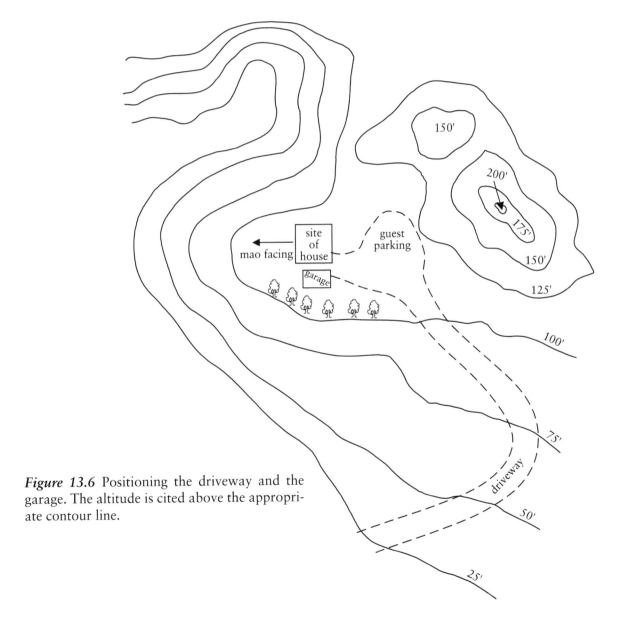

Figure 13.6 Positioning the driveway and the garage. The altitude is cited above the appropriate contour line.

Positioning the Garage

Once the driveway or access road is positioned, we can begin to locate the garage. Because there is adequate space in this example, the garage can be detached from the house (figure 13.6). To protect the occupants from unpredictable and possibly destructive energy carried by the vehicles, there are no parking areas near the house.

Planning the Usage of Space in the House

When a specific orientation is chosen (based on the most desirable geomantic chart), we can begin to work on the floor plan. Using the geomantic chart generated from the facing direction of mao, we will design a general plan for situating the rooms in the house. Figure 13.7 shows the geomantic chart and personal data of the occupants.

POSITIONING THE MAIN ENTRANCE

We will start with the lower level of the house (figure 13.8). First, we put the main entrance in the square with an extremely powerful group of auspicious stars—the area occupied by the combination six-six-one. These are stars of good fortune and prosperity; moreover, in our example, the Earth Base (six-white) of this area is compatible with the guardian star of the head of house, which is also six-white metal.

POSITIONING THE KITCHEN

Next we locate the kitchen, which is also an important area in the house. In our example, the best spot for the kitchen is the square with the combination four-eight-three. This is a benevolent spot; situating the kitchen here will ensure that the family enjoys good health and has enough to eat (that is, a good livelihood). The area does not have any stars associated with fire hazard or injury by fire.

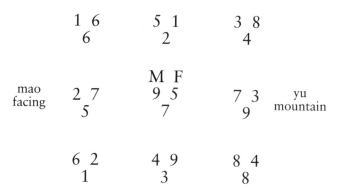

father / male head of household: six-white metal
male child: four-green wood

Figure 13.7 The geomantic chart and the birth data of the occupants.

POSITIONING THE FAMILY ROOM / RECREATIONAL ROOM

There is one viable area left in the lower level—the square with the combination nine-three-seven. Provided that we do not situate a fireplace here, the room can be used as a recreational room for the family.

POSITIONING THE STAIRS

Next we need to position the stairs. Stairs carry energy to the upper level and are used frequently. For these reasons, they should not be situated in harmful areas. The square with the combination one-two-six is better than the square with the combination three-nine-four. It is not desirable to locate a stairway in a square with nine-purple fire as the Facing Star. Although the Facing Star in the area cho-sen for the stairway is two-black, the star is neutralized by the presence of one-white in the Earth Base and six-white in the Mountain Star. The area can be improved if we place countermeasures to offset two-black. Metal objects are ideal, because the earth energy of two-black will be dissipated to create or nourish metal. Metal will also nourish or create the water of one-white in the Earth Base, thus strengthening it as a natural countermeasure against two-black earth (figure 13.8).

POSITIONING THE LIVING ROOM AND DINING ROOM

Since these rooms are used infrequently by the family in our example, they can be located in areas with neutral or even not-so-desirable stars (figure 13.8).

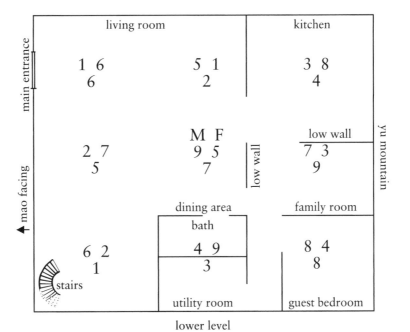

Figure 13.8 Planning the usage of space in the lower level of the house.

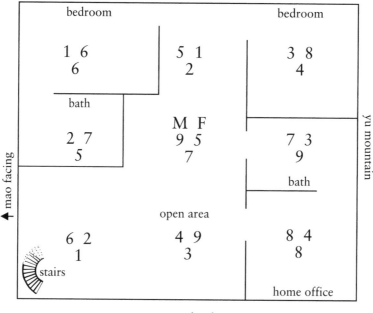

Figure 13.9 Planning the usage of space in the upper level of the house.

POSITIONING THE BEDROOMS

When we design the usage of space for the upper level (figure 13.9), the first thing to do is to select the location for each occupant's bedroom. The main factor determining the selection of bedrooms for the occupants is the interaction of their guardian stars with the Earth Base of the room. If you need a review of this material, refer to chapter 8.

In our example, the best location for the father's bedroom is the one with the combination six-six-one. These stars are associated with good fortune and good health. Moreover, the Earth Base, six-white metal, is compatible with the father's guardian star (which is the same). The areas with four-green wood and three-jade wood as Earth Base are not suitable for him, because metal is weakened when it destroys wood. The area with nine-

purple fire as the Earth Base is dangerous for anyone except those with nine-purple fire and earth-type stars as their guardian star / element. Areas with two-black and five-yellow as the Earth Base (even with neutral Facing and Mountain stars) are viable only for people with two-black and five-yellow as guardian stars / elements. Rooms with combinations of five-two, two-five, and five-five are dangerous for everyone, regardless of their guardian star / elements.

The child, who has four-green wood as his guardian star / element, can have his bedroom in the square with the combination four-eight-three, because the combination four-eight-three is associated with good health and good fortune. Moreover, the Earth Base Star (four-green wood) in that space is compatible with the child's guardian star / element (which is also four-green wood). The other spaces in the upper level all have Earth Base stars that are harmful to his guardian star / element. These stars include nine-purple fire (wood is weakened to create fire), two-black earth, and five-yellow earth (wood is weakened to destroy earth). The child's bedroom should not be situated in the square with the combination eight-four-eight, because the star combination eight-four is associated with children's illnesses.

POSITIONING THE STUDY/ HOME OFFICE

I would make the room with the combination eight-four-eight the home office and make sure that only the father uses this room. The child's study area should be in his room.

POSITIONING THE LESS-USED ROOMS

Once the bedrooms and the home office are positioned, we can fill in the rest of the space with bathrooms, open areas, and other rooms. Notice that in our example, the bathrooms are situated in the least desirable areas, because compared with the other rooms, they are used the least (figure 13.9).

Once you have determined the general usage of space in the house, the next step is to discuss the plan with the architect. Notice that in our general plan, there is sufficient flexibility for the architect to design a floor plan that takes into account your feng-shui needs. You may need to be assertive with your architect and/or builder and not let them make you conform to their preferences. After all, it is *your* house, not theirs.

PLACEMENT OF FURNITURE

Although furniture is moved in after the house is completed, you should have a general idea of where the furniture is to be positioned while you are working on the floor plan. Some areas within a room are optimal for the placement of desks, beds, dining table, and so on, while other areas should be left dormant. Having an idea of the ideal placement of specific furniture will spare you the problem of finding out later that the optimal space for a desk, for example, is occupied by the closet.

When we plan furniture placement, we need to examine the microcosm of each room and identify the type of energy, positive or negative, that flows in each area. We do this by superimposing the geomantic chart for the house onto each room. (Refer to chapter 9 if you need a review.) Let's look at an example of planning the placement of furniture. Refer to figure 13.10. Continuing with the same house, we have superimposed the geomantic chart we have chosen onto the two bedrooms for reference.

Bedrooms

As pointed out earlier, bedrooms are the most important rooms in the house. From chapter 9, you will recall that beds and desks should be placed in areas where the conditional interactions of the Facing Star and/or the Earth Base or the additive interactions of the three stars are benevolent. Specifically,

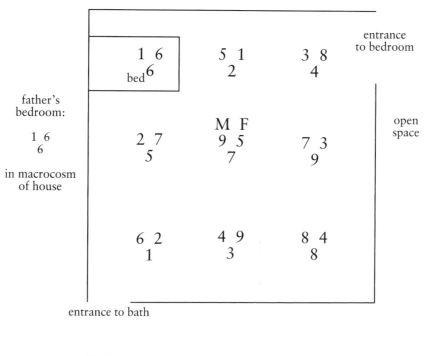

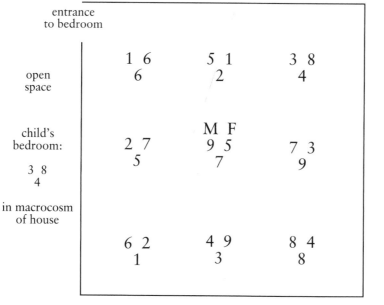

Figure 13.10 Planning the placement of furniture in the bedrooms. Possible spots for the child's bed are the squares with the combinations four-eight-three and three-nine-four.

areas with interactions associated with health, success, and good fortune are the best locations for beds and desks. The worst areas are those occupied by conditional and additive interactions associated with illness. Closets and other seldom-used areas should occupy areas with inauspicious Facing stars, such as five-yellow and two-black. Fireplaces should not be located in areas where nine-purple fire is the Facing Star or the Earth Base. Mirrors should not face the bed, windows, or doors, and the bed should not be placed under an exposed beam.

We will work first with the bedroom with the combination six-six-one. The first thing to do is to determine where to position the entrance to the room, because the entrance puts many constraints on the placement of furniture. The doorway should occupy an area where there are auspicious stars.

In our example, superimposing the geomantic chart onto the room for the father, we find that the best location for the door is the square four-eight-three (figure 13.10). The placement of the bed should be the next priority. Within the same room, the square with the combination six-six-one is the ideal spot (figure 13.10). The stars and the combinations are associated with good health and good fortune. After you have selected the spot for the bed, you should make sure that there are no exposed beams in the ceiling above that area and that mirrors do not face the bed, windows, or doors.

After the most important pieces of furniture are placed, you can decide where to put the closets and the bathroom door. These can be situated in any of the other spots in the room, given the constraints of the general floor plan.

Kitchen

The kitchen is the next most important room in the house. The kitchen's feng-shui governs the health and livelihood of the occupants. Moreover, owing to the presence of fire associated with cooking (even if the stove is electric), we need to be careful that cooking appliances (the stove and microwave oven) are not placed in the location of the star nine-purple fire. If there is an informal dining area within the kitchen, we need to consider the placement of the dining table. Ideally, the cooking and eating areas should be located in spots where there are stars of good health and livelihood; they should not be in places occupied by the stars of illness or disharmony. The dining table should not be put under exposed beams.

Using our previous example, let's look at the positioning of the appliances and the kitchen table. Figure 13.11 shows the geomantic chart superimposed on the microcosm of the kitchen. The best spot for the stove is the square with the four-eight-three combination. This combination is associated with good health and good fortune; using this area for cooking will ensure that the occupants have good health and a good livelihood. Another excellent spot in the kitchen is the area occupied by six-six-one. This is an appropriate place for informal dining. There are two locations that are unacceptable for the stove. These are the squares where nine-purple is located in the Facing Star and in the Earth Base. Placing cooking appliances in these areas will create fire hazards and promote injuries associated with fire. I suggest that sinks and/or cabinets be placed in the areas where nine-purple is the Facing Star, so that the fire element can be neutralized. Once the important pieces of furniture and appliances are posi-

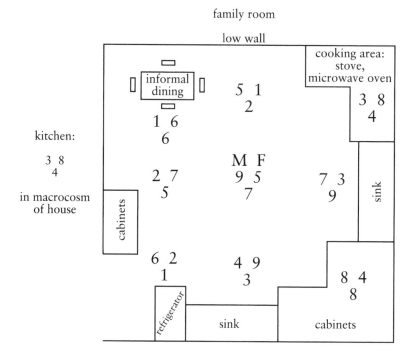

Figure 13.11 Planning the placement of furniture and appliances in the kitchen.

tioned, you can choose locations for the areas that are used infrequently, such as the storage closets.

Family Room / Recreation Room

This room becomes important if it is used frequently by the occupants of the house. Because activity enhances energy, furniture and recreational equipment need to be placed in areas that are occupied by auspicious stars. Using the same example again, let's see how furniture and recreational equipment are situated in the family room (figure 13.12).

Assuming that there are no exposed beams and ceiling edges, we should place the couch in the square with the combination three-nine-four. The best spot, occupied by the com-

bination six-six-one, should be the entryway into the kitchen, since frequent use of this passageway will enhance the auspicious stars. I would place the home entertainment equipment in the square with the combination four-eight-three. The benevolent energy carried by the Earth Base and the Facing Star will be enhanced by movement in the television and the sound system.

Home Office and Study Area

Desks and computer workstations should be placed in areas occupied by the stars of success and prosperity—specifically, Earth Base / Facing Star combinations of one-four, four-one, six-eight, eight-six, and four-six. Areas occupied by Earth Base / Facing Star com-

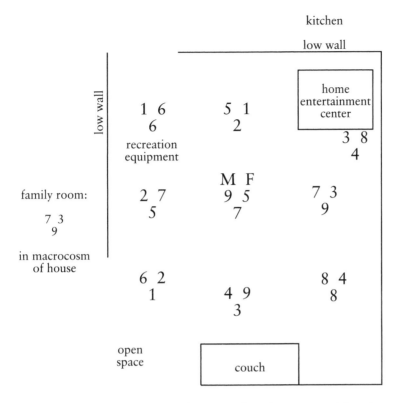

Figure 13.12 Planning the placement of furniture in the family room.

binations of seven-six, six-seven, two-three, and three-two, as well as combinations of two and five, are not desirable. If possible, the person working at the desk should face an area occupied by the stars of success.

Using our current example, let's look at how furniture in a study or home office is arranged (figure 13.13). Looking at the Nine Palaces superimposed onto the microcosm of the home office, we find that the best positions for the desk are the squares with the Earth Base / Facing Star combinations of six-six and four-eight. We can put a desk or computer workstation in the space occupied by the combination eight-four, facing the doorway, where the combination six-six is located.

Since doorways are constrained by the layout of the other rooms, sometimes we do not have much choice. In our example, things seem to work out well, because we can place the doorway in the square occupied by the combination six-six-one. The filing cabinet, photocopier, and fax can be put in the area with the combination one-two-six.

The child's study area should be located in his bedroom. In the microcosm of the room, I would place the desk in the square with the combination three-nine-four and have it face the doorway, which has the combination six-six-one.

Once you have completed the exercises, you will realize that there is more flexibility in

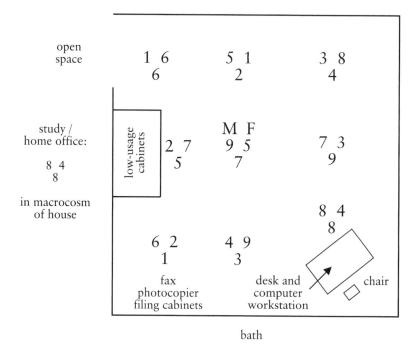

Figure 13.13 Planning the placement of furniture in the study / home office.

working with a new house than with an existing house. The positions of doorways and the placement of fireplaces, stoves, sinks, and built-in furniture can be planned while you are working on the architectural design of the house and the floor plan. The perfect geomantic chart is rare; sometimes, even after you have found the best possible use of space, you will need to put countermeasures and enhancers in place to lessen the impact of inauspicious stars and enhance all the auspicious areas. If you need to review the use of countermeasures and enhancers, refer to chapters 10 and 11.

EXERCISES

EXERCISE 13.1

Identify possible building pads and the general orientations for the new houses shown in figure 13.14. Then mark the building pads and point out the possible facing directions with an arrow. The maps in nos. 2 and 7 show four properties in a subdivision. The partitions are indicated by dashed lines. The maps in nos. 3 through 6 show one piece of property. No. 1 is a worked example.

1.

The building pads for properties A, C, and D are marked by a square with an X in the middle. The general orientation of each building pad is indicated by an arrow. Property B does not have a suitable building pad. The area to the right is too near cliffs, and a road runs straight toward the area to the left.

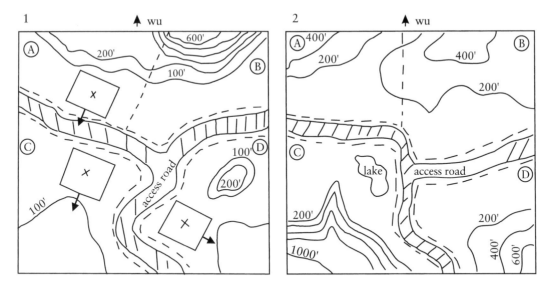

Figure 13.14 Choose the building pads and general facing directions for properties. Dashed lines denote property lines. Sample building pads are marked by a square with an **X**. The asterisk in example 7 indicates a peak (continued on next pages).

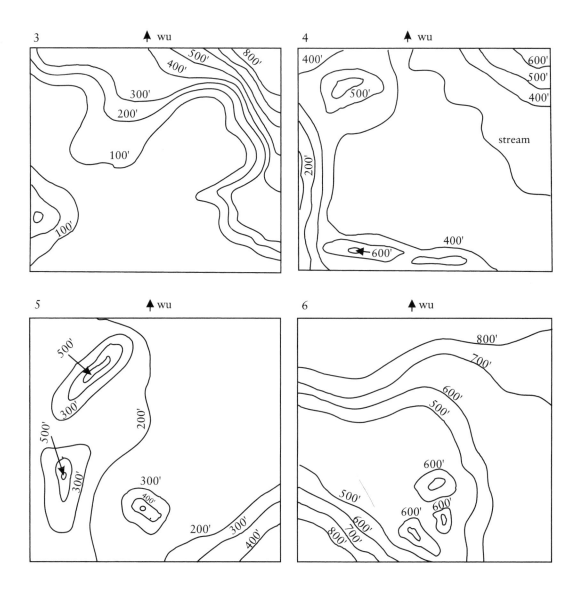

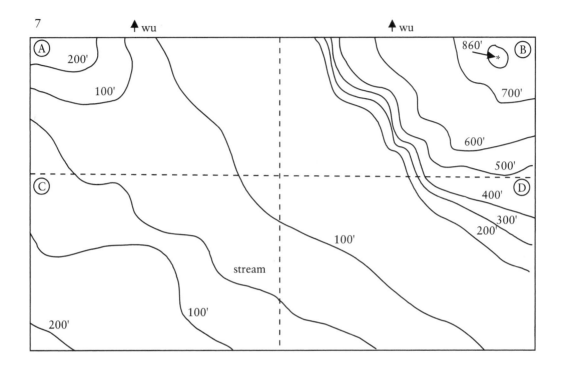

EXERCISE 13.2

Choose a specific orientation between the following possible facing directions in each example. Assume the houses will be built within the seventh cycle.

1. Possible facing directions: tzu and mao

Hints: First, generate the geomantic charts for the two facing directions. Then compare the auspicious and inauspicious Nine Palace squares of the charts. Finally, select one and give the rationale for your choice of the facing direction.

2. Possible facing directions: chia and keng

ANSWERS

EXERCISE 13.1

Refer to figure 13.15 for answers to exercise 13.1.

2.

There are two viable facing orientations for property B—facing the access road or facing the lake. There is no desirable building pad for property C. The flat areas are too close to steep slopes.

3.

There are two viable building pads—X_1 and X_2. Each pad has only one possible facing orientation because of the restrictions imposed by the Black Tortoise formation at the back of each house.

4.

There is one ideal building pad. It is surrounded by all four protection animals. Notice the gentle rising of the land toward the front (the Red Raven), the ridge at the back (the Black Tortoise), and the ridges to the left and right (Green Dragon and White Tiger).

5.

There is one ideal building pad. Although the Red Raven formation is absent, there are good features forming the Black Tortoise, Green Dragon, and White Tiger.

6.

There is one ideal building pad. The site is located in a valley, with the valley sides acting as the Green Dragon and White Tiger. The small, rounded hills toward the back of the house constitute the Black Tortoise formation. The front of the house should face the mouth of the valley.

7.

There is one possible building pad for property A. The gentle upward slope should be at its back, and the house should face the direction of the valley. The building pad for property B is not very desirable because it is a bit too close to the steep slope. There is one possible building pad for property C, and the house should face the downward slope toward the stream. Property D has a very large building envelope. Any pad chosen from the envelope should face the downward slope toward the stream.

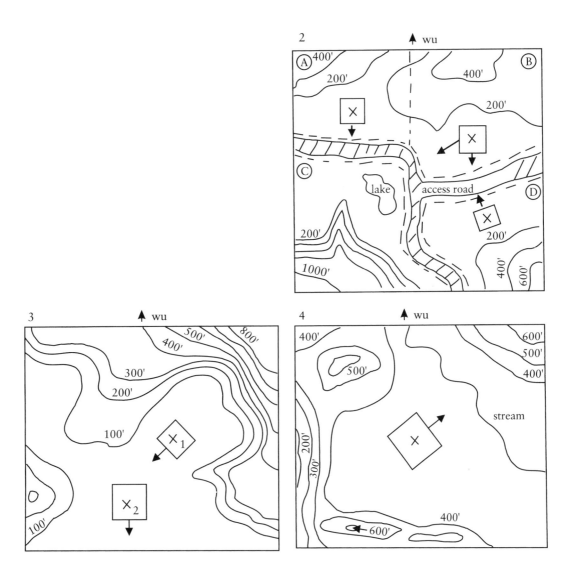

Figure 13.15 Answers to exercise 13.1 (continued on next page). The altitude is cited above the appropriate contour line.

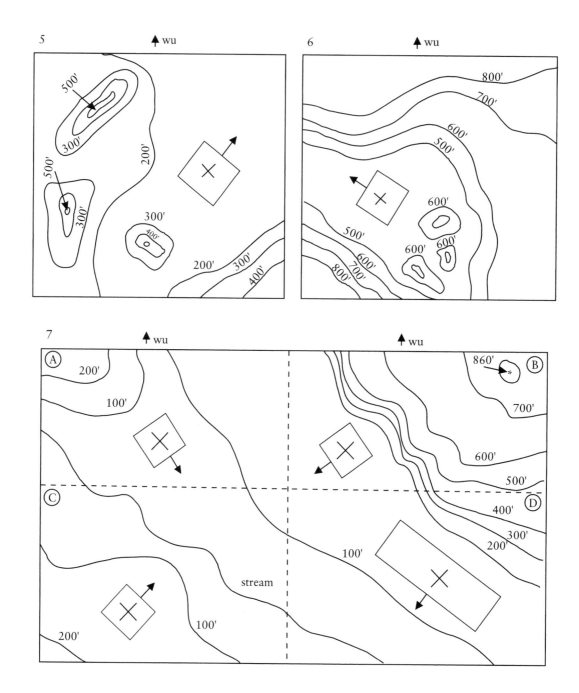

EXERCISE 13.2

1.

These are the geomantic charts:

A.

wu mountain

```
  1  4        6  8        8  6
    6            2            4

              M   F
  9  5        2  3        4  1
    5            7            9

  5  9        7  7        3  2
    1            3            8
```

tzu facing

B.

```
  6  1        1  5        8  3
    6            2            4

              M   F
mao   7  2    5  9    3  7 yu
facing   5       7       9 mountain

  2  6        9  4        4  8
    1            3            8
```

The tzu-facing chart is a Combination of Ten chart. I would choose this chart and make sure that all the palaces are present in the house.

2.

These are the geomantic charts:

A.

```
  8  4        4  9        6  2
    6            2            4

              M   F
chia   7  3    9  5    2  7 keng
facing   5       7       9 mountain

  3  8        5  1        1  6
    1            3            8
```

B.

```
  4  8        9  4        2  6
    6            2            4

              M   F
chia   3  7    5  9    7  2 keng
mountain 5       7       9 facing

  8  3        1  5        6  1
    1            3            8
```

The chia-facing chart has two excellent squares (6/4/8 and 1/6/8), one good square (1/8/3), three squares that can be made viable by installing countermeasures (4/2/6, 3/1/5, and 5/3/7), and three unfavorable squares (9/7/2, 2/9/4, and 7/5/9). The keng-facing chart has two excellent squares (6/8/4 and 8/1/6), one good square (1/3/8), one square that can be made better with countermeasures (4/6/2), three squares that can be made suitable with countermeasures (4/6/2, 3/5/1, and 5/7/3), and two inauspicious squares (7/9/5 and 9/2/7). I would choose the keng-facing chart, because there are fewer troublesome areas. These two charts are almost identical in terms of excellent squares, good squares, and squares that can be made viable by installing countermeasures.

14

Choosing an Apartment

In this chapter, you will learn how to evaluate the feng-shui of an apartment. I use the term *apartment* to refer to a residential unit within a housing complex or a multistory building. Condominiums and town houses that fit this description are classified as apartments, regardless of whether they are owned or rented by the occupants. Duplexes and town houses that are connected to each other are considered houses, and their feng-shui is evaluated in the same way as that of detached houses (see box 14.1).

Although the general principles for evaluating the feng-shui of houses and apartments are similar, there are details that are specific to apartments, including the architectural layout of the main entrance of the apartment building, the arrangement of the units within the building, and the position of elevators, stairways, landings, fire escapes, and areas of common use in relationship to the unit in question.

Before we begin to evaluate the feng-shui of an apartment, we first need to determine whether the unit in question should be classified an "apartment." In traditional apartment buildings this is not a problem, because the apartments clearly are units within a larger building. In newer complexes, especially those built in suburban North America, it is sometimes difficult to tell whether the unit should be considered an apartment or a single house. Let's look at the examples shown in figures 14.1 through 14.5.

The traditional type of apartment building is pictured in figure 14.1. This is a building with three or four stories, a small foyer, and no elevator. The units are well defined and are clearly part of the larger building. In figure 14.2, we have a high-rise apartment building. The only difference between this one and the older type of apartment building is the number of levels and the presence of an elevator and perhaps a larger foyer. Here, too, the units are well defined and are clearly part of the larger building.

When we come to the building shown in figure 14.3, we find that each unit has an independent entrance and there is no main foyer. This is the "motel" type of apartment building. The units still form a cohesive structure within the larger complex and fall within the category of apartment, not house.

How about the building illustrated in figure

BOX 14.1

TOWN HOUSES THAT RESEMBLE HOUSES

Some town houses resemble houses, and their feng-shui should be evaluated as if they were single homes. These types of town houses are typically multistoried homes joined to each other. Usually, each town house has an entrance that opens onto a common courtyard or the road. The independent entrance is probably the most important factor in determining whether a town house is a house or an apartment. (The exception is the motel-type apartment complex.) In fact, we can think of these town houses as a group of duplexes or semidetached houses linked together. Look at figure B14.1, which shows town houses joined together with independent entrances opening onto a common space. These homes are considered houses rather than apartments.

Ultimately, the best way to judge whether a home should be considered a house or an apartment is by its ambience. Does the home feel like a house or like a unit within a larger complex? Do you get a sense that the entrance to your home is your own, or do you share a common entryway with your neighbors? You should try to develop an intuition for whether a town house should be considered a house or an apartment by visiting town house subdivisions and complexes.

Figure B14.1 Town houses treated as single homes with independent entrances.

Figure 14.1 A traditional apartment building.

14.4? This is a low, multistory complex spread across an enclosure. At first glance, the complex resembles a string of houses typical of the suburban subdivisions emerging in many North American bedroom communities. On closer examination, the units in this complex do not qualify as single houses, because there are separate units occupying different levels (see also figure 14.5a and b). For this reason, the feng-shui of the units should be evaluated as apartments and not as houses. If a unit occupies all three levels instead of just one, the unit would be classified as a house and not an apartment. This may seem to be a trivial distinction at first, but the error in classification can lead to inaccurate analysis of the apartment's feng-shui.

Finally, let's consider the loft apartment in a warehouse. Such units are classified as apartments, even though they have been converted from industrial to residential use. The

Figure 14.2 A high-rise apartment building.

Figure 14.3 A motel-type apartment building.

Figure 14.4 A multistory apartment complex spread across an enclosed subdivision.

entrance, stairway, and elevators may not be laid out like those of conventional apartments; nonetheless, there are well-defined units within the larger building.

Now that you have learned to recognize the characteristics that constitute an apartment in the context of feng-shui, you are ready to learn how to choose an apartment.

Figure 14.5a A multistory apartment building in which the upper levels are accessed by the covered stairway in the middle.

Figure 14.5b A multistory apartment building complex in which the upper levels are accessed by stairways on the side of the building.

EVALUATING THE EXTERNAL ENVIRONMENT OF A BUILDING

The external environment of an apartment includes the landscape and buildings in the vicinity of the apartment building; the pattern of roads leading up and into the building complex; and the location and layout of the garage and parking area.

Landscape and Buildings in the Vicinity of the Apartment Building

We begin by examining the features of the landscape and buildings in the area around the apartment building. The procedure is similar to that described in chapter 1.

First, we see if there are harmful features and objects directed at the building, including buildings with knifelike edges, transmission towers, satellite dishes, destructive objects painted on billboards or designed as sculptures, and so on. You may wish to go through the list in chapter 1 for a review of the types of features that carry malevolent energy. Remember to check for harmful objects outside the grounds of the apartment complex as well as inside.

Second, we need to identify features that carry benevolent energy. These features are a bonus and are desirable to have in the vicinity of the apartment building. They include rotundas, domes, round pools with fountains, trees, lawn, and flowers.

Third, we need to check use of land in the neighborhood. Are there undesirable types of land use, such as dumps, power stations, cemeteries, mortuaries, hospitals, and the like? You can turn to chapter 1 for reference.

Road Patterns

The pattern of roads in the surrounding area, including those leading up to and inside the grounds of the apartment complex, should be examined. See if there are road patterns that carry benevolent energy. These patterns include winding (but not mazelike) streets with gentle curves. Avoid apartment buildings that are encircled by a road that forms a loop, that stand at the end of a T junction, or that are squeezed between the arms of a Y junction. For a review of benevolent and destructive road patterns, refer to chapter 1. The pattern of access roads inside the grounds of the apartment complex is also important in determining the selection of the apartment unit. This is especially true if there are several apartment buildings spread out within the grounds. Look at figure 14.6.

Figure 14.6 shows a complex with six apartment buildings, access roads, and parking areas. This type of apartment complex is becoming very common in suburban North America. Assuming that there are no destructive features in the surrounding area, which apartment building in the complex has the best feng-shui? Looking at figure 14.6, we find that buildings 1 and 2, being near the main road, are not well protected from destructive energy carried by the busy traffic along that road. It is not desirable to choose an apartment in these two buildings. Buildings 3 and 4 are more suitable, because they are located in an area with better protection. Building 5 is situated on the convex side of the curving road. Besides being pressed by the bulge in the road, the building is also buffeted by fast destructive energy carried at the curve. We should not consider choosing a unit in building 5. Building 6 has the best feng-shui. It is located near a gentle curve and is far enough from the main road. Moreover, because it is at the end of the access road, traffic is minimal. Thus, building 6 has the best feng-shui in the entire complex.

Choosing an apartment building within a large complex that has many buildings can be tricky. Chances are that if you are not interested in living in high-rise buildings or in tra-

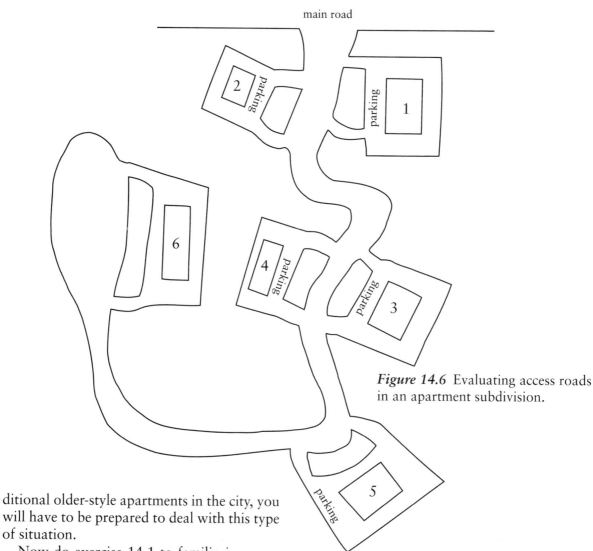

Figure 14.6 Evaluating access roads in an apartment subdivision.

ditional older-style apartments in the city, you will have to be prepared to deal with this type of situation.

Now do exercise 14.1 to familiarize yourself with evaluating access roads and choosing an apartment building within a large housing complex.

Parking Area

Vehicular traffic can bring unpredictable energy into an area. We need to examine the location of the parking area in the apartment grounds before we can choose a unit or even the building itself. The following types of parking areas are desirable, because they are removed from the apartment building and therefore do not bring unpredictable energy into the residential areas:

• A parking area that is isolated from the apartment building

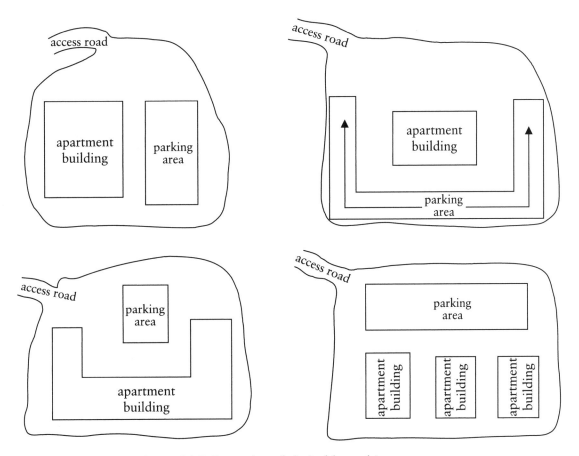

Figure 14.7 Examples of desirable parking areas.

- Parking space in an underground garage, but not directly under the apartment building
- Parking on the street, if the street is not too near the entrance of the apartment building
- A bowl-like enclosure in front of the apartment building

Some examples of desirable parking areas are shown in figure 14.7.

The following kinds of parking areas are undesirable:

- A garage that is located underneath the apartment building, whether above or below ground, which will destabilize the energy in the apartment building as well as bring unpredictable energy into the residential area
- A parking area where the cars drive up toward the apartment units

The worst type of parking area is one that is located beneath the apartments, where the apartments themselves are perched on pillars (figure 14.8).

Figure 14.8 Example of undesirable parking area located underneath an apartment building.

EVALUATING THE INTERNAL ENVIRONMENT OF A BUILDING

The internal environment of the building includes the layout of the entrance area, elevators, stairways, hallways, landings, and fire escapes and the position of the apartment unit itself.

The Entrance to the Apartment Building

The entrance area of the apartment building determines how positive and negative energy will be routed inside. The following types of entrances are desirable, because they can conduct and enhance benevolent energy and minimize the flow of malevolent energy:

- An entrance area with a large square or round foyer

- An entrance area where there are fountains and plant life in the foyer
- An entrance with spacious doors
- An entrance that is sheltered from driveways and streets

The following kinds of entrances are undesirable, because they tend to churn up negative energy and prevent benevolent energy from moving into the building:

- An entrance area that is a long, narrow corridor
- An entrance with a very small foyer or no foyer
- Entrance doors to the apartment building that are small
- An entrance exposed to traffic from driveways and streets

Layout and Design of Elevators, Stairways, Hallways, Landings, and Fire Escapes

Elevators, stairs, hallways, landings, and even fire escape ladders are passageways that affect and direct the flow of energy to the units in an apartment building. The way in which they are designed and laid out within the building is important in evaluating the feng-shui of the apartment building. These are the points to remember when examining the layout of elevators, stairways, hallways, landings, and fire escapes:

- Do not live in an apartment building where there are long hallways.
- Do not live in an apartment building where the stairs to the upper floors are not buffered by a spacious landing.
- Do not live in an apartment building where there is little space between the units and the elevator.
- Do not live in an apartment building with narrow and steep stairs.
- Do not live in an apartment building where the hallways are arranged like a maze.
- Landings, elevator waiting areas, and fire escapes should be buffered from the units themselves.
- Hallways should be spacious, and the units should open into a common square or a round area rather than a narrow corridor.
- There should be ample space between the doors of each unit.
- Fire escape ladders (found in older apartments in large cities) should be located at the back of the apartment building, rather than the front, because they obstruct incoming energy.

Figures 14.9 and 14.10 show examples of desirable and undesirable passageways.

Position of the Apartment Unit in the Building

The position of the apartment unit in the building relative to elevators, stairs, hallways, landings, and entrance foyer affects the kind of energy that flows into the unit. It is possible that any or all of the units in an apartment building with good feng-shui will still have individual problems.

The following kinds of units in an apartment building have undesirable feng-shui:

- A unit located at the end of a hallway with the corridor running straight to it
- A unit with a door facing the stairs or elevator
- A unit that is immediately adjacent to the stairway or elevator

Units with desirable feng-shui are the ones protected from stairways and elevators and not located along narrow and long hallways. In a high-rise apartment building, the best levels are the ones in the middle. Positive energy tends to rise, and negative energy tends to settle at the bottom. The highest levels have the least protection. Figure 14.11 shows examples of desirable, undesirable, and neutral units within one floor of an apartment building.

You should now gain some field experience by walking through apartment buildings and getting a feel for the layout of the hallways and the positions of the units.

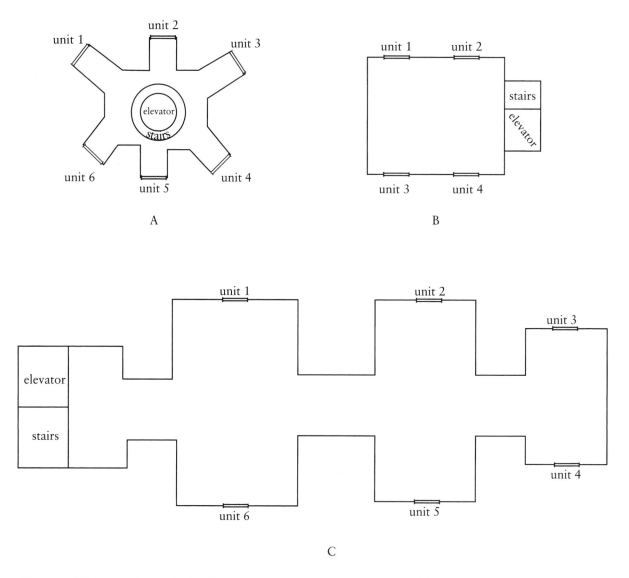

Figure 14.9 Examples of desirable passageways in an apartment building. A: Passageways are short, and the area around the elevator and stairway is spacious. B: There is no passageway. The units open into a spacious area. C: The passageway is short and wide and is broken up by spacious areas.

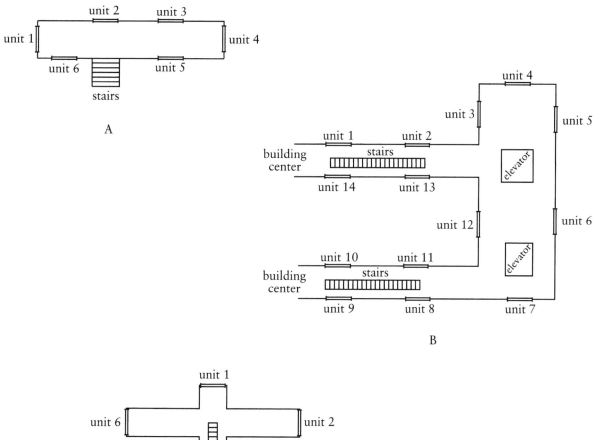

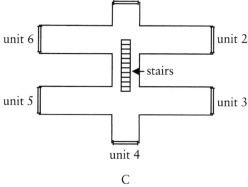

Figure 14.10 Examples of undesirable passageways in an apartment building. A: The passageway is long and narrow. B: The already long and narrow passageway is crowded further by the presence of the stairway. C: A stairway blocks the already long and narrow passageways.

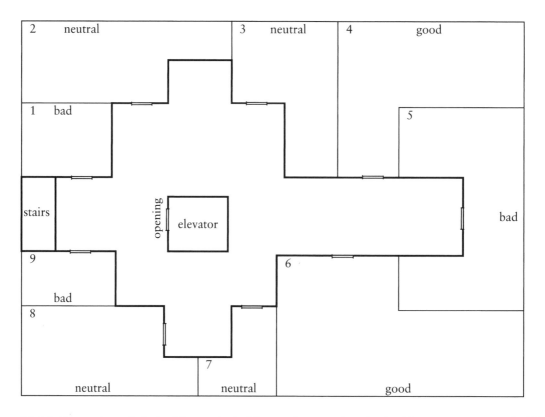

Figure 14.11 Examples of desirable, undesirable, and neutral units inside an apartment building. Units 1 and 9 are bad because they are located next to the stairs. Unit 5 is bad because it is at the end of a corridor. Units 4 and 6 are good because they open into a spacious area. Units 2, 3, 7, and 8 are neutral because the positive effect of opening into a spacious area is canceled by their proximity to the elevator.

EVALUATING THE INTERNAL ENVIRONMENT OF AN APARTMENT UNIT

Once you have selected the apartment building and the unit, the next step is to examine the interior design and the floor plan of the apartment. Here you would apply all the principles of feng-shui in evaluating the internal environment of a house, including assessment of the shape of the unit, the shape of the rooms, the general floor plan, and the interior design features. For a review of desirable and undesirable floor plans and interior designs, you can refer to chapter 2.

Figures 14.12 and 14.13 show examples of apartments with desirable and undesirable floor plans. Notice that units that have "good" locations within the apartment building may not have desirable floor plans. For example, both units in figure 14.13 are in a protected area of the building (in the middle, with other units on both sides) but have problems in their floor plans. The best way to make sure that you have all the necessary information to evaluate the position of the unit and its floor plan is to look at a blueprint. If the management is unwilling to show you one, something is wrong, and you should not choose that building in any case.

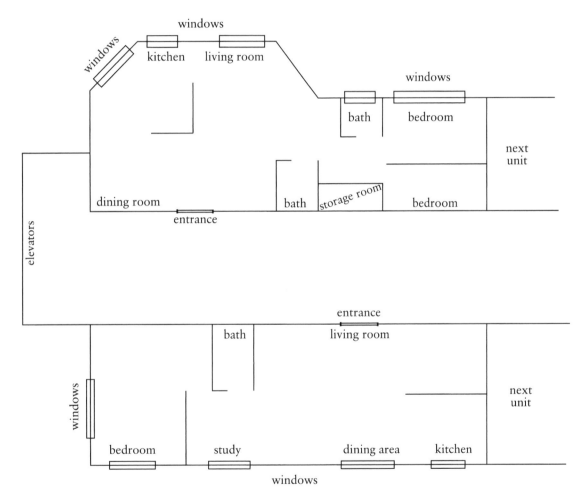

Figure 14.12 Examples of apartments with desirable floor plans. Notice that the shapes of the rooms are regular, the units are well lit by natural light, and there are no long corridors inside the apartment. The units also open into a wide passageway.

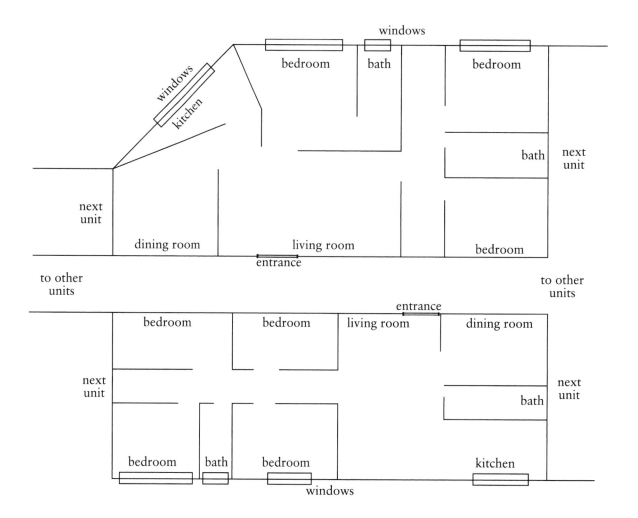

Figure 14.13 Examples of apartments with undesirable floor plans. Notice that the kitchen in the unit shown at the top has a triangular and irregular shape. Also, both units have long corridors, and both open into a long and narrow passageway.

SETTING UP THE GEOMANTIC CHART FOR AN APARTMENT

Once you have selected an apartment building and unit, the next step is to generate the geomantic chart for that apartment. The general procedure is the same as that for a house, but there are a few particulars that you need to take into account.

Determining the General Orientation of an Apartment

Determining the facing direction of an apartment can be difficult. The units may have facing directions different from the general facing of the building. Moreover, not all units will have the same facing direction. In the more traditional approach to the feng-shui of apartments, the procedure is to take two directional readings when the unit and the building have different facing directions. After living in the apartment for a period of time, choose the chart with the better predictive power and plan the usage of space and installation of countermeasures accordingly. This method is cumbersome and requires that both charts be viable. It also assumes that if things do not work out, you have the luxury of moving to another apartment at short notice. This procedure was feasible during the years just before and after World War II in the large cities of China (when this method was first used), because apartments were always rented and not purchased and there were no leases. Today we do not have the luxury of testing the feng-shui of an apartment for six months before settling in. In fact, this flexibility is impossible when you are buying a condominium.

When using multiple charts and testing each one's accuracy, it has been my experience that it is the facing direction of the apartment unit and not that of the building that determines the feng-shui of the apartment. I believe that we need to generate only one geomantic chart—the one that is based on the facing direction of the unit itself. Having decided that we need only one geomantic chart, let's address the procedure of identifying the front facing of the apartment before we take a compass reading.

We can usually get a feel for the facing direction of the apartment by walking around in it. Take note of where the windows with unblocked views are located. If you were sitting inside the apartment, which direction would you want to face? If you can't get a clear answer, you should go outside the building, locate the apartment, and see if you can determine which way it faces. If you are at a loss, the following set of guidelines may help you determine the facing direction of the apartment. Developing an intuition for recognizing the front facing is ultimately the best method. It also turns out to be the most accurate when you become proficient.

- The front of the apartment is the side that has the most views, usually the side with the most windows.
- The front facing of the apartment is not determined by the front of the building, though the building and the unit may have the same facing.
- The front door of the apartment does *not* determine the front facing of the unit, although the entrance may be located in the front facing direction.

The best way to cultivate an intuition for identifying the front facing of an apartment is through experience. Look at figure 14.14. Let's say that the apartment building shown in figure 14.14 lies on an east–west axis with the front door facing due west (yu). Unit A, the one-bedroom apartment on the southeast corner of the building, has a wu facing (south), because the view from that side is unblocked. For the same reason, unit B, on the northeast corner of the building, has a tzu facing. Units C and D, the studio apartments, both have a yu facing, because the west side of

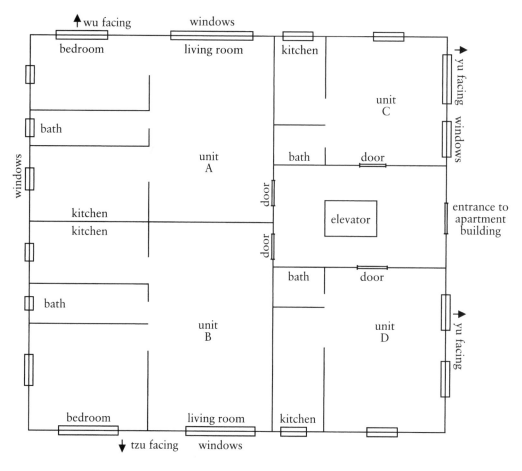

Figure 14.14 Determination of the facing direction of a unit in a traditional apartment building. (See text for more complete explanation.)

these units has the most unblocked views. The important thing to notice here is that the entrances into the units do not necessarily lie at the front of the apartments and do not determine their facing directions.

Even if there are buildings to the north of the apartment building, unit B still would have a tzu facing, because that is the side with the exposed view. (The western and southern sides of the apartment are solid walls, and the eastern side has small windows and small rooms.) Similarly, the front facing of unit A is

wu, regardless of the presence of buildings on the south side.

Let's look at one more example. Figure 14.15 shows the layout of a modern apartment complex typically found in North American suburbs. Unlike traditional or older apartment buildings (shown in figure 14.14), this kind of apartment complex does not have a large common entrance. Moreover, the upper levels are accessed by an exterior stairway.

In figure 14.15, unit A can be oriented toward the south (wu) or the west (yu). There

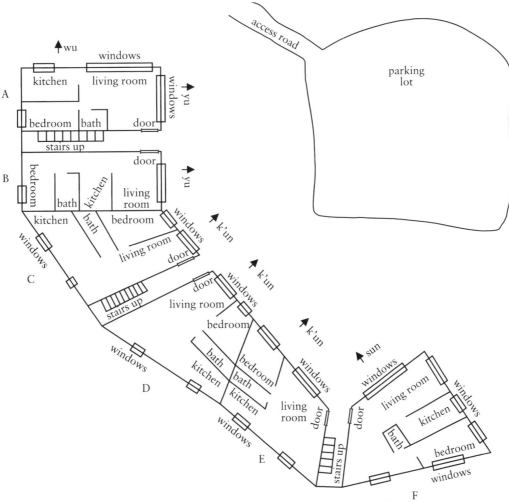

Figure 14.15 Determination of the facing direction of a unit in a modern apartment complex. (See text for explanation.)

are large windows on both the southern and western sides of the living room that give unobstructed views. In this case, we generate geomantic charts for the two facing directions and choose the one that is best. Then we orient the apartment toward the chosen facing direction and arrange furniture to define the orientation of the apartment (see box 14.2).

Unit B has a yu facing, because yu (west) is the side with the large windows and the unobstructed views. The facing direction of unit C

is k'un (southwest), because there is a large window on the southwest side of the living room. If we look at the structure of the entire apartment complex, we notice that unit C is cradled by the two arms of the complex. This creates the sense that the apartment is oriented toward the southwest. In this case, the shape of the apartment complex together with the unobstructed view to the southwest determine the front facing of the unit. The situation is the same for units D and E.

Unit F has a southeast (sun) facing direction, because the southeast side of the apartment has the most unobstructed view. Because the southwestern side has smaller windows and is partitioned into rooms, the southeastern side of the living room has the most unobstructed view from any given room.

Determining the general facing orientation of an apartment is not easy. Competence comes from experience in working with apartments of all shapes and sizes. You should go into apartments and get hands-on experience. Most developers and rental agencies will allow you to walk through apartment units, especially in new buildings that have many vacancies.

Some apartments have ambiguous or competing facing directions that cannot be clarified by the placement of furniture. These types of apartments should be avoided, because when there are competing facing directions, the flow of energy will be unpredictable. The pattern of energy in the space will fluctuate between the two possible facing directions, and it will be difficult to plan the use of space and to install countermeasures and enhancers.

Obtaining the Specific Orientation of an Apartment

To fix the specific orientation of an apartment, we align the geomantic compass with the front facing of the apartment and take a reading. The procedure is the same as that for obtaining the facing direction of a house. For apartments that are not at ground level, you may have to take the compass reading inside the apartment. In this case, identify the front facing wall and take the reading using that wall as a reference. Make sure that you do not put the compass against the wall or near the windows, because metal fittings may disturb the magnetic response of the needle.

Generating the Geomantic Chart for an Apartment

The procedure is the same as that for a house. Find out when the apartment complex was built. Using the Nine Cycles diagrams in the appendix, locate the cycle and set up the Earth Base. If the apartment building was originally a large single house, you will need to find out when the house was partitioned. The renovations involved in converting a single house into apartment units would have been major. In this case, the year the renovations were completed should be used to determine the Earth Base. Complete the geomantic chart by filling in the Mountain and the Facing stars in each square of the Nine Palaces. Refer to chapters 3, 4, and 5 if you need to review the method for taking readings from the compass and setting up a geomantic chart.

Superimposing the Geomantic Chart onto the Apartment

Once the chart is superimposed onto the apartment unit, you should identify the conditional interaction (in the Facing Palace), the unconditional interactions, and the additive interactions of the stars of the Nine Palaces and plan the usage of space accordingly. The procedures are the same as those for a single house. Refer to chapters 6 and 7 if you need to review the interpretation of the interactions of the stars in the Nine Palaces. Next, evaluate the interactions of the heads of household with the Earth Base of the Nine Palace square where the front door is located and then

BOX 14.2

USING FURNITURE PLACEMENT TO ANCHOR THE FRONT FACING OF AN APARTMENT

It is possible to anchor the front facing of an apartment by arranging furniture. Figure B14.2 shows an apartment with two competing facings—tzu (north) and yu (west). By arranging the living room furniture, we can anchor the facing direction. The couch and coffee table are arranged so that the occupants will plan their activities and orient themselves toward a certain facing.

Figure B14.2 Arranging furniture to disambiguate the facing direction of an apartment.

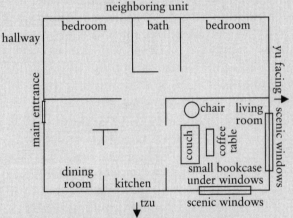

furniture arranged to define yu facing

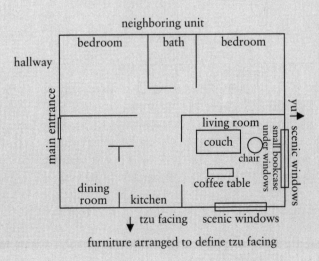

furniture arranged to define tzu facing

match the occupants to the bedrooms. (Refer to chapter 8 if you need a review.) Usually, the smaller the apartment, the less flexibility there will be in planning the usage of space. For example, for a one-bedroom apartment, there is not much choice as to where you would sleep. With a studio apartment, you have only one room.

After evaluating the auspiciousness of each room of the apartment, the next step is to superimpose the Nine Palaces onto each room and work out the placement of furniture. (Refer to chapter 9 if you need a review.) The studio apartment is treated as one room, and the space within it is evaluated as if it were a single room in a multiroom apartment or house.

Figure 14.16 shows an example of a geomantic chart superimposed onto a two-bedroom, a one-bedroom, and a studio apartment. In this example, the one-bedroom apartment (shown in panel B in figure 14.16) clearly has more constraints in the usage of space than the two-bedroom apartment (panel A). In the two-bedroom apartment, we can exclude the room with the inauspicious combination seven-five-nine as a bedroom, which is not possible for the one-bedroom apartment. Because the studio apartment (panel C) is essentially one large room, we can avoid the corner with the seven-five-nine combination simply by not placing the bed or a desk there. If the Earth Bases of the front door area and the Central Palace of the studio apartment are not compatible with the guardian star / element of the occupant, and if countermeasures cannot neutralize the Earth Base or strengthen the occupant, there is not much choice but to move out or not to move in.

Now do exercise 14.2.

Because there is less flexibility in the usage of space in apartments, countermeasures and enhancers are more common in apartments than in houses. This is especially true in smaller apartments, where you are stuck with one bedroom. If you are renting and don't have the time to look around, you should settle for an apartment with viable feng-shui and work to enhance the benefits and neutralize the problems. (Methods of installing countermeasures and enhancers are described in chapters 10 and 11.) Of course, it is better to avoid apartments with many unfavorable areas, because installing countermeasures may be harder than finding another apartment.

To summarize, these are the points to remember when you are setting up the geomantic chart for an apartment:

- The geomantic chart is based on the facing direction of the apartment.
- The facing direction of the apartment is the side with the most unobstructed view.
- The facing direction of the apartment is not necessarily the front of the apartment building.
- The facing direction of the apartment is not necessarily where the entrance of the unit is located.
- You need to generate only the geomantic chart for the apartment; it is not necessary to generate the geomantic chart for the entire building.
- The Three Combinations and the Combination of Ten charts apply to apartments if all the Nine Palaces are inside the apartment.

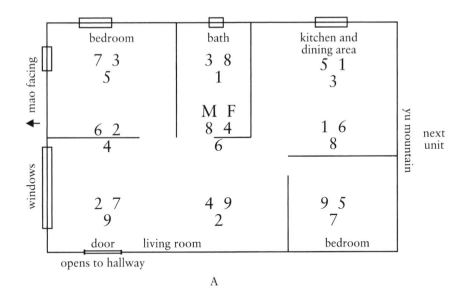

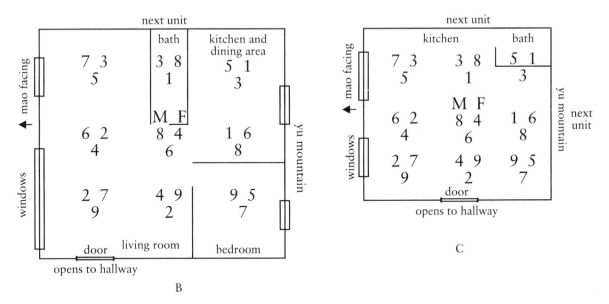

Figure 14.16 The geomantic chart superimposed onto a two-bedroom (A), a one-bedroom (B), and a studio apartment (C).

EXERCISES

EXERCISE 14.1

Evaluate the feng-shui of the apartment buildings (good, bad, or neutral) shown in figure 14.17 and give reasons for your choice. No. 1 is a partially worked example.

1.

- *Building 1 has bad feng-shui because it is located at the end of a road.*
- *Building 2 has good feng-shui because it is away from intersections and is protected from busy streets by other buildings.*

(Continue with the analysis.)

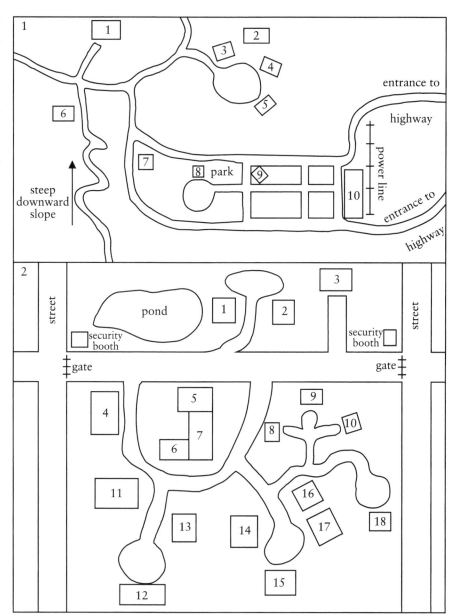

Figure 14.17 Evaluating the feng-shui of apartment buildings.

EXERCISE 14.2

Identify the facing direction, generate the geomantic chart, and superimpose the chart onto the floor plan for each of the seven units in the apartment building shown in figure 14.18. Then choose the one with the best feng-shui (giving reasons for your choice) and plan the placement of furniture, countermeasures, and enhancers. The apartment building is built on a direct north–south axis, has a mao facing, and was completed in the fifth cycle.

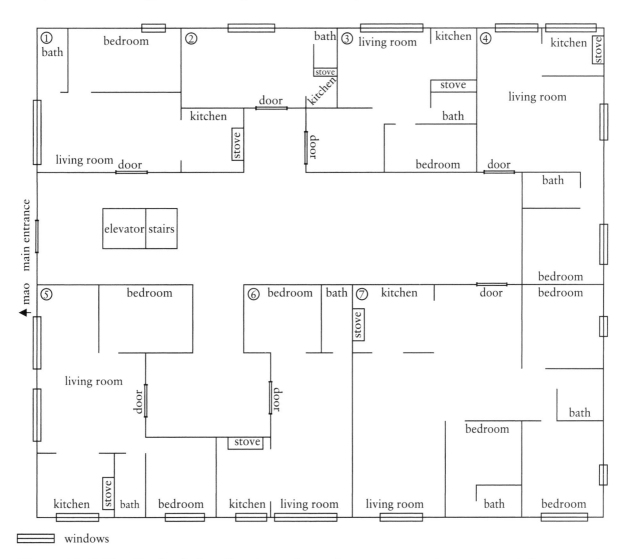

Figure 14.18 Identify the facing directions of sample apartment units, generate their geomantic charts, choose a unit that you would want to live in, and plan the placement of furniture, countermeasures, and enhancers.

ANSWERS

EXERCISE 14.1

1.
- Building 3 has bad feng-shui because it is situated at the entrance (or the neck) to the cul-de-sac.
- Building 4 has good feng-shui because it is situated in a section of the cul-de-sac that is away from the neck; it also is not directly in front of the road entering the cul-de-sac.
- Building 5 has bad feng-shui because it is situated directly in front of the road entering the cul-de-sac.
- Building 6 has bad feng-shui because it is located on a steep slope with a steep and winding road running along its side.
- Building 7 has bad feng-shui because it is squeezed by two roads.
- Building 8 has good feng-shui because it is near a park.
- Building 9 has bad feng-shui because it faces diagonally into an intersection.
- Building 10 has bad feng-shui because it is near a power line and also is close to a high-speed road.

2.
- Buildings 1 and 2 have bad feng-shui because they are at the neck of a cul-de-sac.
- Building 3 has bad feng-shui because it is at the end of a road.
- Building 4 has bad feng-shui because it is too close to the main street and the gate.
- Buildings 5, 6, and 7 have good feng-shui because the buildings protect each other; they also are situated within a loop that is not constricting.
- Buildings 8, 9, and 10 have bad feng-shui because they all are situated at ends of roads.
- Building 11 has neutral feng-shui. The negative effect of being close to the main street cancels the positive effect of being located in the concave curve of the access road.
- Building 12 has bad feng-shui because it is directly in front of the road entering the cul-de-sac.
- Buildings 13 and 14 have good feng-shui because they are in a protected part of the apartment subdivision.
- Building 15 has good feng-shui because it is in a section of a cul-de-sac away from the entrance. The road entering the cul-de-sac also misses the apartment building.
- Building 16 has bad feng-shui because it is at the end of a T junction in the road.
- Building 17 has good feng-shui because it is in a protected part of the apartment subdivision.
- Building 18 has bad feng-shui because it is directly in front of the road entering the cul-de-sac.

EXERCISE 14.2

Refer to figure 14.19 for answers to exercise 14.2.

Unit 1	mao facing
Unit 2	wu facing
Unit 3	wu facing
Unit 4	wu facing
Unit 5	mao facing
Unit 6	tzu facing
Unit 7	tzu facing

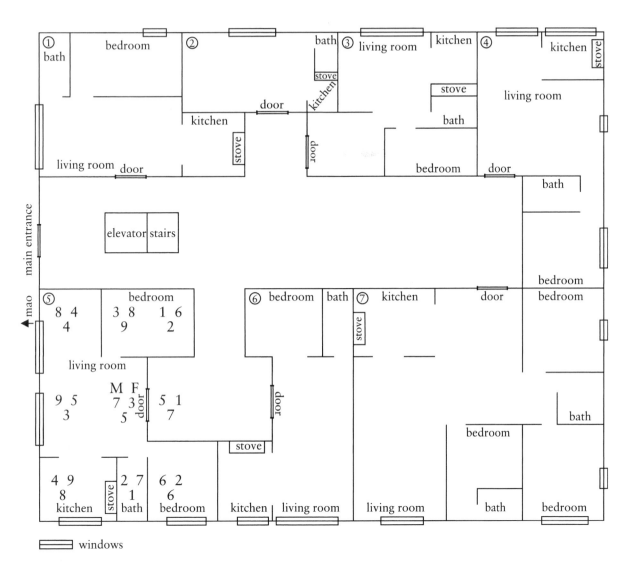

Figure 14.19 Answers to exercise 14.2.

The geomantic chart for both units 1 and 5 is this:

```
        8  4      3  8      1  6
          4          9         2

                   M  F
mao    9  5      7  3      5  1   yu
facing   3          5         7   mountain

        4  9      2  7      6  2
          8          1         6
```

The geomantic chart for units 2, 3, and 4 is this:

```
              wu facing

        2  1      6  5      4  3
          4          9         2

                   M  F
        3  2      1  9      8  7
          3          5         7

        7  6      5  4      9  8
          8          1         6
             tzu mountain
```

The geomantic chart for units 6 and 7 is this:

```
              wu mountain

        1  2      5  6      3  4
          4          9         2

                   M  F
        2  3      9  1      7  8
          3          5         7

        6  7      4  5      8  9
          8          1         6

              tzu facing
```

The mao-facing chart (units 1 and 5) has three excellent squares (4/4/8, 9/8/3, and 8/9/4). The rest of the palaces are either neutral or can be made viable by installing countermeasures.

The wu-facing chart (units 2, 3, and 4) has three good squares (4/1/2, 8/6/7, and 6/8/9), four harmful squares (2/3/4, 9/5/6, 3/2/3, and 5/9/1), one fairly good square (7/7/8), and one square that can be made viable by installing countermeasures (1/4/5).

The tzu-facing chart (units 6 and 7) has one disadvantageous square (9/6/5). The rest of the palaces either are neutral or can be made viable by installing countermeasures.

Based on the feng-shui depicted in the geomantic charts, units 1 and 5 are the best. The front door of unit 1, however, is too close to the elevator and stairs. The rest of the units have good locations within the apartment building, but their geomantic charts are not very desirable compared with the chart for unit 5. When the geomantic chart is superimposed onto unit 5 (figure 14.19), we find that one bedroom has an excellent combination of stars (9/8/3) and one has a viable combination (6/2/6), the living room has an excellent combination (4/4/8), and the kitchen has an excellent combination (8/9/4). The rest of the space can be made viable by installing countermeasures.

Given these reasons, I would choose unit 5. Having selected unit 5, these are the points to note when placing furniture, countermeasures, and enhancers:

- Make sure to match the guardian star / elements of the occupants to the bedrooms.
- Place countermeasures in the bedroom with the combination 6/2/6 to neutralize the Facing Star two-black.

- Place countermeasures in the living room to neutralize five-yellow in the Facing Star and nine-purple in the Mountain Star.
- Place enhancers in the section of the living room with the auspicious combination 4/4/8.
- Although the kitchen has an auspicious combination (8/9/4), you should be careful about the presence of nine-purple in the Facing Star. Do not put red objects in the kitchen to aggravate the fire element. Use predominantly blues and greens for decor in the kitchen.
- In the microcosm of each bedroom, place the bed in the area occupied by the stars of health, prosperity, and good fortune (4/4/8).
- If you wish to place a desk in the bedroom, put it in the area occupied by the stars of celebration (8/9) and have it face the stars of fame (9/8) or vice versa.
- If you wish to make part of the living room a work area, put the desk in the section with the combination 4/4/8. Within the microcosm of that palace, put the desk in the area occupied by the stars of celebration (8/9) or fame (9/8) and have it face one of these spots.
- In the microcosm of the living room, put furniture and entertainment systems in areas with auspicious stars.

15

*Choosing and Designing
a Business Office*

In this chapter, you will learn how to choose and design an office suite for a small business. In general, the feng-shui of business offices is similar to the feng-shui of residences. What is not good for residences also is not good for the business office and vice versa. In addition to the factors that determine the feng-shui of residences, there are particular points specific to business offices. This chapter introduces you to them and shows you how to situate your business office, plan the usage of work space, and place the office furniture. First we will choose the commercial building. Then we will choose a suite within the building.

The principles applied to choosing your of-fice suite are similar to those used for selecting a residence. First, we need to identify the destructive and benevolent features in the surrounding environment by looking at the neighboring buildings, road patterns, and parking lots. Second, we must look at the relationship of the building to the surrounding environment, its shape and design, the layout of its main entrance, and the positions of elevators, stairs, and hallways. Third, we need to consider the position of the suite within the building and evaluate the floor plan of the suite. Last, we should draw up the geomantic chart for the office and plan the usage of space.

CHOOSING AN OFFICE BUILDING

In choosing an office building, we need to consider the external environment and the general design of the building.

Evaluating the External Environment

NEIGHBORING BUILDINGS AND STRUCTURES

When choosing a building to locate a busi-ness office, we first must see if there are destructive features in the surrounding buildings. If there are none, we will look for benevolent features. Always identify the destructive features first, because if they exist there is no reason to continue the exploration. In my experience, it is safer to identify the benevolent features after the destructive features, because enthusiasm about the benevolent features often can blind you to the troublesome ones. Presented here is a set of guidelines for identifying destructive and benevolent features of neighboring buildings and structures.

Destructive Features

BUILDINGS WITH SHARP, KNIFELIKE EDGES

Buildings with sharp edges act like knives or axes. The business as well as the workers inside the target building will be hit with economic disasters and health problems. An example of this kind of building is shown in figure 15.1.

BUILDINGS WITH REFLECTIVE GLASS WINDOWS

A reflective building sends waves of energy crashing against the target building. The business and the workers in the target building will be hit with unending economic disasters. An example of this type of building is shown in figure 15.2. A reflective building also can harm businesses inside a target building if images of objects of destruction are cast on it. There are other dangerous effects in the types of reflections that these buildings can throw onto other buildings. Figure 15.3 depicts a building that appears to be on fire as a result of the reflections cast on it by a neighboring building. Some reflections are obvious only at certain times of the day. You should examine the buildings at various times of the day and in sunny as well as overcast conditions.

Figure 15.1 A commercial building with blade-like edges (*top*).

Figure 15.2 A reflective building with the potential to harm neighboring buildings (*bottom*).

Figure 15.3 A commercial building that appears to be on fire as a result of reflections cast on it by a neighboring building.

Figure 15.4a A building with protruding wedges.

Figure 15.4b Irregular blocks of a building perched on pillars.

Figure 15.5a,b Buildings with protruding iron beams.

IRREGULARLY SHAPED BUILDINGS

Buildings with irregular shapes trap energy and disrupt its flow in a neighborhood. Their irregularities create eddies and vortexes, transforming benevolent energy into malevolent energy. Figure 15.4a and b shows two examples of irregularly shaped buildings.

SHARP AND POINTED STRUCTURES

Sharp and pointed features protruding from buildings, cranes, and large sculptures act like spears aimed at the target building, skewering and impaling everything in their path (figure 15.5a,b). Business projects and ventures inside the target building will be sabotaged and destroyed before they can get off the ground. Moreover, workers will feel oppressed and exploited by management.

OBJECTS OF DESTRUCTION AND THEIR IMAGES

Weapons of destruction, their images, and sculptures of such objects are all detrimental. (See figures 15.6 and 1.8a–f for examples.) Images on billboards can change. A friendly face promoting dairy products may become a jet fighter flying toward you when it changes to an advertisement for military recruitment. My advice is to stay away from areas with billboards, because the images on them are unpredictable.

Benevolent Features

PARKS AND GARDENS

Parks and gardens provide benevolent greenery, growth, and open space, assuming that pesticides are not used on the lawns. They allow energy to gather and be transformed into gentle, positive forces. Plant growth is associated with life, and life energy in an area that usually is dominated by concrete and glass will diffuse much of the destructive force that accumulates in urban streets. A garden can introduce benevolent energy into a business district (figure 15.7).

WATERFALLS AND FOUNTAINS

Waterfalls carry benevolent energy if they do not drop from great heights (figure 15.7). The best types of waterfalls are those connected to a water channel that winds around an area. Fountains spurting upward also carry benevolent energy (figure 15.8). If the waterfall and water channels are located within a garden or park, the effect is enhanced as a result of the added presence of trees and grass.

Figure 15.6 A structure resembling a machine gun perched on a building.

PLAZAS

Plazas can diffuse destructive energy, because the open space acts as a buffer between tall buildings. A circular structure is the best shape to absorb and neutralize malevolent energy. Plazas that form wind tunnels, however, are destructive.

ROUND BUILDINGS

Buildings with round edges (figure 15.9) and dome-shaped roofs transmit benevolent energy and diffuse destructive energy. These buildings include planetariums, sports stadiums with a circular arena, and basilicas.

Figure 15.7 Gardens with a waterfall in the business district can introduce benevolent energy into the area.

Figure 15.8 Fountains in the business district can introduce benevolent energy into the area.

Figure 15.9 A commercial building with rounded edges has the best kind of protection against buildings with sharp edges, pointed structures, and other destructive features.

Figure 15.10 A road pattern associated with bad feng-shui. The section of town on the right is wedged in by highways.

SURROUNDING ROAD PATTERNS

Roads in the vicinity of a building affect its feng-shui. Recall from chapter 1 that some road patterns carry destructive energy, while others carry benevolent energy. Figures 15.10 and 15.11 show road patterns in business districts with bad and good feng-shui, respectively.

PARKING AREAS

The location and design of parking areas can affect the feng-shui of a commercial building.

Undesirable Parking Areas

The following types of parking areas carry destructive energy and are undesirable:

- Parking areas where vehicles drive into a building, as if the cars are trying to crash into the offices, are destructive (figure 15.12). Businesses in the building will meet with frequent financial disasters. The health of the workers will be in jeopardy.

- Parking areas that are located below a building that is standing on pillars also are harmful (figure 15.13a). The building is unstable because it is perched on stilts. If we add to it the movement of cars underneath, the situation is doubly dangerous. Businesses in the building will not be financially stable.

- The situation just cited is worsened when the building is perched on several levels of parking, especially when the levels are structurally rickety in appearance (figure 15.13b and c). Such rickety structures are associated with business instability.

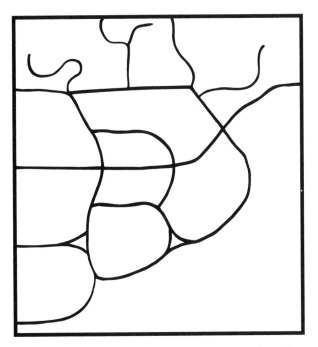

Figure 15.11 A road pattern associated with good feng-shui. The roads wind around gently and smoothly.

- Parking areas that are situated underground below a building are not as bad as those that are above ground, but the instability is still present.

Desirable Parking Areas

The following types of parking areas do not carry destructive energy and are therefore desirable:

- Open-air parking areas that are not attached to the building that they serve are desirable. They confine unpredictable energy carried by the cars to an area away from the building.
- Multilevel parking garages that form separate structures are also beneficial, because they, too, confine to an isolated area energy carried by cars.

Figure 15.12 The cars "drive" into the building. The building is also top-heavy, because its front end is sitting on two pillars.

Figure 15.13a–c *Undesirable parking areas.*

Figure 15.13a Parking lot located underneath a building that is standing on pillars.

Figure 15.13b A parking garage that intrudes into the office building. It looks as if the garage is taking a bite out of the building.

Figure 15.13c A rickety-looking parking garage.

Evaluating the Office Building

Once you have examined the structures in the vicinity of the commercial building, look at the building itself. The two factors we need to consider are the shape of the building and its overall design. With respect to the overall design, we must look at the frontage, the design of the foyer and main entrance, the architectural and interior features, and the locations of elevators, stairs, and hallways.

SHAPE

The shape of the building affects the flow of energy inside. Some shapes facilitate the flow of energy, some hinder it, some create beneficial energy, and some carry destructive energy.

Undesirable Building Shapes

Typically, businesses located in buildings with undesirable shapes have high risks of financial problems, employee disharmony, and health hazards (figures 15.14a–j and 15.15a, b). There are several shapes associated with destructive energy:

- Buildings shaped like pyramids trap energy at the top levels. As the space decreases, energy is compressed. When energy compresses, it becomes constricted and oppressive. In general, because the flow of energy is distorted in the building, the feng-shui of offices in the entire building will not be good. In a pyramid building, offices at the highest levels have the most problems.
- Buildings with triangular shapes squeeze energy at the apexes. Here, too, as the space decreases, energy is compressed. The most disadvantaged offices will be the ones located at the apexes.

- Buildings with irregular shapes hinder the flow of energy. Irregular energy flow causes erratic profits and losses.
- Buildings in which the upper levels are larger than the lower levels are called *top-heavy buildings*. This type of structure is associated with business instability as well as management problems. The top-heaviness forebodes an unwieldy upper-level management dominating the rank-and-file workers.
- When a top-heavy building is perched on posts and pillars, the problem of instability becomes even more serious. Businesses inside will find it difficult to maintain a good cash flow and always will be threatened by bankruptcy.
- When the levels of a building form a cascade, like a stepped pyramid, fortunes will "roll down" the building. Businesses inside will lose capital through loopholes, projects will never get off the ground, and there will be a high turnover of employees.
- When the levels of a building form a reverse cascade, we have the effects of a top-heavy building with sharp overhanging edges. The result is an oppressive upper management, low productivity in the rank and file, and the threat of disharmony among workers.
- Buildings with knife-edge ridges are destructive to businesses in other buildings as well as to the workers inside. Their aggressive feng-shui may benefit the business within, but at the expense of its own workers as well as those in the neighboring buildings.
- When a building is capped by a lidlike structure or surrounded by bars, the businesses inside will find it difficult to expand.

Figure 15.14a–j Examples of commercial buildings with shapes that are associated with bad feng-shui.

Figure 15.14a A top-heavy building.

Figure 15.14b A building that is completely supported by pillars.

Figure 15.14c A bowl-like building on top of pillars.

Figure 15.14d A cascading building.

Figure 15.14e A reverse cascade building.

Figure 15.14f A building in which the upper levels are squeezed and the lower levels form a cascade.

Figure 15.14g A building capped by a lid.

Figure 15.14h A building surrounded by bars.

Figure 15.14i The upper levels of this building are caged in.

Figure 15.14j A building with a sawtooth roofline.

• Buildings with overhangs, supported or unsupported by pillars, are associated with oppression from upper management.

Desirable Building Shapes

Typically, businesses located in buildings with desirable shapes experience good growth and productivity and harmonious relationships among employees. There are several shapes associated with benevolent energy:

• Buildings shaped like a horseshoe have the most auspicious feng-shui. Because the shape is circular, it not only imparts benevolent energy but also offers the best protection against buildings with sharp edges. The most desirable offices in a horseshoe-shaped building are in the middle, where they are enclosed by the two arms of the semicircle.

• Round buildings are carriers of benevolent energy, as are buildings with domed

Figure 15.15a,b Examples of undesirable features in commercial buildings.

Figure 15.15a Unsupported overhanging roofs.

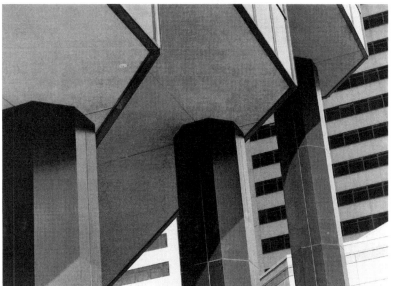

Figure 15.15b Overhanging roofs on pillars.

roofs and rounded edges. These structures offer a degree of protection against buildings with sharp edges.

- The old-fashioned symmetrical, rectangular building is also desirable for situating a business office. The flow of energy in this type of building is regular and steady. Businesses in these kinds of buildings will grow slowly but steadily and will not be subjected to sharp rises and falls in their fortunes.

GENERAL DESIGN

In examining the general design of the building, we need to consider the frontage, the structure of the foyer or main entrance, the architectural features (including types of windows), and the positions of elevators, stairways, and hallways.

Frontage

The design of the frontage is an important consideration when choosing a building in which to locate a business office. If the space in front of the building is constricted, benevolent energy will not be able to grow. As a result, businesses located inside will not receive forces associated with prosperity, harmony, and health. The best types of frontage are plazas and squares that form a part of the building.

The worst kind of office building is one situated along a narrow street and surrounded by tall buildings. Narrow streets confine the flow of energy, and tall buildings cast shadows onto the street, transforming neutral energy or even positive energy into destructive energy. Commercial buildings in city centers tend to fall into this category.

What about suburban commercial buildings? These buildings usually have no more than three levels and are built to house small businesses. Because there is more space in the suburbs, the frontage of these types of commercial buildings is typically more open than the ones in the city center. It is not unusual for suburban commercial buildings to be surrounded by greenery, landscaping, and parking lots that are removed from the building. This type of frontage obviously is more desirable than that of a narrow street. The openness of the building's frontage not only allows benevolent energy to be collected but also helps tame wild and destructive forces. All things considered, a smaller commercial building in a suburban setting tends to have better feng-shui than a high-rise commercial building in a congested city center.

Foyer and Main Entrance

The foyer and main entrance to the building are considered the first entrance of the business offices located in the building. (The second entrance of the business is the doorway into the office suite.) If energy cannot pass through the first entrance, it will not enter the offices inside the building. Even worse, if energy becomes transformed into destructive forces here, it will affect all the offices inside in the building.

The most desirable types of foyers and main entrances are those that are spacious and well lit by natural light. Ideally, the doors should be wide, so that traffic in and out of the building will not be constricted. Revolving doors are acceptable, but they need to be wide. Otherwise, the movement of the doors will not allow benevolent energy to enter and gather inside the foyer. If an indoor fountain and plants are inside the foyer, benevolent energy is enhanced, and destructive energy is minimized. Most modern office buildings tend to have spacious foyers, but some of them have architectural structures that are not beneficial to the businesses inside. (See later discussion on architectural features.)

The worst types of foyers and main entrances are those that are narrow and cramped. Some commercial buildings have no real foyers—you open the front door and walk right up to the elevators. These buildings do not offer a buffer to cushion and neutralize destructive energy, they do not provide a space for positive energy to accumulate, and they seem to push individuals into the building when they enter and throw them out when they leave. Small doors are undesirable, because they restrict the flow of energy and create congestion when people leave the building at the end of the workday. Diagonal entrances can turn positive into negative energy. Figure 15.16 shows an example of a disadvantageous entrance, and figure 15.17 compares entrances with good and bad feng-shui.

Architectural and Interior Features

Some architectural features enhance the feng-shui of a building, while others destroy it. In a commercial building, the first architectural feature that we need to consider is the windows. A building with a bank of windows from ceiling to floor makes a poor feng-shui environment. Benevolent energy (and thus prosperity) leaks out through the large windows, and there is little protection against destructive and wild forces.

Next, we want to see if there are exposed beams throughout the building. Some interiors of modern buildings are crisscrossed with iron beams. Others have irregular roofs and walls. Iron beams impart negative feng-shui, because they "crush" the people underneath. Irregular roofs and walls carry destructive en-

Figure 15.16 A diagonal entrance.

ergy and hinder the circulation of benevolent energy.

We also must evaluate the color of the walls of the building. Dark colors enhance malevolent energy and make the space feel constricted. Black marble or dark stonework are not beneficial interior wall facades. Light colors, on the other hand, enhance positive energy and create the sense of an open, friendly space. Light-colored marble, stonework, or natural drywall are all viable interior wall facades for a commercial building. Mirrored walls are highly undesirable, because they reflect energy out of the building.

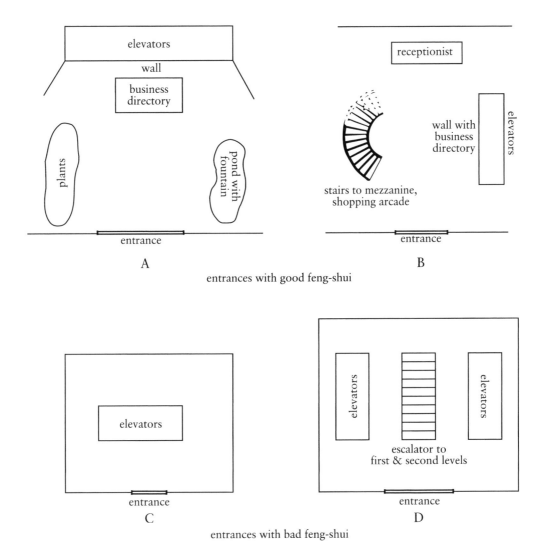

Figure 15.17 Commercial building entrances. A, B: Entrances with good feng-shui. C, D: Entrances with bad feng-shui.

Elevators, Stairways, and Hallways

Elevators, stairs, and hallways are conduits and transformers of energy. Well-designed and well-placed elevators, stairs, and hallways not only facilitate the flow of positive energy (and thus prosperity) but also can transform malevolent energy into beneficial energy. Wide hallways that lead to open spaces are good conductors as well as collectors of benevolent energy (figure 15.18a). Stairways with spacious landings allow energy to slow down as it descends, thereby preventing its transformation into destructive energy. Spacious elevators (and therefore larger shafts) do not constrict the flow of ascending energy or trap destructive energy in the area around the elevator. Finally, it is advisable to have a large open area at the elevator entrances, so that energy carried by the elevator can be calmed and transmuted into positive energy before reaching the offices (figure 15.18a).

Badly designed and poorly placed elevators, stairs, and hallways can hinder the flow of positive energy (and thus prosperity) and convert neutral and even positive energy into malevolent energy. Narrow, mazelike hallways carry destructive forces (figure 15.18b), and narrow stairways with small landings force energy to rush down the stairs, thereby

transforming neutral and even positive energy into harmful energy. Small elevators (and small shafts) constrict the flow of ascending energy as well as trap destructive energy in the area around the elevator. Finally, if the space around the elevator entrance is small and constricted, energy carried by the elevators cannot be changed into positive energy and cannot collect and amplify before reaching the offices (figure 15.18b).

In general, when you are evaluating the interior design and architectural features of a commercial building, you need to be aware of discontinuities. Discontinuities are features that have the appearance of abruptness and sharpness, and they are associated with de-

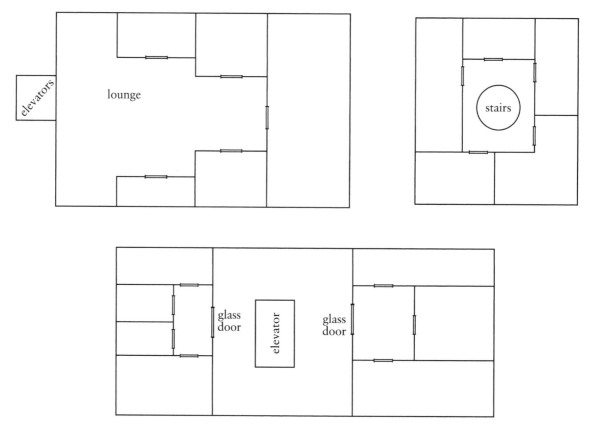

Figure 15.18a Elevators and hallways with good feng-shui.

structive energy. When there is no gradual transition or neutral space between two spaces with different uses, we have a discontinuity. One type of discontinuity is the abruptness in the transition between elevator space and office space illustrated in figure 15.18b. Another type of discontinuity is the abrupt transition between the entrance to the office building and the elevators and escalators shown in figure 15.17 (panels C and D).

CHOOSING AN OFFICE SUITE

Once you have selected a viable commercial building for your business office, the next step is to choose the suite itself. As we shall see, some suites have better feng-shui than others;

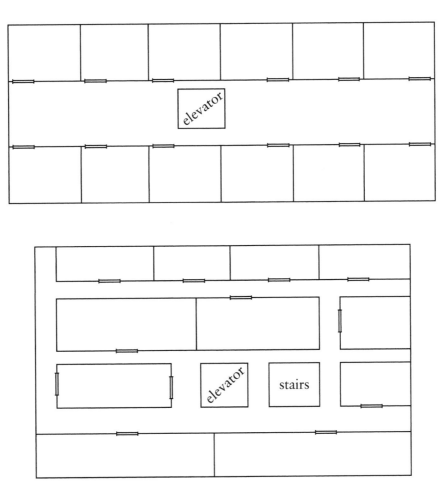

Figure 15.18b Elevators and hallways with bad feng-shui.

to discriminate the good suites from the bad ones, we need to consider the following four factors:

- The position of the suite in the building
- The location of the office in the scheme of the Nine Palaces of the building
- The partitions within the suite (that is, the floor plan)
- The flow of energy and the usage of space inside the suite

Position of the Suite

The position of the suite in the building affects its feng-shui. First, because positive energy expands as it rises, suites located at the upper levels of a commercial building generally have better feng-shui than those at the lower levels. There is a ceiling effect, because energy expands only up to a certain height. In my experience, for commercial buildings, the limit is about twenty stories. Above that level, you don't find any difference. Regardless of the number of stories, however, the top three or four levels are too exposed and therefore are not protected from destructive energy.

Second, within a given level, the suites located in the corners of the building are the least protected. The ones found in the middle, along the side of the building, have the best protection. If the building has a circular or horseshoe shape, the suites situated in the center are the best, because they are protected by the two arms of the building. Suites positioned deep in the center of the building have no windows and so do not receive the yang energy of the sun. These spaces are not desirable, because destructive energy tends to collect in areas with no natural light.

Third, the position of the office suite relative to the elevators, stairs, and hallways is important. As we noted earlier, these access structures are conduits and transformers of energy. We need to choose a suite that takes optimal advantage of the positive effects created by the access structures.

UNDESIRABLE POSITIONS

The following is a set of guidelines for identifying undesirable positions of office suites in a commercial building (see figure 15.19):

- Do not select a suite next to the elevator. Raw and untamed energy rising in the elevator and the shaft will rush into the suite, causing disruption and disharmony. Any positive energy generated within the suite will drop down the elevator and the shaft.
- Do not choose a suite next to the stairway or the fire escape, for the same reasons.
- Do not select a suite in front of the elevator or a stairway, for the same reasons.
- Do not choose a suite at the end of a hallway. The hallway has the same effect as a road. Positioning an office at the end of a hallway is like locating a house at the end of a street. Energy rushes toward the office like waves crashing onto the shore. The business will be buffeted constantly by business storms and will spend most of its effort and time bailing out of difficult situations.
- Do not select a suite with a door that opens diagonally into a hallway or an open space. Diagonal doors twist energy entering the suite, cause fluctuations in positive energy, and can increase the destructiveness of malevolent energy.

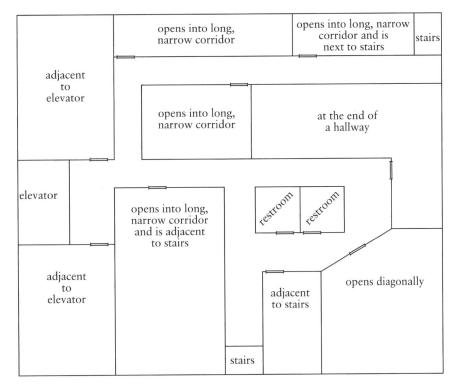

Figure 15.19 Undesirable locations for office suites.

DESIRABLE POSITIONS

The following is a set of guidelines for identifying desirable positions of office suites in a commercial building (see figure 15.20):

- The most protected suites are those with a buffer between them and any access structure.
- Suites that are not located in the corners of the building are protected.
- Suites that open into a spacious area are desirable, because the open space collects positive energy and tames destructive energy.
- Suites located in the middle segment along a hallway are better than suites located toward the ends of the hallway.

Now that you have an idea of what to look for when you are selecting a space for an office suite, try exercise 15.1.

Location of the Office Suite in the Scheme of the Nine Palaces of the Building

To figure out where the suite is located in the scheme of the Nine Palaces of the building, we must take the geomantic compass reading for the office building itself. (Later, we also will need to take a geomantic compass reading for the suite.) We obtain the facing direction of the building in the same way as we did for houses. (Refer to chapter 3 if you need a review.) Walk around the building

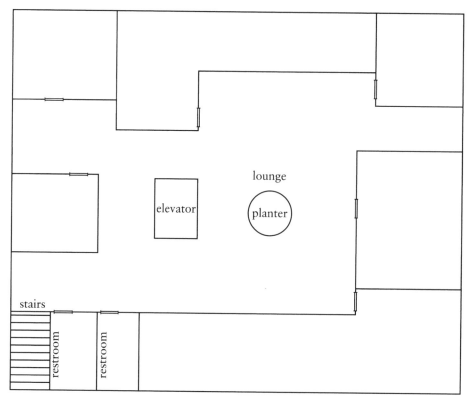

Figure 15.20 Desirable locations for office suites. All the suites open into a spacious area, and none of them is adjacent to the elevator.

and get a feel for which direction it faces. For most conventional office buildings, the facing direction is quite obvious—it is the side with an unblocked exposure. In older commercial buildings, the front of the building is very well defined—pillars, large doors, wide steps, unblocked views, and so forth. Determining the front facing of newer and smaller commercial buildings may not be easy. We will study several examples, to identify the front of a commercial building.

In example 1 (panel A of figure 15.21), the main doorway of the building is oriented southwest (k'un), but the general orientation of the building is west (yu)—the side of the building that faces the street. Which is the fac-

ing direction of the building? In this case, it is yu, not k'un. In this example, the facing direction of the building is determined by the presence of the alley, loading docks, and garbage dumpsters—which are usually located at the back of the building (in our example, on the eastern side, mao).

In example 2 (panel B of figure 15.21), we have a building that is trapezoidal. The main entrance, which opens onto a small landing, faces northwest (ch'ien), but it is the northern side (tzu) of the building that fronts on the street. The long side of the trapezoid, which appears to be the back side of the building (it has the garbage dumpsters), faces south (wu). Which is the front facing of the building? In

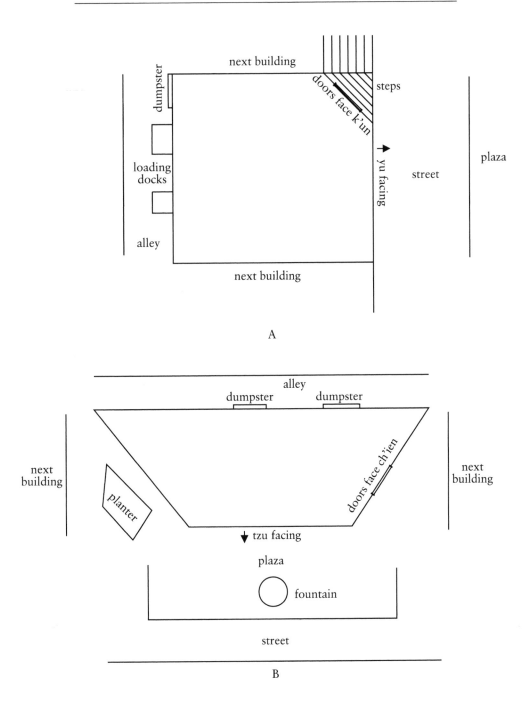

A

B

Figure 15.21 Determining the facing direction of a commercial building. (See text for more complete explanation.)

this case, it is tzu (north), because that is the side of the building that is not blocked. Although the main entrance is on the northwest side, its presence is not strong enough to give the impression that the building faces that direction. The small entrance and the small landing are insufficient to define the front facing of the building. On the other hand, the large plaza and the unblocked exposure on the north side of the building clearly impart the feeling that this is the front of the building.

In example 3 (panel A of figure 15.22), the building has a large doorway on the western side (yu, or west) that opens onto the parking lot. There is also another door on the side of the building that faces the street (wu, or south). Which is the facing direction of the building—yu or wu? This is a tricky case. The side of the building with the large doors and foyer faces yu, but if we look at the building's surrounding environment, we see that there are tall trees to the north, east, and west of the building. Only the side facing the street (wu) is not blocked. Moreover, if you look at the entrance to the parking lot, you will find that the access to the parking area is from the south. The southern side of the building, however, has a small entrance and almost no foyer. In other words, it does not feel like the front of the building. Which, then, is the facing direction of the building—yu (west, facing the parking lot) or wu (south, facing the street)? This is a real dilemma, because it represents a case of ambiguous or competing facing directions. (See box 3.1 in chapter 3 if you need a review of this topic.)

To solve the problem, we need to disambiguate the competing facing directions of the building. In other words, we must put in features to indicate that one side is unmistakably the front. My suggestion is that we make wu the facing direction, because it is the side of the building that is unblocked. For a business, it is very important to have a facing direction that is free of obstacles, because energy associated with prosperity and productivity must enter from the front of the building. Having decided that wu will be the facing direction, we will proceed to make the south side of the building look more like the front. First, if the building houses a single business, I suggest that an awning with the name of the business be installed over the front door. If the building houses several businesses, the street number of the building should be placed on the awning. Second, I suggest that the foyer on the south side be enlarged. Third, we should install a light on either side of the doors, to improve its frontal image. Fourth, we should landscape the driveway into the parking area, putting up a sign with a small flower garden around it. (These modifications are shown in panel B of figure 15.22.)

Now that you have a sense for how to identify the facing direction of a commercial building, we will proceed to take the compass reading for a building and generate the Nine Palaces. Figure 15.23 shows the floor plan of a commercial building built in 1989 with ping as the facing direction. Superimposing the chart onto the floor plan of the building, we can see that some suites have good stars, some have bad stars, and some have viable stars.

The Three Combinations and the Combination of Ten charts do not apply to the geomantic chart of the commercial building as a whole, but they do apply to the geomantic chart of the office suite itself, provided that all the palaces are included in the office space.

Now do exercise 15.2.

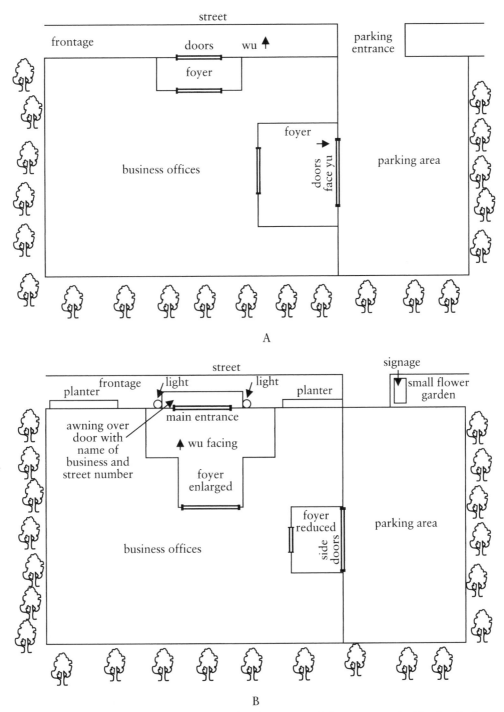

Figure 15.22 Using renovations and landscape modification to clarify the facing direction of a commercial building.

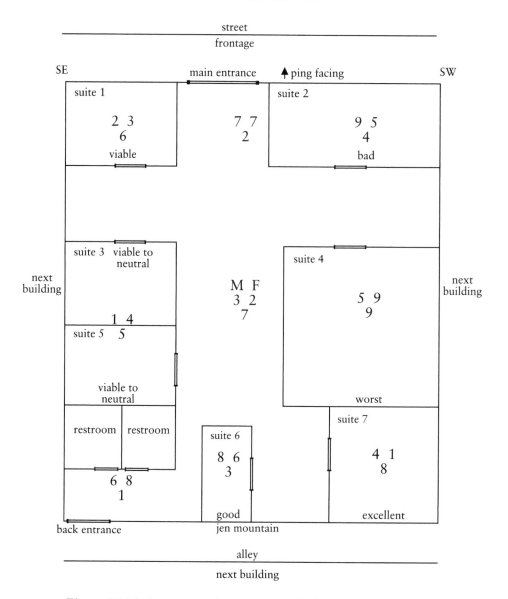

Figure 15.23 Superimposing a geomantic chart onto a commercial building. SE, southeast; SW, southwest.

Floor Plan of the Office Suite

The floor plan and the arrangement of rooms in the suite affect the flow of energy in that space. To judge whether the floor plan of the suite has good feng-shui, we need to ex-amine the layout of the entrance to the suite and the arrangement of rooms inside. To illustrate, let's look at an example of a floor plan with good feng-shui (figure 15.24).

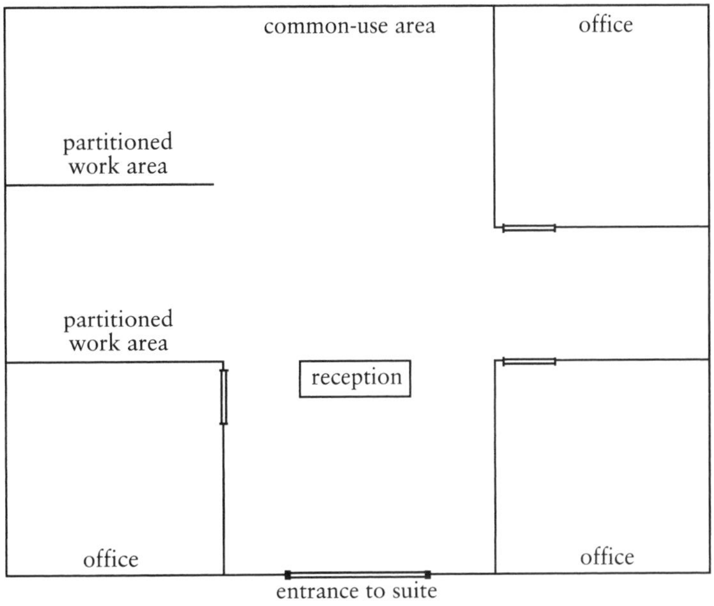

Figure 15.24 Example of a good floor plan for an office suite. The rooms open into a spacious area, and there are no long and narrow corridors.

The office suite shown in figure 15.24 has several desirable features. First, there is a spacious entrance area that can collect and amplify positive energy, neutralize malevolent energy, and tame wild energy. The entrance area also provides a buffer between the outside and the inside, making the transition from the external to the internal environment less abrupt. Moreover, the entrance area can be used as a reception area or a waiting room, depending on the type of business. Typically, this space is optimal for initial contact with customers.

Second, the offices in the rest of the suite should open into a common space instead of long, narrow hallways. This layout allows energy to accumulate before entering the offices. Although space may be at a premium in many office buildings, we should avoid filling "energy collector" spaces with cubicles and partitions. Cubicles can scatter and block energy so that positive forces amplified in the entrance area will be broken up and lost.

Now let's look at an example of a floor plan with bad feng-shui (figure 15.25). First, notice that the entrance to the suite opens into a small space, so that there is no effective buffer between the outside and the inside.

Second, the rooms open into a long, maze-like hallway. Any positive energy that enters the suite will be transformed into destructive energy as it squeezes through the winding maze. Third, the open space that can potentially turn negative energy into benevolent energy is crowded with cubicles. This cluttering can break up, scatter, and block any positive energy that may have entered the suite.

The floor plan of an office suite usually can be modified. Partitions can be removed, and the entire floor plan can be redesigned. Most businesses remodel a suite completely to suit their needs, and the remodeling costs typically are covered in part by the property owner(s). The amount that the owners are willing to pay will depend on how desperate they are to rent the space. If the feng-shui of the location

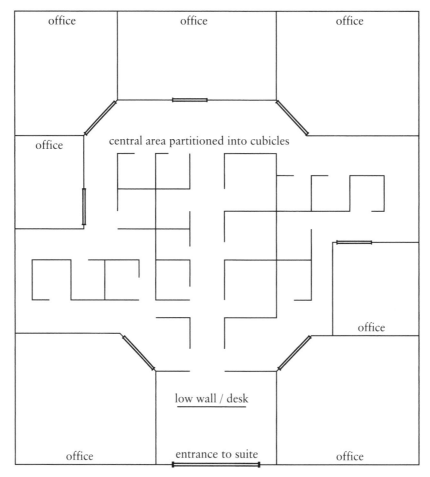

Figure 15.25 Example of an undesirable floor plan for an office suite.
The work space is crowded, and the passageways are mazelike.

of the suite in the building is good but the partitions are untenable, you can change the floor plan of the suite.

Planning the Usage of Space

Whether or not you are keeping the original floor plan, you will need to generate the geomantic chart for the suite in order to plan the usage of space. These are the steps in planning the usage of space in an office suite.

Step 1: *Generate the geomantic chart for the office suite.*

To generate the chart of the suite, we need to identify its facing direction, that is, the direction the front entrance faces. This orientation may or may not be similar to the facing direction of the commercial building itself. *Do not confuse the facing direction of the building with the facing direction of the suite.*

If the suite occupies less than one-third of the entire square footage of the building (remember to figure in the square footage of all the levels), the Earth Base of the geomantic chart is based on the year the commercial building was completed, regardless of when the suite was partitioned. If the suite occupies more than one-third of the total square footage of the building, the Earth Base in the geomantic chart for the suite will be based on the year the partitions were completed.

Step 2: *Superimpose the geomantic chart onto the office suite.*

When you superimpose the Nine Palaces of the geomantic chart onto the suite, you will be able to identify the areas with the best and worst stars and plan the usage of space accordingly.

Step 3: *Superimpose the geomantic chart onto each room of the suite.*

Superimposing the Nine Palaces onto each room will allow you to plan the placement of furniture, avoiding the areas with inauspicious stars and taking advantage of the areas with auspicious stars.

Step 4: *Install countermeasures and enhancers.*

Not all suites have perfect feng-shui. Even the ones in which the floor plan has been redesigned will have untenable areas. The placement of countermeasures and enhancers can enhance areas with good feng-shui, improve the areas with passable feng-shui, and neutralize the areas with bad feng-shui.

EXAMPLES

Let's apply steps 1 through 4 to two examples. In the first example, we will work with an existing floor plan, and, in the second example, we will design a new floor plan.

Example 1: Working with an Existing Floor Plan

In this example, the floor plan of an office suite and the usage of space based on evaluating the stars of the Nine Palaces are shown in figure 15.26.

STEPS 1 AND 2: GENERATING THE GEOMANTIC CHART AND SUPERIMPOSING IT ONTO THE FLOOR PLAN

In our example, the suite occupies less than one-third of the total square footage of the building, and major remodeling was not possible. The building was completed in 1979, and the facing direction is chia (easterly). The geomantic chart for the suite is superimposed onto the floor plan of the business suite. Because one palace is missing, we need to treat it as a regular geomantic chart instead of a Combination of Ten chart.

First, we notice that the front door is situated in an extremely good position, an area occupied by the combination four-six-one, the stars of prosperity. When stars of prosperity are located at the front door of a business, their positive effects are enhanced if the entrance is wide and spacious. A spacious entrance also allows benevolent energy to enter, gather, and be enhanced. In our example, the area at the entrance should not be cluttered with furniture.

Second, notice that a low wall that also functions as a desk is installed near the center of the suite. This prevents the energy of the auspicious stars six-four-eight in the center of the suite from flowing out the doors to the hallway. The desk is where the receptionist sits. Since the receptionist is the first contact between the business and potential customers or clients, the business's fortunes are en-

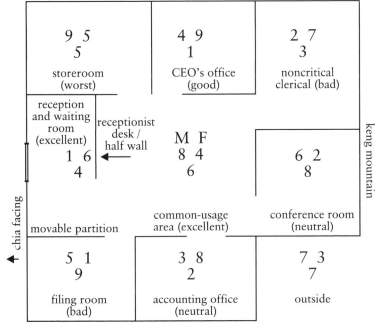

Figure 15.26 Floor plan of an office suite with the geomantic chart superimposed onto it. The usage of space is shown (see text, example 1). The Combination of Ten chart is treated as a regular chart because one of the palaces lies outside the suite.

hanced when the receptionist works in an area where the stars of prosperity are found.

Third, we need to find a tenable room for the chief executive officer (CEO). Since the CEO is the most important person in the business, his or her room must occupy a space with one or two auspicious stars. In our example, this is the room with the combination one-nine-four.

Fourth, we need to find a room for employees whose work is critically linked to the finances of the business, for example, the comptroller, the financial planner, and the accountant. This room should not be exposed to the entrance and should have at least one auspicious star. The room with the combination two-eight-three will suffice.

Fifth, we must find a suitable conference room. The space with the combination eight-two-six is viable as the meeting room. The Facing Star two-black can be neutralized by the eight-white of the Earth Base and six-

white of the Mountain Star, making this area neutral.

Now we will plan how to use the rest of the space. The area with the most malevolent stars—five-five-nine—should be used as storage room for old files and documents, office supplies, and unused furniture. This space should be entered infrequently.

The space with the combination nine-one-five has a small residual negative effect after evaluating the additive interactions of the three stars of the palace. Because nine-purple is in the presence of five-yellow, the positive energy of the Facing Star one-white water cannot counter completely both malevolent stars. The space can be made better with countermeasures (see step 4); however, given its position and the stars, it is best used as a room to store files.

The space with the combination three-seven-two does not have desirable feng-shui. (You should know what this unconditional

Earth Base / Facing Star interaction means by now.) With countermeasures installed to weaken the destructive effect of the combination (see step 4), the area can be used as an office for clerical work that is not critical to the finances of the business.

Finally, we have the excellent space in the center of the office suite—the area with the combination six-four-eight. This area should be used as shared space. Equipment commonly used by all the employees—photocopy machines, common computer, faxes—should be placed here. The frequent usage of the space enhances the energy of the prosperity stars and induces interpersonal harmony among the employees. We need to make sure that we do not clutter this space with equipment. The room should be open, and equipment should be positioned along the walls.

STEP 3: SUPERIMPOSING THE GEOMANTIC CHART ONTO EACH ROOM

Once we have decided how to use the space, the next step is to determine placement of furniture in the rooms. We will begin by superimposing the geomantic chart onto each room. Figure 15.27 shows the Nine Palaces superimposed onto two rooms—the CEO's office and the common room in the center.

Let's look at the CEO's office first. The most important piece of furniture is the desk. The desk and the chair should be situated in a spot occupied by prosperity stars. Ideally, the desk also should face an area with prosperity stars. In our example, we should place the desk in the area occupied by either six-four-eight or four-six-one in the microcosm of the room. I recommend positioning the desk in the area with the combination six-four-eight facing the area with the combination four-six-

one. The corner with five-five-nine should not be used at all. We can put bookcases or objects that are not used frequently here. The areas seven-three-seven and three-seven-two also should be used as little as possible. The area with one-nine-four is a fairly good spot. We can place a computer workstation or a secondary worktable there. The area with two-eight-three is a neutral spot and would be a good space for extra chairs for visitors. The doorway, which has the combination nine-one-five, presents a slight problem. Because it is a doorway, its frequent use will churn up the destructive energy carried by the Earth Base nine-purple and the Mountain Star five-yellow. Because it is also the entrance to the most important room in the office suite, we will need to place countermeasures to neutralize the problem (see step 4).

Second, we will consider the placement of furniture and equipment in the shared space. Equipment should be positioned in the areas occupied by auspicious stars or at least neutral stars—along the middle segment of the room (figure 15.27). Another good space for shared equipment is immediately behind the receptionist—the area occupied by four-six-one in the microcosm of the room. The area with the combination one-nine-four is also viable. No equipment or objects with moving parts should be placed in the corner with the five-five-nine combination.

Third, we will look at the design of the reception area and the common-use area. I suggest a long worktable and a counter forming a low wall that separates the center of the suite from the front door. This low wall will act as a buffer against destructive energy and allow benevolent energy to flow into the other offices. The receptionist should sit facing the front entrance toward the center. Phones and other desktop equipment should

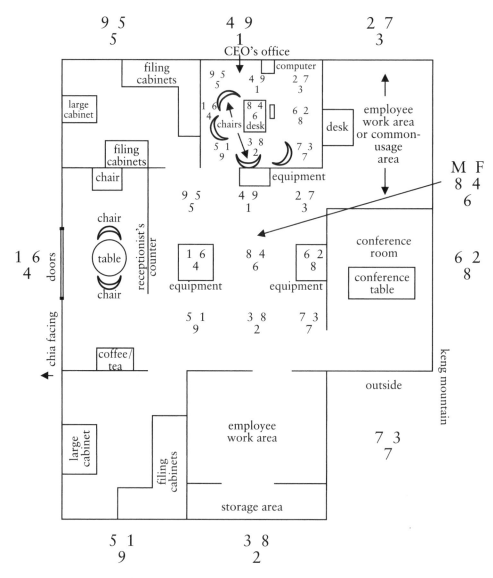

9 5
5

4 9
1
CEO's office

2 7
3

M F
8 4
6

1 6
4

6 2
8

5 1
9

3 8
2

Figure 15.27 Floor plan of the office suite in Figure 15.26 with the geomantic chart superimposed onto it. The placement of furniture is shown.

be placed as close as possible to the center of the long counter.

We will now plan the usage of space in the other rooms. We need to superimpose the geomantic chart onto the microcosm of each room. If you have problems visualizing the arrangement of the Nine Palace stars in the rooms, put a transparent sheet over figure 15.27 and write in the numbers for each room.

First, let's look at the room with the combination two-eight-three. In the microcosm of this room (figure 15.27), we should place the desk(s) in the areas occupied by the combinations four-six-one and six-four-eight, because the employees in this room are involved with the finances of the company. My suggestion is to partition this room with a screen, so that the rear third of the space is used for storage. Telex machines, faxes, and telephones should be placed in the middle of the rear third of the room, in the area with the two-eight-three combination. Again, the dangerous corner with the five-five-nine combination should be dormant. If the room is to be occupied by more than one employee, cubicles can be installed. In this case, the cubicles should occupy the two optimal squares—six-four-eight and four-six-one—and the neutral square with the combination eight-two-six. The inauspicious stars in the entrance—the three-seven-two combination—should be neutralized by countermeasures (see step 4).

Next, we will look at the room occupied by employees engaged in noncritical clerical work—the room with the combinations three-seven-two in the macrocosm of the suite. Again, within the microcosm of the room, the desks and workstations should be placed in the squares with the auspicious stars, toward the middle of the room. Because activity in these rooms is not as critical to the finances of the business, all we need to do is to make sure that the desks are placed in the areas with auspicious stars.

Next, we will consider the waiting room, which in the macrocosm of the suite is occupied by the combination four-six-one. I suggest that we place chairs in the area of the room with the combination one-nine-four. We should put a low table with reading material in the middle of the room and perhaps a table serving water, tea, or coffee in the spot with the combination two-eight-three.

Furniture should be situated in the middle of the conference room, which is occupied by the combination eight-two-six in the macrocosm of the suite. (Refer to figure 15.27.) Finally, the storeroom should contain only shelves, cabinets, and storage-type furniture (figure 15.27). It is assumed that no one will be in this room for a lengthy period of time.

STEP 4: INSTALLING COUNTERMEASURES AND ENHANCERS

Countermeasures. In our example, there are several areas with undesirable combinations of palace stars, and these troublesome spots need to be neutralized with countermeasures. The room with the worst combination—five-five-nine—should be dormant space. Moreover, no red-colored objects should be present in that room (figure 15.28).

The room with the combination three-seven, stars that are associated with mental anxiety and illness, needs countermeasures. When installing countermeasures for the entire room, the artifacts can be placed anywhere. To optimize the effect of the countermeasures, we should position them so that they also will neutralize the local problem areas inside the room (figure 15.28). Fire is the element that will neutralize both three-jade wood and seven-red metal. (If you need to review the principles of the interactions of the five elements in the design of countermeasures, refer to chapter 10.) In this case, bright lights, like spotlights, can be installed on some of the walls of the room.

The room with the combination nine-one-five needs a countermeasure to neutralize the nine-purple fire of the Earth Base and the five-yellow earth of the Mountain Star. Water is the best countermeasure here. The presence of water also will take the burden off the one-white water of the Facing Star in countering the Earth Base and Mountain Star. I recommend that we put a fish tank and/or a small waterfall-type fountain in this room. The fish can be of any color except red or orange, and the water from the fountain should not flow toward the front door. The best position for the fountain is in the southeast corner of the room, which in the microcosm of the room is occupied by the combination five-five-nine.

The room with the combination one-nine-four also needs the presence of water to counter the nine-purple fire of the Facing Star as well as to free up the energy of the auspicious Earth Base Star one-white water. An added benefit of placing water in this room is that it nourishes four-green, the auspicious

Mountain Star. A small waterfall-type fountain or pictures of water images are both suitable countermeasures for this room.

Last, we need to install countermeasures in the conference room. To prevent two-black earth from gaining strength, no red-colored objects should be placed in the room. We cannot use wood, water, or metal to counter the earth of two-black, because these elements also will harm the auspicious Earth Base eight-white earth. The best option is not to introduce colors that will enhance two-black.

Enhancers. Recall that enhancers are used to increase the strength of auspicious stars. Enhancers work best when all three stars in the palace are auspicious. Enhancers placed in areas where only the Earth Base and Facing

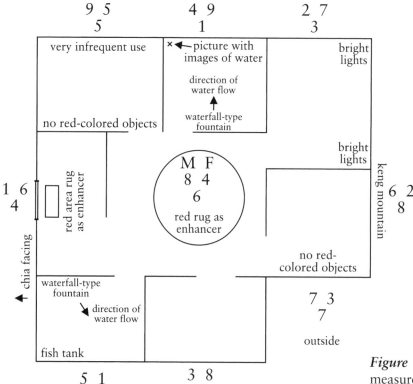

Figure 15.28 Placement of countermeasures and enhancers in example 1.

Star are favorable must be chosen with care, so that the enhancer does not magnify the destructiveness of the Mountain Star.

In our example, there are two areas that will benefit from enhancers—the entrance (with the combination four-six-one) and the middle of the suite (with the combination six-four-eight). To enhance the entrance, we would place red-colored objects in the area. Paintings, photographs, posters, and wall hangings with red and orange colors will work, as will a red-colored area rug at the entrance. (Refer to figure 15.28.)

The work area in the middle of the suite can be enhanced with the color red carried in paintings, posters, and the like. Because this space is located in the center of the suite and has access to the offices, we should put a red-colored circular rug in the middle of the room. The red enhances the auspicious stars, and the circular shape helps gather and increase the positive energy associated with those stars (figure 15.28).

To help plan the usage of space, you should rank the feng-shui of the squares of the Nine Palaces after you have generated the geomantic chart. A simple five-step scale—excellent, good, neutral, bad, worst—will do. Next, you should rank the business activities in terms of critical, important, noncritical, neutral, and dormant. Figure 15.29a and b shows the rankings of the Nine Palace squares and the business activities based on example 1.

Example 2: Designing a New Floor Plan

There is much more flexibility in planning the usage of space when you are working with a new floor plan. Areas occupied by malevolent stars can be turned into storage rooms, and areas occupied by stars associated with prosperity and productivity can be optimized. Moreover, we can design the partitions so that the doorways of the most important rooms are occupied by the auspicious stars in the microcosm of the room. Let's now follow steps 1 through 4 again as we design a new floor plan and plan the usage of space in the suite.

STEPS 1 AND 2: GENERATING THE GEOMANTIC CHART AND SUPERIMPOSING IT ONTO THE FLOOR PLAN

We obtain the facing and mountain directions and the Earth Base in the same way as the previous example. Let's suppose that the suite occupies less than one-third of the building, that the building was completed during the seventh cycle (1991), and that the facing direction of the suite (based on the front entrance of the suite) is ping (southerly). The geomantic chart is shown in figure 15.30. Because we plan to design a new floor plan, essentially we are superimposing the Nine Palaces of the geomantic chart onto an empty space. We will

FENG-SHUI RATING	PALACE
excellent	4/6/1
excellent	6/4/8
good	1/9/4
neutral	8/2/6
neutral	2/8/3
bad	3/7/2
bad	7/3/7 (outside the suite)
bad	9/1/5
worst	5/5/9

Figure 15.29a Ranking the feng-shui of the Nine Palaces (example 1 in text).

ACTIVITY RATING	ROOM	ACTIVITIES	PALACE
critical	reception	customer contact	4/6/1 (excellent)
critical	CEO's office	business planning	1/9/4 (good)
important	common area	communications (internal and external)	6/4/8 (excellent)
important	finance office	financial planning, billing, accounting	8/2/6 (neutral)
noncritical	office	noncritical clerical work	3/7/2 (bad)
noncritical	office	noncritical clerical work	7/3/7 (bad)
neutral	conference	meetings and parties	2/8/3 (neutral)
dormant	filing room	very little activity	9/1/5 (bad)
dormant	storage room	very little activity	5/5/9 (worst)

Figure 15.29b Listing the activities of the business and planning the usage of space in an already partitioned suite. Palaces with small positive effects are ranked as neutral (example 1 in text).

even assume that there is a certain degree of flexibility in the position of the entrance along the south side of the suite. Architectural constraints do not allow us to put an entrance on any of the other three sides.

Looking at the three squares of the Nine Palaces on the southern end of the suite, we find that the area with the combination six-three-two is the best. The square with the Earth Base / Facing Star combination two-seven forebodes fire caused by natural conditions. Since movement amplifies the effects of the stars, we should not place the entrance there. The square with the combination four-five-nine also is not desirable as a location for the entrance. The five-yellow in the Facing Star is associated with illness, the nine-purple in the Mountain Star enhances the strength of the five-yellow, and the four-green in the

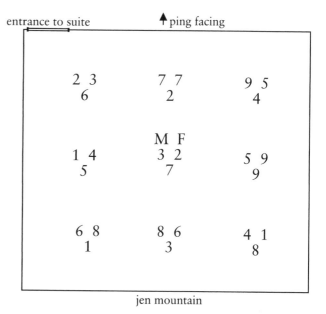

Figure 15.30 The geomantic chart superimposed onto an open space (example 2 in text).

Earth Base is not strong enough to counter the malevolent stars. Even if we put countermeasures here, movement through the doorway will strengthen the destructiveness of the malevolent stars. When everything is considered, the existing front entrance, in the area with the combination six-three-two, is the best of the three options. It has no destructive effects and is basically a neutral position.

Our next task is to plan the usage of the workplace. We will start by ranking the feng-shui of the Nine Palaces and the activities in terms of their importance to the business. Let's say that in this example the business is a law firm. The rankings are shown in figure 15.31a, and the proposed plan for the usage of space is shown in figure 15.31b. Using the rankings shown in figure 15.31a, we will design and partition the workplace. (In this discussion, refer to figure 15.32.)

First, we will select the spaces with the best feng-shui to house activities that are critical to the finances of the business. In this example, these would be the offices of the three part-

FENG-SHUI RATING	PALACE
excellent	1/8/6
excellent	8/1/4
good	3/6/8
neutral	5/4/1
neutral	6/3/2
bad	7/2/3
bad	4/5/9
worst	2/7/7
worst	9/9/5

Figure 15.31a Ranking the feng-shui of the Nine Palaces (example 2 in text).

ners of the law firm and the accounting office. The locations in the suite with the best feng-shui are in the northeast and northwest corners. They are occupied by the stars of prosperity, good fortune, and health. Thus, the lawyers' offices and the accounting and

ACTIVITY RATING	ROOM	ACTIVITIES
critical	3 lawyers' offices	legal consultation
important	finance office	accounting, billing
important	reception	client contact
important	meeting room / library	legal research
noncritical	2 offices	noncritical clerical work
neutral	waiting room	client waiting area
neutral	file room	filing
dormant	storage room	very little activity

Figure 15.31b Listing the activities of the business and planning the usage of space for an open space (example 2 in text). Palaces with small positive effects are ranked as neutral.

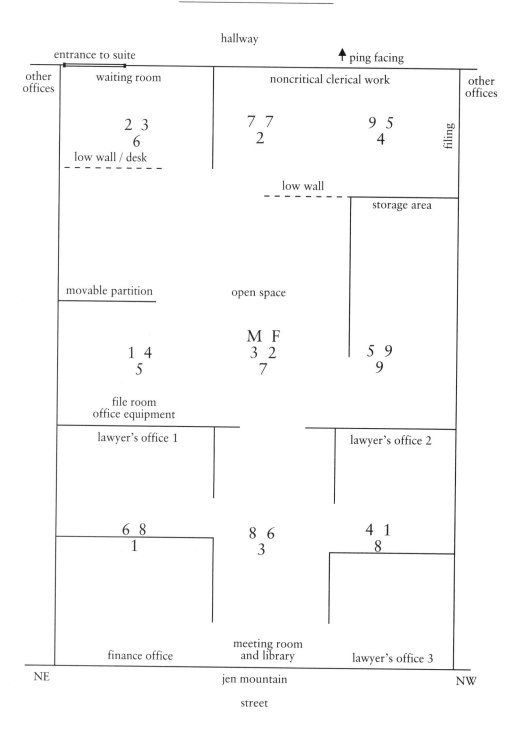

Figure 15.32 Proposed floor plan for office suite and usage of space. NE, northeast; NW, northwest.

billing department should be situated in either the space with the combination one-eight-six or the space with the combination eight-one-four. Notice that the spaces occupied by these two squares are large enough to be partitioned into two rooms (figure 15.32).

Second, we see that the area with the combination three-six-eight is also favorable. In our list, the meeting room / library is important, so we will designate this space for legal research and in-house meetings among employees.

Third, we see two areas with neutral feng-shui—those spaces with the combinations six-three-two and five-four-one. Of the two, the second one is slightly better, because it has a net positive effect after the Facing Star four-green and Mountain Star one-white have countered the five-yellow of the Earth Base. I suggest that we designate this area as general work space. We also can put common-use equipment in this area, such as mailboxes, filing cabinets, fax, and photocopier.

The entrance area, with the combination six-three-two, can be used as a waiting room, but we need to make sure that it is not crowded with furniture. The area in the center of the suite, with the combination seven-two-three, should be left as open space. The Facing Star two-black should be neutralized with countermeasures (see step 4).

Now we come to the areas with bad feng-shui—the squares with the combinations four-five-nine and two-seven-seven. Filing cabinets and shelves can be put here. Both areas can be used as work space for people engaged in noncritical clerical work, if the fire hazard (two-seven) and the risk of illness (five-yellow in the Facing Star) are neutralized by countermeasures (see step 4). Finally, the worst spot in the suite—the area with the combination nine-nine-five—should be used

as a storage room for office supplies and inactive files.

STEP 3: SUPERIMPOSING THE GEOMANTIC CHART ONTO EACH ROOM

We will now position the doorways of the rooms and work out the placement of furniture. We first need to superimpose the Nine Palaces of the geomantic chart onto each room. Figure 15.33 shows the Nine Palaces superimposed onto two of the rooms in the suite. If you have problems visualizing how the numbers of the Nine Palaces are arranged in the rooms, place a transparent sheet over figure 15.33 and write in the numbers for each room.

First, let's look at the offices of the three partners in the law firm. For office 1, the best position for the doorway is the area with the combination eight-one-four in the microcosm of the room. Since the doorway affects the energy entering the room, it is beneficial that the stars of prosperity, good fortune, and health be in that location. Moreover, constant traffic through the doorway will enhance the auspiciousness of the already benevolent stars. The best location for the desk is the position occupied by the combination one-eight-six in the microcosm of the room. Positioning the desk there also will allow the worker to face the other set of auspicious stars (eight-one-four). The areas with the combinations nine-nine-five and four-five-nine should be used infrequently. Bookcases and ornaments are best placed there. The center of the room has an inauspicious Facing Star (two-black), but we can neutralize it with countermeasures. This is a good spot to place chairs for visitors. A small worktable or computer station can be situated in the area occupied by the combination five-four-one, where the residual effect of

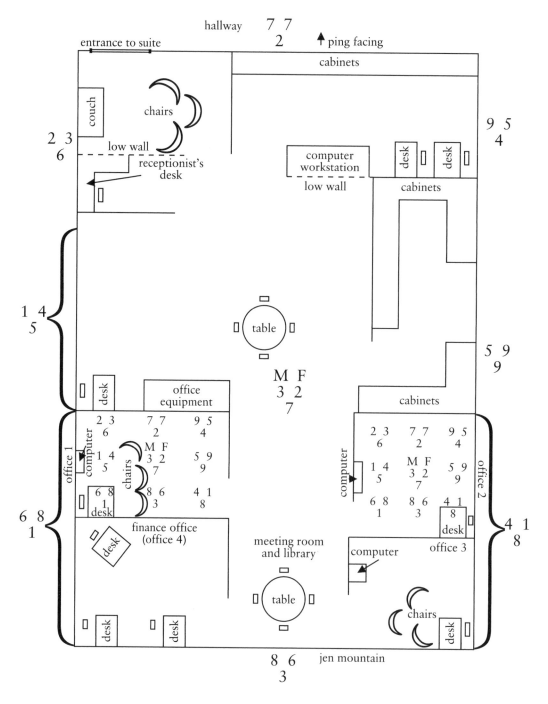

Figure 15.33 Superimposing the Nine Palaces onto two rooms in the office suite and planning the placement of furniture.

the auspicious Mountain Star can be felt after the four-green of the Facing Star has been used to neutralize the five-yellow of the Earth Base.

For office 2, the best position for the doorway is in the area occupied by the combination one-eight-six. The best location for the desk is the spot with the combination eight-one-four. For the reasons stated earlier (office 1), the desk should face the area with the auspicious combination one-eight-six. The areas with the combinations nine-nine-five and four-five-nine should be used infrequently. The central space of the office is a viable place for clients to sit, after two-black has been neutralized. A small worktable or computer station can be placed in the square occupied by the combination five-four-one.

Office 3 is identical to office 2, and the finance office occupied by the accounting and billing department (office 4) is identical to office 1. We can use offices 1 and 2 as guides to place furniture in offices 3 and 4 (figure 15.33).

Second, let's superimpose the geomantic chart onto the microcosm of the meeting room / library. The best location for the table is toward the north end of the room, where the auspicious stars are found. I suggest that we place a circular table in the area with the combination three-six-eight, so that people will be seated primarily in the areas occupied by the combinations eight-one-four and one-eight-six. The rest of the space can be an open area.

Third, we will look at the receptionist's area and the small work space behind it. I suggest putting the shared equipment and perhaps a desk toward the back of that space, where frequent use of the equipment will enhance the benevolent effects of one-eight-six, eight-one-four, and three-six-eight in the mi-

crocosm of the room. The receptionist should have a work area in the square with the combination six-three-two. Make sure that the receptionist's desk does not overlap with the square with the four-five-nine combination. I suggest an L-shaped desk, which would confine the work space to the area in the microcosm with at least neutral stars.

Fourth, we will consider the waiting room and the entrance to the suite. Superimposing the geomantic chart onto this room, we find that the best space for clients to sit and wait is the area occupied by the combination eight-one-four. The area where the receptionist receives the clients also is occupied by auspicious stars—one-eight-six. The rest of the area should not be used actively. In fact, as we shall see later, countermeasure artifacts need to be placed in some of these spots.

Finally, we will plan the placement of furniture in the remaining rooms. Remember, within the microcosm of a room, areas occupied by the auspicious stars should be used, and areas taken up by malevolent stars should be left dormant. Look at figure 15.33 to see how the furniture is placed in the rest of the rooms in the suite. Notice that even within the microcosm of the less important rooms, desks and workstations for employees are positioned in spots occupied by the auspicious stars within the rooms.

STEP 4: INSTALLING COUNTERMEASURES AND ENHANCERS

Countermeasures. In our example, there are several areas where we need to install countermeasures to neutralize the malevolent stars. The placement of countermeasures is shown in figure 15.34. First, the storage room with the combination nine-nine-five needs pictures with water images to neutralize the

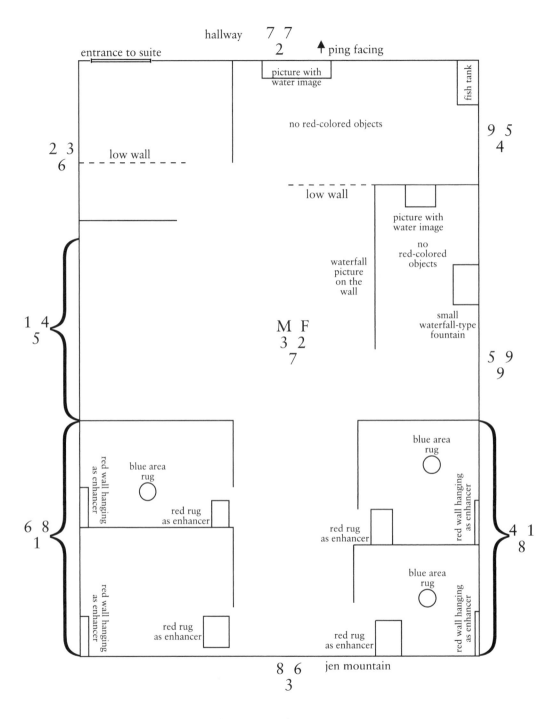

Figure 15.34 Placement of countermeasures.

threat of fire from the nine-purple stars. Also, no red-colored objects should be in this room. Second, in the work area occupied by the combination two-seven, we need pictures with water images to neutralize the fire hazard associated with that combination.

Third, in the corner of the suite that is occupied by the combination four-five-nine, we need to put countermeasures in place to neutralize the five-yellow earth in the Facing Star. The element water is the best countermeasure here, too, because it simultaneously dissipates the earth energy of five-yellow and nourishes the wood energy of the Earth Base four-green.

Fourth, a picture of a waterfall should be hung on the western wall of the space in the center to neutralize the Facing Star two-black. Finally, in the center of each of the business partners' offices, we should place a small blue area rug to neutralize the Facing Star two-black in the microcosm of the room.

Enhancers. Several areas in the office suite will benefit from enhancers. These rooms are the offices of the partners of the law firm and the office of the accounting and billing department. Red-colored objects will enhance the auspicious stars of these offices, but within the microcosm of the office, these objects should not be positioned in the areas occupied by the combinations nine-nine-five and two-seven-seven. The positions of the enhancers are shown in figure 15.34.

Although it is easier to plan the usage of space for a new floor plan than for an existing floor plan, you should not demolish the original partitions without working out the feng-shui of the existing plan. The following is a set of guidelines that I use when working on the feng-shui of business offices:

1. Examine the existing floor plan. If the arrangement of the partitions is not tenable, you should plan to remodel the suite.
2. If the floor plan is tenable, you need to work out the geomantic chart for the suite. If the space can be optimized given the layout of the Nine Palaces, there is no need to demolish the original partitions.
3. If the geomantic chart turns out to have problems, or if there are too many areas with bad feng-shui, you should consider remodeling and designing a new floor plan.

Remember, if the office suite occupies less than one-third of the entire commercial building, remodeling does not affect the Earth Base, regardless of when the renovations are completed. Moreover, remodeling will not give you new Facing and Mountain stars if the orientation of the suite is not changed in the remodeling. The new floor plan will allow you to optimize the usage of areas occupied by auspicious stars and avoid the ones with malevolent stars.

In summary, these are the points to remember when you are generating geomantic charts for a business:

- You need to generate geomantic charts for the commercial building as well as for the office suite itself.
- The front facing of the commercial building is the side with the most unobstructed view.
- The front facing of the office suite is the side where the entrance to the suite is located.
- The Three Combinations chart and the Combination of Ten chart do not apply to the geomantic chart of the commer-

cial building. They *do* apply to the geomantic chart of the office suite, provided that all the palaces are included in the office space.

- Conditional interactions do not apply to commercial buildings and office suites.

In this chapter our focus has been offices of small and medium-size businesses. The feng-shui of large businesses is more complex and is beyond the scope of a do-it-yourself project. If you need to evaluate the feng-shui of banking offices, corporate headquarters of large businesses, warehouses, manufacturing plants, university campuses, transportation terminals, government buildings, and the like, you should employ the services of a feng-shui expert.

EXERCISES

EXERCISE 15.1

Evaluate the feng-shui of the office suites (good, bad, or neutral) shown in figure 15.35 and give reasons for your choice. Unit 1 is a worked example.

Unit 1 is bad because it is situated next to the stairway and is at the corner of the building.

(Continue with the analysis.)

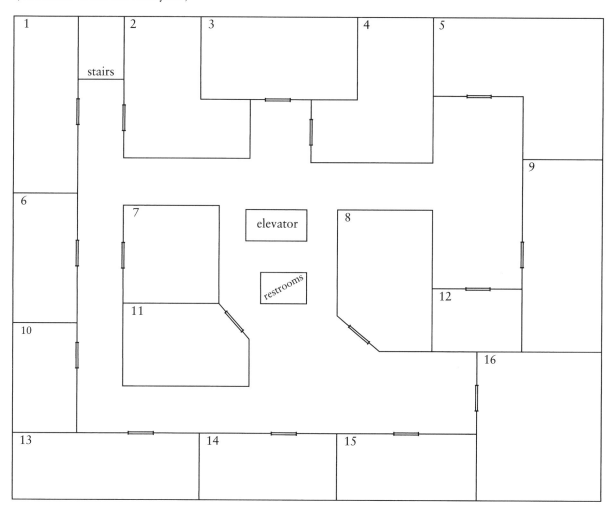

Figure 15.35 Evaluate the feng-shui of these office suites based on the floor plan of the building.

EXERCISE 15.2

Generate the geomantic chart for the building, superimpose it onto the building, and evaluate the feng-shui of the suites shown in figure 15.36. Use everything you have learned to evaluate the sites, including the floor plan of the building and the arrangement of the Nine Palaces in the building. The building was completed in the sixth cycle, and the facing direction is ch'en.

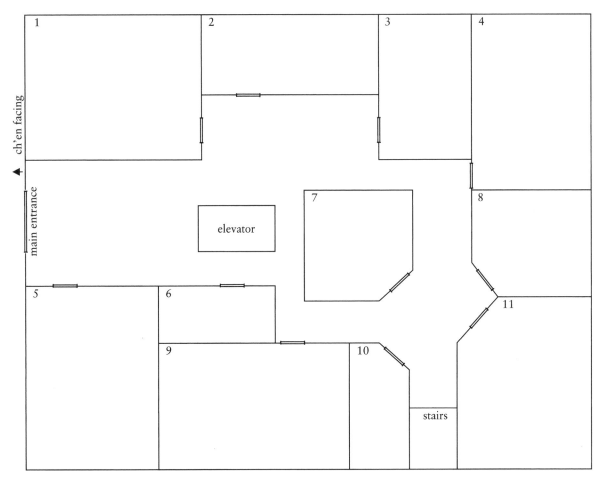

Figure 15.36 Evaluate the feng-shui of these office suites based on the geomantic chart and the floor plan of the building.

EXERCISE 15.3

Generate the geomantic chart, plan the usage of space, place the furniture, and install the countermeasures and enhancers in the office suites shown in figure 15.37. Assume that each suite occupies less than one-third of the total square footage of the building.

A. The building was completed in the sixth cycle, and the facing direction is ting. The suite should have one room for the CEO, one common-use area, one shared office for critical clerical work, two shared offices for noncritical clerical work, and a filing/storage room.

B. The building was completed in the fourth cycle, and the facing direction is mao. The suite should have private offices for two equal partners in the business, one common-use area, one shared office for critical clerical work, a conference room, one shared office for noncritical clerical work, and one waiting area for clients.

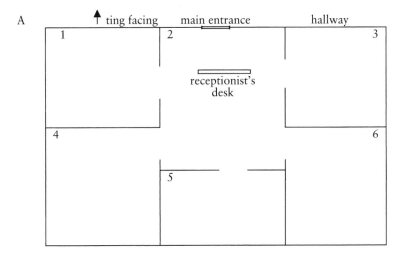

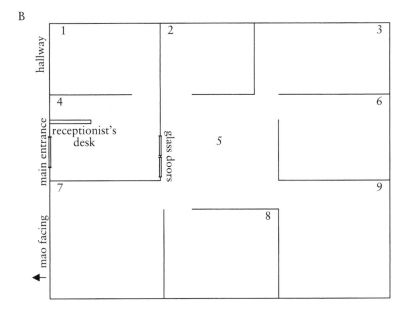

Figure 15.37 Plan the usage of space in these office suites using the existing floor plans.

ANSWERS

EXERCISE 15.1

- Unit 2 is bad because it is next to the stairs and opens into a narrow hallway.
- Units 3 and 4 are good because they are in a protected part of the building and they open into a spacious area.
- Unit 5 is neutral. The negative effect of being at the corner of the building cancels the positive effect of opening into a spacious area.
- Unit 6 is neutral. The negative effect of opening into a narrow hallway cancels the positive effect of being in a protected part of the building.
- Unit 7 is bad because it opens into a narrow hallway, it is near the elevators, and it has no windows.
- Unit 8 is bad because it is near the elevator, it has a diagonal entrance, and it has no windows.
- Unit 9 is good because it is in a protected part of the building and it opens into a spacious area.
- Unit 10 is neutral because the negative effect of opening into a narrow hallway cancels the positive effect of being in a protected part of the building.
- Unit 11 is bad because it has a diagonal entrance and has no windows.
- Unit 12 is neutral because the negative effect of having no windows cancels the positive effect of opening into a spacious area.
- Unit 13 is bad because it opens into a narrow hallway and is in the corner of the building.
- Units 14 and 15 are good because they open into a spacious area and are in a protected part of the building.

- Unit 16 is neutral because the negative effect of being in the corner of the building cancels the positive effect of opening into a spacious area.

EXERCISE 15.2

Refer to figure 15.38 for answers to exercise 15.2.

- Suite 1 is good. There are two positive aspects: it opens into a spacious area, and it has a residual benevolent effect carried by the Facing Star one-white after the Earth Base Star (one-white) is used to counter the two-black in the Mountain Star. There is a negative effect attached to its location in the corner of the building. Overall, the two positive aspects balance out the negative effect, with a small benevolent effect left over.
- Suite 2 is excellent. There are four positive aspects: it opens into a spacious area, it is in a protected part of the building, and the Facing and Mountain stars (eight-white and four-green) are both auspicious.
- Suite 3 is good. There are three positive aspects: it opens into a spacious area, the Earth Base Star (eight-white) is auspicious, and it is in a protected area of the building.
- Suite 4 is bad. There are three negative aspects: it is at the end of a long hallway, the hallway points directly at the entrance, and it is in the corner of the building. The only positive aspect is eight-white in the Earth Base.
- Suite 5 is bad. There are three negative aspects: its entrance is too near the main

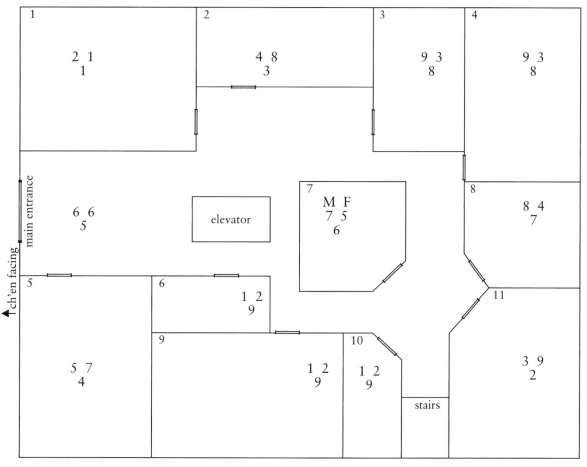

Figure 15.38 Answers to exercise 15.2.

entrance to the building, it is a corner unit, and its Mountain Star is five-yellow. There is only one positive effect—the Earth Base four-green. This star, however, is used up to counter the five-yellow of the Mountain Star.

• Suite 6 is very bad. There are four negative aspects: it is close to the elevators, it opens into a narrow hallway, it has no windows, and the malevolent Facing Star two-black is enhanced by the Earth

Base nine-purple. There is nothing positive about this space.

• Suite 7 is very bad. There are four negative aspects: it is close to the elevator, its entrance opens diagonally, there are no windows, and there is a negative effect carried by the Facing Star five-yellow.

• Suite 8 is fairly good. The one negative aspect is that the doors open diagonally. There are four positive aspects: the doors open into a spacious area, the suite is in a protected part of the building, and both the Facing Star (four-green) and the Mountain Star (eight-white) are auspicious.

- Suite 9 is bad. There are three negative aspects: the hallway points directly at the entrance, the Facing Star is two-black, and this star is enhanced by the presence of nine-purple. The only positive aspect is that it is in a protected part of the building. The small benevolent effect of one-white in the Mountain Star is negligible.
- Suite 10 is bad. There are three negative aspects: it is situated next to the stairs, its doors open diagonally, and the Facing Star two-black is enhanced by the presence of nine-purple. There are two positive effects: it opens into a spacious area, and it is in a protected area of the building.
- Suite 11 is very bad. There are four negative aspects: it is situated next to the stairs, it is in the corner of the building, the doors open diagonally, and the combination 2/9 forebodes obstacles in business. The only positive effect is that it opens into a spacious area. This effect is canceled by the diagonal entrance.

EXERCISE 15.3

Refer to figure 15.39 for answers to exercise 15.3.

For the positioning of furniture, equipment, enhancers, and countermeasures, refer to figure 15.40.

A.
- Room 1 (5/2/1): shared office for non-critical work. No red-colored objects should be placed in this room. Install water- and metal-type countermeasures against the combination 5/2. These

countermeasures preferably should be moving objects.
- Room 2 (1/6/6 and 6/1/2): common-use area in the section occupied by 6/1/2. Enhance the area with 1/6/6 with red carpet and other red objects. Do not put red-colored objects in the area with 6/1/2, because red may aggravate the Mountain Star two-black.
- Room 3 (3/4/8): CEO's office. Enhance the office with red-colored objects.
- Room 4 (4/3/9 and 9/7/5): Partition this room into two sections. Use the section with the combination 4/3/9 as a shared office for noncritical clerical work. Use the other section (9/7/5) for storage. Do not place any red-colored objects in either room. Install water-type countermeasures in both rooms to counter the fire element of nine-purple.
- Room 5 (2/5/7): storage and filing room. Install water- and metal-type countermeasures against the combination 2/5. The countermeasures preferably should be moving objects.
- Room 6: Partition this room into two sections. Use the section with the combination 8/8/4 as a shared office for critical clerical work. Use the section with the combination 7/9/3 for storage. Put in place water-type countermeasures against nine-purple and the combination 7/9.

B.
Refer to figure 15.39.
- Room 1 (3/1/5): waiting room. Install water-type countermeasures against the Mountain Star five-yellow.
- Room 2 (8/6/1): office for one of the business partners. Enhance with red-colored objects.
- Room 3 (1/8/3): shared office for critical

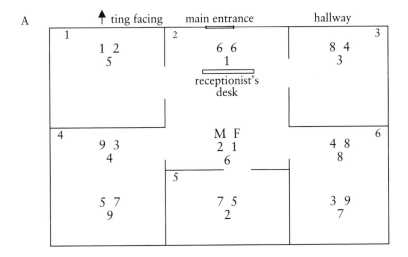

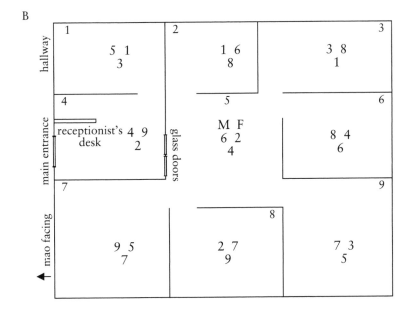

Figure 15.39 Answers to exercise 15.3.

clerical work. Enhance with red-colored objects.

- Room 4 (2/9/4): receptionist's work area. Install water- and metal-type countermeasures against the combination 2/9. The countermeasures preferably should be moving objects. No red-colored objects should be placed here. The flow of water should be directed away

from the front entrance and into the suite.

- Room 5 (4/2/6): common-use area. This is a neutral space.
- Room 6 (6/4/8): office for the other business partner. Enhance with red-colored objects.
- Room 7 (7/5/9): shared office for non-critical clerical work. Install water- and

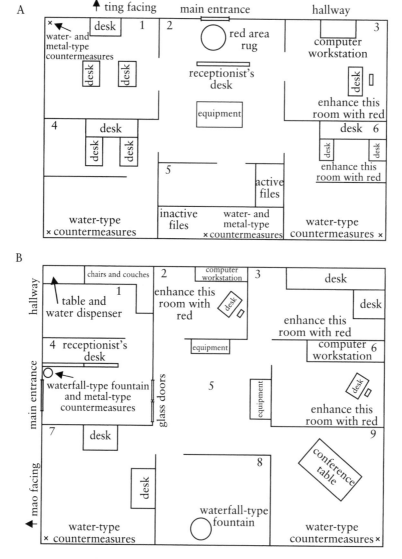

Figure 15.40 Answers to exercise 15.3.

metal-type countermeasures against five-yellow and nine-purple. The countermeasures preferably should be moving objects. No red-colored objects should be placed here.

- Room 8 (9/7/2): storage room. Install water-type countermeasures against the

serious threat of fire associated with the combination 9/7. No red-colored objects should be placed here.

- Room 9 (5/3/7): conference room. Install water-type countermeasures against five-yellow. No red-colored objects should be placed in this room.

16

Choosing and Designing a Retail Space

In this chapter, you will learn how to choose and design a space for a small retail business. In general, the feng-shui of retail businesses is similar to the feng-shui of residences and business offices. If you have studied chapter 15, you will find that some of the information is repeated here. Despite the similarities between the feng-shui of offices and that of retail shops, there are aspects that are specific to the retail space.

There are several steps to take in evaluating the feng-shui of a space for a small retail business. First, we need to identify the destructive and benevolent features in the surrounding area by examining the structures of neighboring buildings, road patterns, and parking lots. Second, we must consider the shape and design of the retail building. In evaluating the design of the building, we need to look at the frontage, the foyer and main entrance, and the position of escalators, stairways, and walkways. Third, we should look at the partitions (floor plan) within the shop, generate the geomantic chart, and plan the usage of space. If the store is located within a retail building or shopping mall, we will have to take into account the position of the store within the building as well.

CHOOSING A RETAIL BUILDING

In choosing a retail building, we must consider the external environment and the overall design of the building itself.

Evaluating the External Environment

NEIGHBORING BUILDINGS AND STRUCTURES

When choosing a building to locate a shop, we must first examine the neighboring build-

ings and see if there are destructive features. If there are none, we will look for benevolent features. Always identify the destructive features first; if they exist, there is no reason to continue the exploration. In my experience, it is safer to identify the destructive features first, because enthusiasm about the benevolent features often can blind you to the less favorable ones. Presented here is a set of guidelines for identifying destructive and benevolent features of neighboring buildings and structures.

Destructive Features

BUILDINGS WITH SHARP, KNIFELIKE EDGES

Sharp-edged buildings act like knives or axes. The business as well as the workers inside the target building will be hit with economic disasters and health problems. An example of this kind of building is shown in figure 15.1.

BUILDINGS WITH REFLECTIVE GLASS WINDOWS

A reflective building sends waves of energy crashing against the target building. The businesses and the employees in the target building will be hit with unending economic disasters. An example of this type of building is shown in figure 15.2. All sorts of dangerous reflections can be thrown onto the target building. Figure 15.3 shows a building that appears to be on fire as a result of the reflections cast on it by a neighboring building. Some reflections are obvious only at certain times of the day. You should examine the buildings at various times of the day and in sunny as well as overcast conditions.

IRREGULARLY SHAPED BUILDINGS

Buildings with irregular shapes trap energy and disrupt its flow in a neighborhood. Their irregularities create eddies and vortexes, transforming benevolent energy into malevolent energy. Figure 15.4 shows two examples of irregularly shaped buildings.

SHARP AND POINTED STRUCTURES

Sharp and pointed features protruding from buildings, cranes, and large sculptures act like spears aimed at the target building, skewering and impaling everything in their path (figure 15.5). Business projects and ventures inside the target building will be sabotaged and destroyed before they can get off the ground.

Moreover, workers will feel oppressed and exploited by management.

OBJECTS OF DESTRUCTION AND THEIR IMAGES

Weapons of destruction, their images, and sculptures of such objects are all harmful. (See figures 15.6 and 1.8a–f for examples.) Images on billboards can change. A friendly face promoting dairy products may become a jet fighter flying toward you when it changes to an advertisement for military recruitment. My advice is to stay away from areas with billboards, because the images on them are unpredictable.

Benevolent Features

PARKS AND GARDENS

Parks and gardens provide benevolent greenery, growth, and open space, assuming that pesticides are not used on the lawns. They allow energy to gather in sheltered areas and be transformed into gentle, positive forces. Plant growth is associated with life energy, and life energy in an area that usually is dominated by concrete and glass will diffuse the destructive forces that are found in constricted urban streets.

WATERFALLS AND FOUNTAINS

Waterfalls carry benevolent energy if they do not drop from great heights (figure 15.7). The best types of waterfalls are those connected to a water channel. The benevolent effect is enhanced when the waterway forms a winding path in an area. Fountains spurting upward also carry benevolent energy (figure 15.8). If the waterfall, fountain, and water channels are located within a garden or park, the benevolent effect is enhanced as a result of the added presence of trees and grass.

PLAZAS

Plazas can diffuse destructive energy, because they provide buffers between tall buildings. A circular structure is optimal in absorbing and neutralizing malevolent energy. Today most shopping centers and malls in suburban areas are designed as plazas. If you are looking for a retail space in a shopping plaza, you will need to consider the access roads into the plaza, in particular. (The feng-shui of shops in a plaza or shopping center is discussed in more detail in box 16.1.)

ROUND BUILDINGS

Buildings with round edges (figure 15.9) and dome-shaped roofs transmit benevolent energy and diffuse destructive energy. These buildings include planetariums and sports stadiums with a circular arena.

SURROUNDING ROAD PATTERNS

Roads in the vicinity of a building affect its feng-shui. You will recall from chapter 1 that some road patterns carry destructive energy while others carry benevolent energy. Figures 15.10 and 15.11 show examples of road patterns with bad feng-shui and good feng-shui, respectively.

PARKING AREAS

The location and design of parking areas can affect the feng-shui of shops in a retail district. You should examine the types of parking available near the store. Presented here is a set of guidelines for evaluating the parking areas in the vicinity of the shop.

Undesirable Parking Areas

The following types of parking areas carry destructive energy and are undesirable:

- Parking areas where vehicles drive into a building, as if the cars are trying to crash into the shop, are destructive (figure 15.12). The store will meet with frequent financial disasters. The health of the workers will be in jeopardy. If there is a sidewalk between the parking spaces and the shop, this destructive effect is neutralized.
- Parking areas that are located below a building that stands on pillars are also harmful (figure 15.13a). The building is already unstable because it is perched on stilts. If we add to it the movement of cars underneath, the situation is aggravated. Shops in the building will be financially unstable, and there will be frequent turnover of employees. This type of condition usually is found in downtown shopping centers, where parking space is at a premium.
- The situation just cited is worsened when the building is perched on several levels of parking, especially when the levels are structurally rickety in appearance (figure 15.13b and c). Such structures are associated with business instability.
- Parking areas that are situated underground below a building are not as bad as those that are above ground, but the instability is still present.

Desirable Parking Areas

The following types of parking areas do not carry destructive energy and are optimal:

- Open-air parking areas are desirable.
- Multilevel parking garages that form a separate structure from the shopping center are also beneficial, because they confine to an isolated area the energy carried by cars.

- Parallel parking on the street in front of the stores is advantageous, because the cars do not drive toward the building.

Evaluating the Retail Building

Once you have examined the surrounding structures, the next step is to look at the building where you want to locate the shop. The two factors we need to consider are the shape of the building and its overall design. With respect to the overall design, we must look at the frontage, the design of the foyer and main entrance, the architectural and interior features, and the locations of escalators, stairs, and walkways.

SHAPE

The shape of the building affects the flow of energy inside. Some shapes facilitate the flow of energy, some hinder it, some create beneficial energy, and some carry destructive energy.

Undesirable Building Shapes

Typically, retail businesses located in buildings with undesirable shapes will have high risks of financial problems, employee disharmony, and health hazards (figure 15.14a–j). There are several shapes associated with destructive energy:

- Buildings shaped like pyramids trap energy at the top levels. As the space decreases, energy is compressed. When energy compresses, it becomes constricted and oppressive. Consequently, the flow of energy in this type of building is distorted. Although it is not typical for retail shops to occupy the higher floors of the pyramid, it is not advisable to put a store in such a building.
- Buildings with triangular shapes squeeze

energy at the apexes. Here, too, as the space decreases, energy is compressed. The most troublesome areas are those located at the apexes.

- Buildings with irregular shapes hinder the flow of energy and make it erratic. Shops located inside these kinds of buildings will experience volatile profits and losses.
- Buildings in which the upper levels are larger than the lower levels are called *top-heavy buildings*. Retail businesses located in the lower levels of the building will be oppressed financially and will not be able to make large profits.
- When the levels of a building form a cascade, like a stepped pyramid, fortunes will "roll down" the building. Retail businesses inside will lose capital through loopholes, projects will never get off the ground, and there will be a high turnover of employees.
- When the levels of a building form a reverse cascade, we have the effects of a top-heavy building with sharp, overhanging edges. The result is an oppressive upper management, low productivity in the rank and file, and the threat of disharmony among workers.

Desirable Building Shapes

Typically, retail businesses located in buildings with desirable shapes experience good growth and productivity and harmonious relationships among employees. There are several shapes associated with benevolent energy:

- Buildings shaped like a horseshoe have the best feng-shui. Because the shape is circular, it not only imparts benevolent energy but also offers the best protection against buildings with sharp edges. The best retail spaces in a horseshoe-shaped building are the ones in the middle, where they are enclosed by the two arms of the semicircle.

- Round buildings are carriers of benevolent energy, as are buildings with domed roofs and rounded edges. These structures offer good protection against buildings with sharp edges.

GENERAL DESIGN

In examining the general design of the building, we need to consider the frontage, the structure of the foyer or main entrance, the architectural features (including types of windows), and the positions of escalators, stairways, and walkways. In large, multilevel shopping centers and malls, these factors become important. If benevolent energy cannot enter the building or if the design of the building generates malevolent energy, the retail businesses inside will suffer.

Frontage

The design of the frontage is an important consideration when choosing a building in which to locate a retail business. If the space in front of the building is constricted, benevolent energy will not be able to grow. As a result, shops located there will not receive forces associated with prosperity, harmony, and health.

The worst kind of retail building is one situated along a narrow street and surrounded by tall buildings. Narrow streets confine the flow of positive energy, and tall buildings cast shadows onto the street, creating destructive energy (figure 16.1).

In suburban areas, retail businesses tend to be located in malls and shopping plazas. The frontage of these retail spaces is typically more open than those in the city center. It is not unusual for suburban shopping areas to be surrounded by greenery and landscaping. Moreover, parking areas usually are located away from the building. This type of frontage is more desirable than that of the narrow streets in the city center. The openness of the building's frontage not only allows benevolent energy to be collected but also can help tame wild and destructive energy. All things considered, a shopping area in the suburbs tends to have better feng-shui than one located in a congested city center.

Figure 16.1 Shops that open into alleys do not have good feng-shui.

Foyer and Main Entrance

If you are considering a retail space in a mall or a multilevel shopping center, you will need to examine carefully the layout of the entrance area in the building, because the mall entrance is considered the shop's first entrance. (The second entrance is the doorway into the store itself.) If energy cannot pass through the first entrance, it will not enter the stores inside the building. Even worse, if energy becomes transformed into destructive forces there, it will affect all the shops in the building.

The most desirable types of main entrances are ones that are spacious and well lit by natural light. The doors to the building or the mall should be wide, so that traffic in and out of the building will not be constricted. Revolving doors are acceptable, as long as they are not narrow and tight. If such doors are not wide enough, the movement of the doors will not allow benevolent energy to gather inside. If indoor fountains and plants are placed inside the foyer and throughout the mall, the positive effects are enhanced. Most newer malls and shopping centers tend to have spacious foyers. Some of them, however, have architectural structures that are not beneficial to retail businesses located inside them. (See later discussion on architectural features.)

The worst types of foyers and main entrances are ones that are narrow and cramped. Some older malls and shopping centers have no real foyers—you enter into a hallway with shops located on both sides. These buildings do not offer a buffer to cushion and neutralize destructive forces. They do not provide a space for positive energy to accumulate, and they seem to push individuals into the building when they enter and throw them out when they leave. Small doors are undesirable, because they restrict the flow of positive

energy. Moreover, they create congestion when people leave the building at closing time. Figure 16.2 compares an entrance of a shopping center with good feng-shui with one that has bad feng-shui.

Architectural and Interior Features

Some architectural features enhance the feng-shui of a building, while others destroy it. In a mall or shopping center, the first architectural feature we need to consider is the windows. A building with a bank of windows from ceiling to floor makes a poor feng-shui environment. Positive energy (and thus prosperity) will leak out through the large windows, and there is little protection against destructive and wild forces. Skylights, however, are acceptable. In fact, skylights provide natural lighting and allow benevolent energy to enter and circulate.

Next, we want to see if there are exposed beams throughout the shopping center. Some interiors of modern buildings are crisscrossed with iron beams. Others have irregular roofs and walls. Iron beams impart negative feng-shui, because they "crush" the people beneath them. Irregular roofs and walls carry destructive energy and hinder the general circulation of benevolent energy.

We also must evaluate the color of the walls of the shopping center. Dark colors enhance malevolent energy and make the space feel constricted and uninviting. Black marble or dark stonework are not desirable wall facades. Light colors, on the other hand, enhance positive energy and create the sense of an open, friendly space. Light-colored marble, stonework, or natural drywall are all viable wall facades for a shopping center or mall.

Escalators, Stairways, and Walkways

Escalators, stairs, and walkways are conduits and transformers of energy. If you are choosing a retail space in a mall or a large shopping center, you will need to evaluate these features. Well-designed and well-placed elevators, escalators, stairs, and walkways not only facilitate the flow of positive energy and prosperity but also can transform malevolent energy into positive energy. Wide walkways

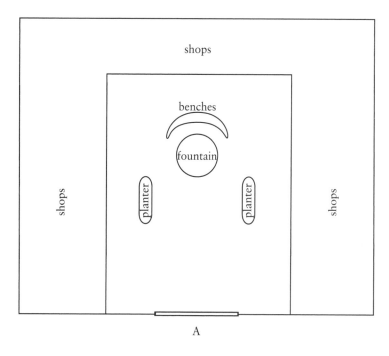

Figure 16.2 Retail building entrances. A: Entrance with good feng-shui. B: Entrance with bad feng-shui.

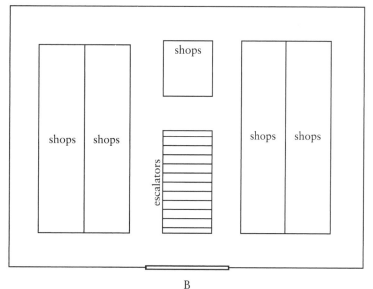

that lead to open spaces are good conductors and collectors of benevolent forces (figure 16.3). Escalators, elevators, and stairways with spacious landings are also beneficial, because they allow energy to slow down as it descends, thereby preventing positive or neutral energy from transforming into destructive energy.

Badly designed and poorly placed escalators, elevators, stairways, and walkways will

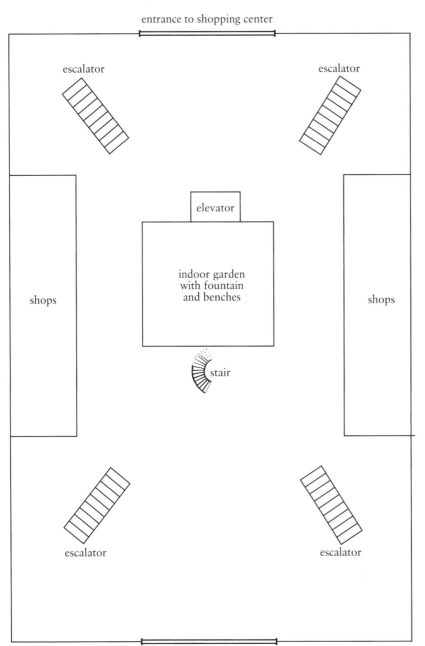

Figure 16.3 Walkways associated with good feng-shui.

hinder the flow of energy and prosperity as well as transmute neutral or positive energy into malevolent energy. Narrow, mazelike hallways carry destructive forces (figure 16.4), and narrow and steep stairways with small landings can force energy to rush down the stairs, changing neutral and even good energy into harmful energy. Beware of steep escalators with narrow steps; they have the same effect as narrow and steep stairways.

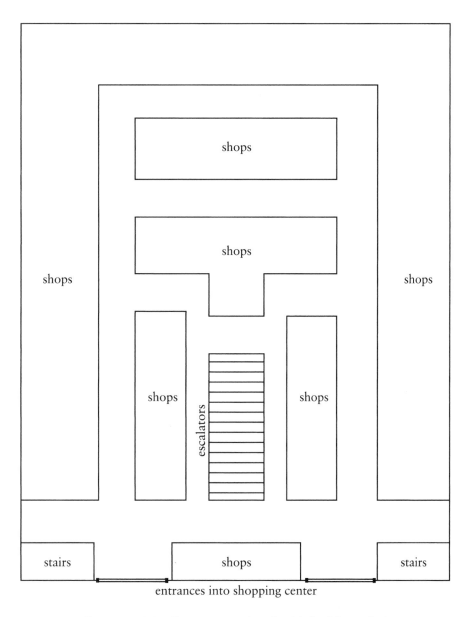

Figure 16.4 Walkways associated with bad feng-shui.

CHOOSING A RETAIL SITE

We will consider two types of retail sites—street-front retail sites and sites inside buildings.

Street-Front Retail Site

If you are choosing a street-front retail site, you will need to be able to distinguish the undesirable sites from the desirable ones.

UNDESIRABLE SITES

The following types of street-front retail sites are undesirable:

- Retail sites along a very busy street have unfavorable feng-shui. The heavy traffic carries away positive energy and churns up negative energy.
- Sites on a narrow street do not receive good circulation of positive energy. Moreover, the constriction tends to trap negative energy in the area.

- A retail site situated underneath a tall building will have its business crushed by the weight on top.
- A retail site with a diagonal door has bad feng-shui, because energy entering the site will be twisted and transformed into destructive energy.
- A retail site with doors opening diagonally onto an intersection may bring in fortunes, but prosperity comes at the expense of the workers' health and well-being.
- A retail site at the intersection of streets will be buffeted by destructive energy associated with the intersection. The situation is analogous to being caught in crosswinds.
- Retail sites on deserted streets have bad feng-shui, because energy tends to be stagnant.
- A retail site positioned on a street with a narrow sidewalk is far too exposed to

Figure 16.5 An example of an undesirable street-front retail site. Notice that its entrance is diagonal and that it faces the intersection.

the street traffic and has insufficient protection.

- A retail site on an extremely wide street with heavy traffic also does not have good protection.

Figures 16.5 and 16.6 show various examples of undesirable street-front sites for a retail business.

DESIRABLE SITES

The following types of street-front retail sites are desirable:

- Retail sites along a moderately busy street are desirable. The traffic brings in positive energy, ensures that there is no stagnant energy, and does not carry away benevolent energy.

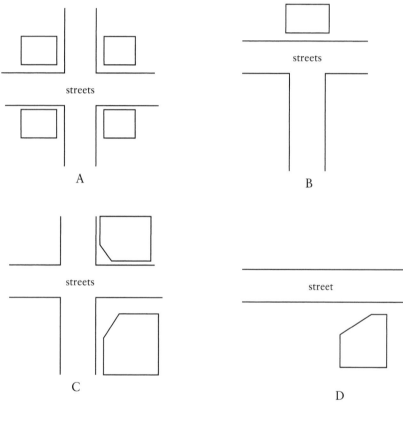

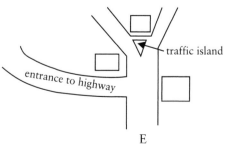

Figure 16.6 More examples of undesirable street-front retail sites. A: Retail sites located at an intersection. B: Retail site with road running straight into it. C: Retail sites with diagonal doorways facing an intersection. D: Retail site with diagonal doorway. E: Retail sites at a Y intersection and adjacent to highway.

- Retail sites along a moderately wide street receive good circulation of energy without being too exposed.
- A retail site in a single-level or at most a two-level building is a good choice, because it is not crushed by the weight on top.
- Sites that have an entrance that is parallel to the street are desirable.
- Sites that are removed from intersections

of streets are advantageous, because they are not exposed to destructive energy associated with intersections.
- Sites on streets that have a moderately wide sidewalk are recommended, because the sidewalk provides a buffer between the business and the traffic.

Figure 16.7 shows examples of desirable street-front sites for a retail business.

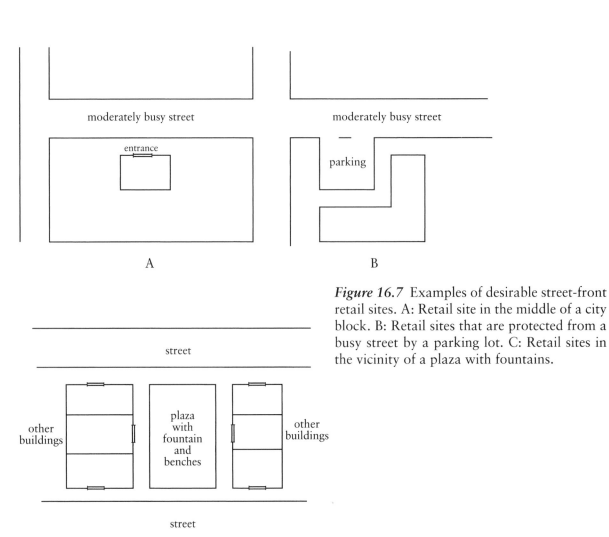

Figure 16.7 Examples of desirable street-front retail sites. A: Retail site in the middle of a city block. B: Retail sites that are protected from a busy street by a parking lot. C: Retail sites in the vicinity of a plaza with fountains.

PLANNING THE USAGE OF SPACE

Once you have selected a site, the next step is to generate the geomantic chart for the space. The geomantic chart and the pattern of stars in the Nine Palaces will determine the design of the usage of space in the shop, including where to place the cash register and how to display the merchandise.

There are three general rules that we need to bear in mind when we design the usage of retail space:

- Never crowd a store with too many objects.
- Always have clearly defined walkways toward and around the merchandise. Mazelike display counters, shelves, or racks constrict the flow of energy and can turn benevolent energy into destructive energy.
- The cash register and the position of the entrance to the store are the most important considerations, followed by the placement of the owner's office (if there is a private office) and then the display of high-priority merchandise.

For a street-front retail space, the procedure of generating the geomantic chart and superimposing it on the space is relatively straightforward. Let's work through the steps with an example. The Three Combinations chart and the Combination of Ten chart apply to the geomantic chart of the street-front retail site, provided that all the palaces are included in the space.

Step 1: *Generate the geomantic chart for the retail site.*

For a street-front site, the facing direction is the side with the front entrance (figure 16.8). To obtain the Facing and Mountain stars, take the geomantic compass reading for the front facing, making sure that your compass is not near any metal fittings on the building. To determine the Earth Base of the chart, find out when the building was completed. Let's look at a retail site that was built in 1978 and has a west facing (yu). Its geomantic chart is shown in figure 16.9.

Step 2: *Superimpose the geomantic chart onto the retail site.*

Retail space is usually open before it is stocked with merchandise. To take advantage of the arrangement of the stars of the Nine Palaces, we will place the most important components of the business in the areas occupied by the most auspicious stars. In the feng-shui of retail businesses, top priority must be given to the position of the entrance and the placement of the cash register.

Looking at the geomantic chart in figure 16.9, we find that in our example, the front door of the retail space is located in a square with the combination eight-one-six. This is an extremely auspicious combination for a front entrance. The traffic in this area will enhance the benevolent effects of the auspicious stars. The stars located at the front door of a retail business are very important. The Facing Star should be auspicious (one-white, four-green, six-white, and eight-white), and the Earth Base and Mountain Star should not be malevolent (two-black, five-yellow).

Next, we will examine the other squares of the Nine Palaces inside the retail space. The best method is to rank the auspiciousness of all the squares of the geomantic chart in a five-step scale—excellent, good, neutral, bad, and worst. The list for our example is shown in figure 16.10. With the list in hand, we can plan the usage of space. In the following discussion, refer to figure 16.11.

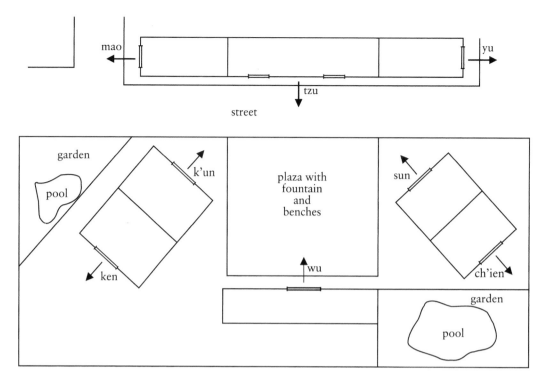

Figure 16.8 Determining the facing direction of a retail site. The facing directions of the retail sites shown are designated by arrows. Notice that the facing direction is determined by the position of the front (or main) entrance into the store.

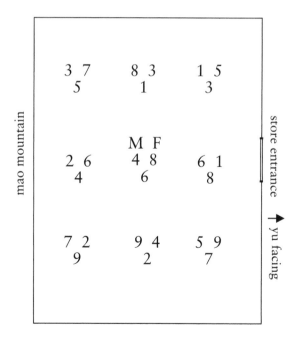

Figure 16.9 The geomantic chart superimposed onto a retail site.

FENG-SHUI RATING	PALACE
excellent	8/1/6
excellent	6/8/4
good	4/6/2
good	1/3/8
neutral	2/4/9
bad	9/2/7
bad	3/5/1
bad	5/7/3
worst	7/9/5

Figure 16.10 Ranking the feng-shui of the Nine Palaces. A palace with a small positive effect is ranked as neutral.

First, we see two excellent areas—squares with the combinations six-eight-four and eight-one-six. These are all combinations of stars of prosperity, health, and harmony. I suggest that these areas be optimized. First, we should place the cash registers in the position occupied by the combination six-eight-four. The cashier should face the square with the combination eight-one-six, so that activity in the area of the registers will magnify the benevolent effects of the auspicious stars. Since this is the center of the store, I also suggest that the cash registers be placed on a circular type of counter, with the cashiers facing the entrance where the auspicious stars are located.

Second, we should place merchandise in the areas with the combinations of four-six-two and one-three-eight. Some merchandise also can be placed near the entrance of the store, to take advantage of the excellent combination eight-one-six. We want to maximize customer traffic and activity in these areas, so that the movement will enhance the benevolent effects of the auspicious stars.

Third, we should place the storage area in the corner occupied by the combination nine-two-seven. The negative effect of two-black in the Facing Star cannot be countered by the neutral seven-red of the Mountain Star. Moreover, the negative effect of two-black is enhanced by the fire of nine-purple in the Earth Base. Given these adverse stars, the space should be used as little as possible.

Fourth, we need to determine what to do with the two trouble spots located toward the front of the store—the areas occupied by the combinations of seven-nine-five and three-five-one. I suggest that they be turned into dormant display areas, because they face windows. (A dormant display is one where goods are looked at rather than picked up and examined by customers.) In using this area for a dormant display, we will minimize activity in the unfavorable areas.

Finally, we have an inauspicious combination in the corner occupied by five-seven-three. As the Earth Base, the effect of five-yellow is not very strong. With a few countermeasures, we can turn this into a neutral spot and place merchandise there. Moreover, after we have a better idea of which types of merchandise are of high and low demand, we can position the low-demand items in this area.

Step 3: *Install countermeasures and enhancers.*

Countermeasures. In our example, we need to position countermeasures in several areas of the store. First, we will hang pictures of water in the areas where nine-purple is the Facing Star or the Earth Base. Decor in these areas should be bluish and greenish in color. No red or orange-colored objects should be placed in these spots. In fact, the best countermeasure for the area occupied by the combination seven-nine-five is a small waterfall-type fountain with water flowing toward the center of the store. A similar fountain can be placed on the other side of the door, in the position occupied by the combination three-five-one. The presence of water will drain the earth energy of the Facing Star five-yellow, enhance the wood element of the Earth Base three-jade, and add strength to the one-white water of the Mountain Star (figure 16.11).

In the corner with the combination five-seven-three, we should place metal objects, preferably ones that have moving parts. The metal will help dissipate the earth element of five-yellow in the Earth Base. A picture with

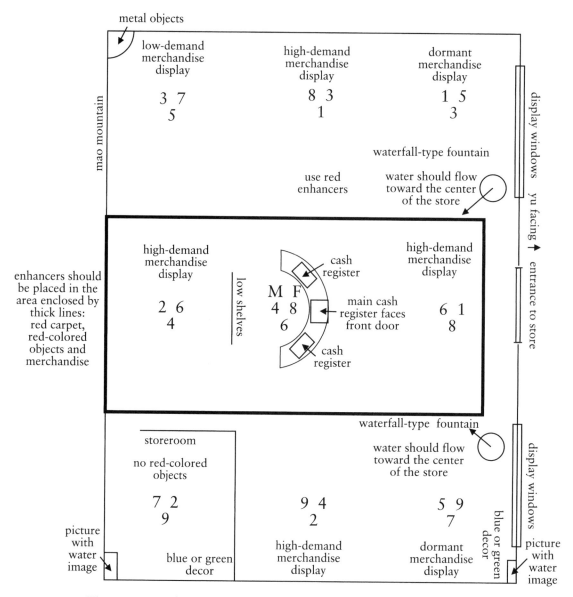

metal objects

low-demand
merchandise
display

3 7
5

high-demand
merchandise
display

8 3
1

dormant
merchandise
display

1 5
3

mao mountain

waterfall-type fountain

use red
enhancers

water should flow
toward the center
of the store

display windows   yu facing →   entrance to store

enhancers should
be placed in the
area enclosed by
thick lines:
red carpet,
red-colored
objects and
merchandise

high-demand
merchandise
display

2 6
4

low shelves

cash
register

M F
4 8
6

main cash
register faces
front door

high-demand
merchandise
display

6 1
8

cash
register

waterfall-type fountain

water should flow
toward the center
of the store

storeroom

no red-colored
objects

7 2
9

high-demand
merchandise
display

9 4
2

dormant
merchandise
display

5 9
7

blue or green
decor

display windows

picture
with
water
image

blue or green
decor

picture
with
water
image

Figure 16.11 Planning the usage of space in a street-front retail site.

images of flowing water should be put in the
storage room, to counter the combination
nine-two-seven (figure 16.11).

Enhancers. Enhancers should be situated in
areas occupied by auspicious stars, to amplify

their benevolent effects. I suggest that we
place a red rug at the entrance and in the middle of the store. We also should put red-colored objects along the cash register counter.
Merchandise with red as the dominant color

should be positioned in the areas with the combinations one-three-eight and eight-one-six (figure 16.11).

Now do exercise 16.1.

Site Inside a Retail Building

In this section, you will learn how to choose a retail space inside a mall or a shopping center. The feng-shui of retail sites inside a building is more complex than that of street-front sites. We need to consider the feng-shui of the position of the site within the building as well as the site itself. Here is the procedure for evaluating the feng-shui of a retail site.

POSITION OF THE STORE

First, because positive energy expands as it rises, the sites in the upper levels of a mall or shopping center generally have better feng-shui than those at the lower levels. If a shopping center or mall has more than one level, we should examine the sites at the upper levels before we consider space in the lower levels.

Second, within a given level, the sites located in the corners of the building and near the entrances are the least protected. The ones found in the middle, toward the center of the building, are the best. Sites that are farthest from the entrance are also not desirable, because positive energy entering the building will lose its strength by the time it reaches those areas. We should narrow our search within the areas in the middle of the mall or shopping center.

Third, we need to examine the position of a retail site relative to the escalators, stairways, and open spaces (sometimes called courts) within the mall or shopping center. As we saw earlier, access areas are conduits and transformers of energy, and open spaces are collec-

tors of energy. When we are selecting a retail site, we want to choose one that takes optimal advantage of the positive effects created by these areas.

Undesirable Position

The following is a set of guidelines for identifying unfavorable retail sites in a shopping center or mall (see also figure 16.12):

- Do not select a site in front of the escalator landing. Raw and untamed energy rising up the escalator will rush into the store, causing disruption and disharmony. Moreover, since the flow of energy follows a downward gradient, any positive energy generated inside the shop will flow down the escalator.
- Do not select a site next to or in front of a stairway, elevator, or fire escape for the same reasons specified for escalators.
- Do not select a site at the end of a walkway. The walkway has the same effect as a road. A store location at the end of a walkway is similar to a house location at the end of a street. Energy rushes toward the site like waves crashing onto the shore. The business will be buffeted by business storms and will spend most of its effort and time recovering from financial disasters.

Desirable Position

The following is a set of guidelines for identifying favorable retail sites in a mall or shopping center (see also figure 16.12):

- The most protected sites are the ones with a buffer between them and any access structure.
- Sites that are positioned away from the

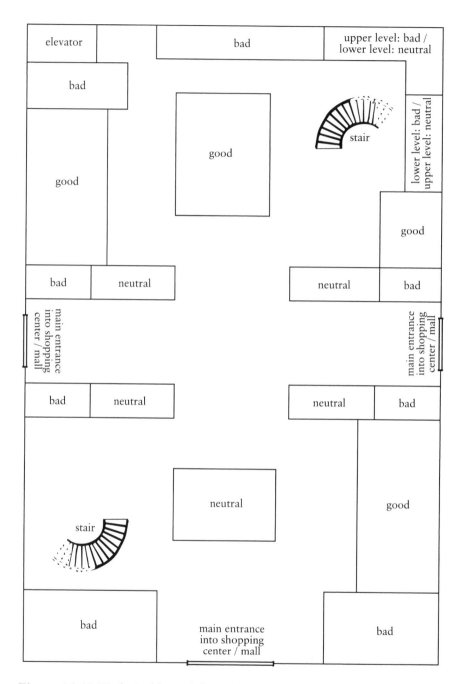

Figure 16.12 Undesirable and desirable locations for retail businesses in a mall. If not specified, the evaluation refers to both levels.

corners of the building have good protection.

- Sites that open into a spacious area are
also desirable, because the open space
collects positive energy and tames destructive energy.
- Sites that are located in the middle segment of a walkway are better than sites
located toward the ends of a walkway.

LOCATION OF THE RETAIL SITE
IN THE SCHEME OF THE
NINE PALACES OF THE BUILDING

The flow of energy inside the mall or shopping center affects the businesses there. We
need to ascertain the position of a retail site
when we superimpose the Nine Palaces onto
the floor plan of the retail building. To do this,
we need to take the geomantic compass reading for the mall or shopping center. (Later, we
will also need to take a geomantic compass
reading for the shop itself.)

Before we can take the geomantic compass
reading of the retail building, we need to identify the facing direction of the building. Walk
around the building and/or look at the blueprint of the building plans. Sometimes the
front facing of the building complex may not
be obvious.

Let's examine a few examples. We will first
look at the typical city-center shopping arcade. The building shown in panel A of figure
16.13 is a commercial building with shopping
arcades in the lower floors and offices in the
upper levels. The main doorway of the building is oriented southwest (k'un), but the general orientation of the building is west (yu),
because this is the side of the building with the
unblocked exposure. Which is the facing direction of the building? In this case, it is yu,
not k'un. Remember from chapters 1 and 3

that the best way to gain a sense for the front
of a building is to imagine the building as a
chair. If you were sitting in that chair, which
direction would you be facing?

The building shown in panel B of figure
16.13 has a trapezoidal shape. The main entrance, which opens onto a small landing,
faces northwest (ch'ien), but it is the north
side that fronts the street. The long side of the
trapezoid, which appears to be the back side
of the building (it has the loading docks),
faces due south (wu). Which is the front facing of the building? In this case, it is tzu (due
north), because this is the side of the building
that is unblocked. Although the main entrance is on the northwest side, its presence is
not enough to give the impression that the
building faces that direction. The small entrance and the small landing are insufficient
to define the front facing of the building. On
the other hand, the large plaza and the unblocked exposure on the north side clearly impart the sense that this is the front of the
building.

Now let's look at a shopping mall. Malls,
especially those in North America, have multiple entrances and are typically built around
a focal point, which is at the center. Figure
16.14 shows the building plan of a mall. From
the plan, we can see that in this example, the
mall has a westerly facing (hsin), where the
main entrance is located. In many North
American malls, the front entrance usually de-
fines the facing direction of the mall, because
the entranceway is a dominating feature.

Some newer malls, however, do not have
dominant front entrances. Looking at the
building plan of the mall shown in figure
16.15, we notice that all the entrances are
equally dominant, and there are no distin-
guishing features in the building plan that

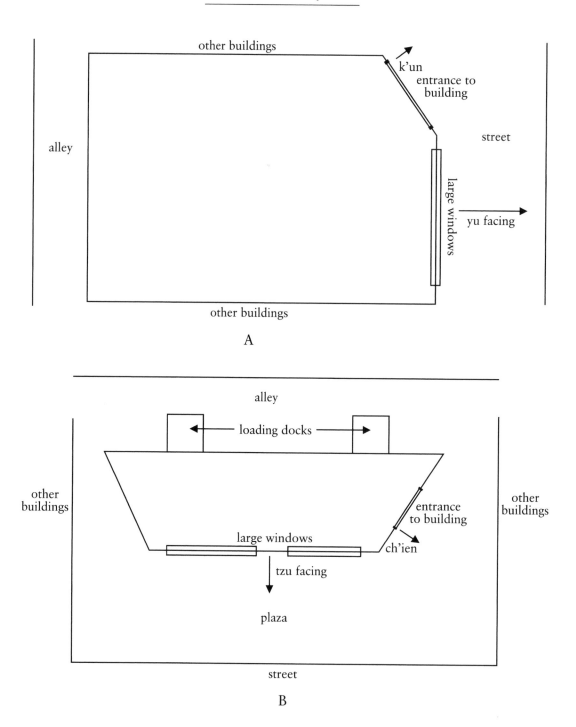

Figure 16.13 Determining the facing direction of a retail building: the shopping arcade.

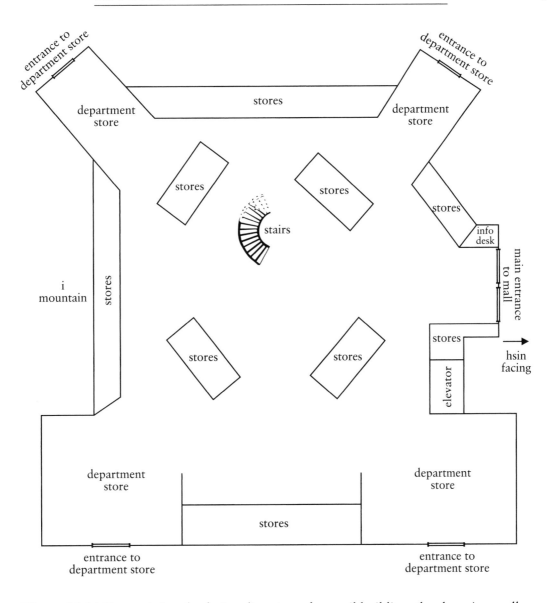

Figure 16.14 Determining the facing direction of a retail building: the shopping mall.

identify the front facing. In this case, we need to look at other features in the surrounding area, such as road patterns. In our example, the mall complex has a main entrance—this is the area with the traffic lights (in the direction tzu, or north). Furthermore, if we look at the general layout of the area around the mall, we

notice that there are two large retail buildings near the main access road serving the shopping complex. There is a large parking lot toward the south, with two smaller access roads nearby. Behind the parking area are trees that form a divider between the mall complex and another building lot. Given these features, the front facing of the mall becomes obvious—it is the side that faces the main access road with the traffic light, in the direction tzu.

After you have identified the facing direction of the retail building, you can take the compass readings and generate the geomantic chart for the building. The facing direction of the building will give you information to identify the Facing and Mountain stars. You can obtain information for the Earth Base star by asking the building manager or leasing agent which year the shopping center was completed. The Three Combinations chart and the Combination of Ten chart do not apply in the geomantic chart of the retail building. They apply only to the geomantic chart of the retail store, provided that all the palaces are included in the space.

Once you have generated the geomantic chart, the next step is to superimpose the chart onto the floor plan of the shopping center. Figure 16.16 shows the geomantic chart superimposed onto the mall shown in figure 16.15.

Examining the stars of the Nine Palaces of the mall, we find that the stars of prosperity, fortune, health, and harmony are located in the southwestern and southeastern sections of the mall—the squares with the combinations four-six-eight and six-four-one. The stores with the best feng-shui in the mall are located in these areas. The worst retail spot is in the northeast section, the square occupied by the combination one-nine-five, the stars of illness and obstruction. The combination of stars eight-two-three, in the northwest section, is not good. The stores in the middle of the mall, in the area occupied by the combination seven-three-two, also do not have good feng-shui, because the combination seven-three encourages gains in business but also indicates that profits will be lost through robbery and treachery.

Of the four entrances, the western one, with the combination nine-one-four, is best, followed by the south entrance, with the combination two-eight-six. The front entrance is occupied by the combination three-seven-seven, which forebodes illness associated with anxieties and worries. Finally, the eastern entrance is occupied by the stars of destruction, obstruction, and illness—the combination five-five-nine. The stars in the entrances affect the general fortunes of the mall itself as well as the businesses inside it. Since the traffic pattern of the shoppers cannot be controlled, the best way for the store owners to counter the undesirable effects of the eastern and northern entrances is not to use those entrances themselves.

Now that you have an idea of what to look for in selecting a retail site, you can try exercise 16.2.

PLANNING THE USAGE OF SPACE

As in the case of the street-front retail site, the geomantic chart and the pattern of stars in the Nine Palaces will determine the design of the space.

Step 1: *Generate the geomantic chart for the retail space.*

After you have selected a retail site, the next step is to generate the geomantic chart for the site itself. The layout of the Nine Palaces within the site will help you plan the usage of space in the store. To generate the geomantic chart for the retail site, we need to know when the retail building was completed. If the shopping mall has undergone major renovations in which more than one-third of the floor plan has been altered, the Earth Base will be derived from the year the remodeling was completed.

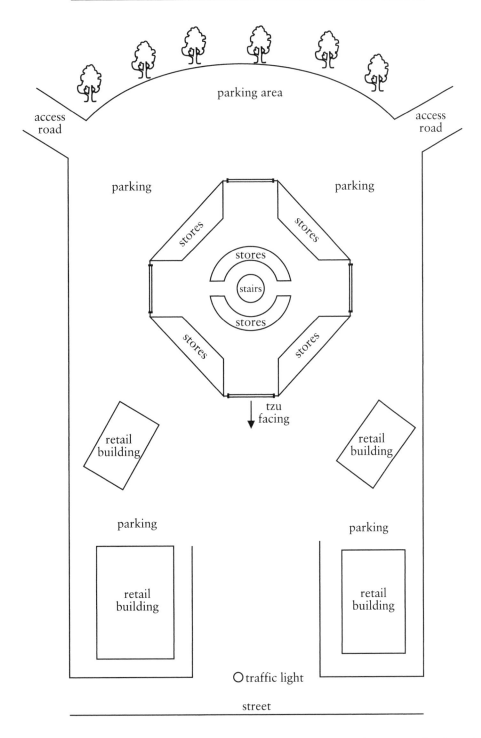

Figure 16.15 Using surrounding features to determine the facing direction of a shopping mall.

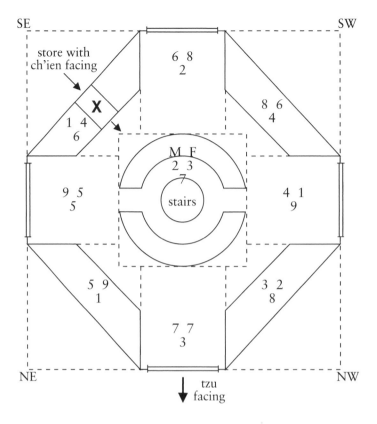

Figure 16.16 The geomantic chart superimposed onto the floor plan of a shopping mall. SE, southeast; SW, southwest; NE, northeast; NW, northwest.

Let's look at an example of the method for generating the geomantic chart of a retail site. Suppose we have chosen the site marked X in the shopping mall shown in figure 16.16. The facing direction of a site inside a retail building is determined by the entrance into the shop. In this example, let's say that using the compass, we have found the facing direction to be ch'ien (northwest). Since the mall was built in the seventh cycle and there have been no major renovations, we have the geomantic chart shown in figure 16.17.

Step 2: *Superimpose the geomantic chart onto the retail space.*

To plan the usage of space in the store, we need to superimpose the geomantic chart onto the retail space. Notice that because the facing direction is at the corner of the chart, we need to reorient it before superimposing it onto the space (figure 16.17).

Looking at the arrangement of the Nine Palaces, we see that the entrance to the store is occupied by the auspicious combination eight-nine, which is associated with celebra-

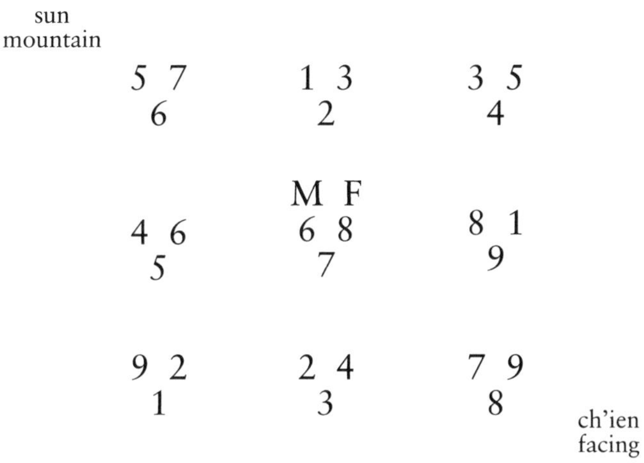

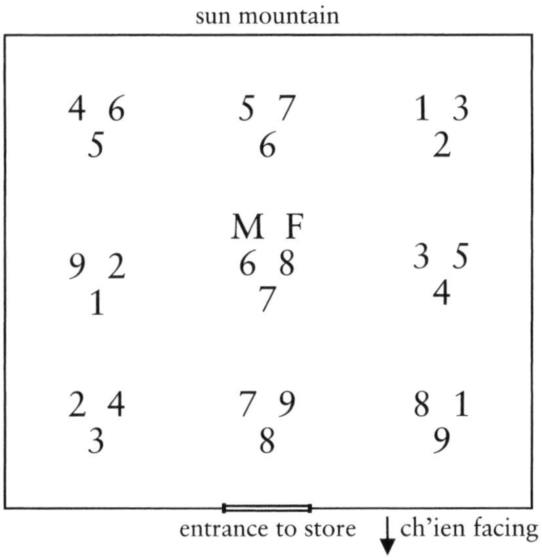

sun
mountain

5 7	1 3	3 5
6	2	4

	M F	
4 6	6 8	8 1
5	7	9

9 2	2 4	7 9
1	3	8

ch'ien
facing

sun mountain

4 6	5 7	1 3
5	6	2

	M F	
9 2	6 8	3 5
1	7	4

2 4	7 9	8 1
3	8	9

entrance to store   ↓ ch'ien facing

Figure 16.17 The geomantic chart superimposed onto the store's space.

need to examine the site further, because we do not want inauspicious stars at the entrance to a retail business.

Continuing with this example, let's look at the rest of the squares of the Nine Palaces. The best way to evaluate the combinations of the stars in the palaces is to rank them. Using a five-step scale of excellent, good, neutral, bad, and worst, we have the rankings of the palaces shown in figure 16.18.

The most important item in a retail space is the cash register. It should be placed in the areas occupied by auspicious stars. In our example, we should place the cash register in the area with the combination nine-one-eight or seven-eight-six. In either case, the cashier should face the front entrance, where the auspicious combination eight-nine is located (figure 16.19).

Next, we will arrange the merchandise. The optimal areas for merchandise are those

FENG-SHUI RATING	PALACE
excellent	8/9/7
good	9/1/8
good	7/8/6
neutral	3/4/2
neutral	5/6/4
bad	4/5/3
bad	1/2/9
worst	2/3/1
worst	6/7/5

Figure 16.18 Ranking the feng-shui of the Nine Palaces. Palaces with a small positive effect are ranked as neutral.

tions. In the context of a retail business, this refers to profits that are worthy of celebrating. Because the entrance to the store is so auspicious, we should continue to evaluate the rest of the space. If the stars at the entrance had been malevolent, we would not with the combinations eight-nine-seven, nine-one-eight, and seven-eight-six. Even if the cash register is located in one of those spots, merchandise can still be placed on the counter and on racks in front of the counter. It is also viable to display merchandise on a table placed near the front entrance (figure 16.19).

Now we come to the areas with the destructive combinations of stars. First, the corner that is occupied by the combination two-three-one should be left dormant, because three-two forebodes disharmony and quarrels among employees and owners. I suggest that this space be used as a storeroom. The area with the combination six-seven-five also should be left dormant, because six-seven presages robbery. The presence of five-yellow as the Mountain Star makes this threat even more serious. In view of this possibility, I suggest that this space be used as a display area. For example, if this is a clothing store, we can put mannequins there (figure 16.19).

The areas occupied by neutral combinations of stars—three-four-two and five-six-four—are also viable spaces to place merchandise, but I suggest that popular merchandise be placed in the areas with the most auspicious stars (figure 16.19).

Finally, the two troublesome areas with the combinations four-five-three and one-two-nine can be turned into usable spaces by installing the appropriate countermeasures (see the next section). Once the countermeasures are put in place, we can arrange low-priority merchandise in these areas (figure 16.19).

Step 3: *Install countermeasures and enhancers.*
Countermeasures. The areas most in need of countermeasures are those occupied by the combinations six-seven and two-three. We can counter the first combination with wood since the metal energy of six-white and seven-red is drained by wood. Wooden objects and plants are good countermeasures for this spot. Do not use water, even though water also can weaken the energy of metal. Water placed in this area is directly opposite the front door. Since water symbolizes wealth, the presence of water in line with the entrance will allow wealth to escape easily out the front door. If the flow of water is directed toward the entrance, prosperity and profits will flow out (figure 16.19).

In the area with the combination two-three, we can use a bright light as a countermeasure. The bright light carries the fire element and will break up the combination by destroying the wood element of the three-jade in the Facing Star (figure 16.19).

The two disadvantageous areas of four-five-three and one-two-nine also need to be neutralized by countermeasures. We will use water to offset the Facing Star five-yellow in the combination four-five-three, because the earth energy of five-yellow can be weakened by water. Moreover, water nourishes wood, so the three-jade wood in the Earth Base and four-green wood in the Mountain Star will be strengthened to counter five-yellow earth. The area in question is not exposed directly to the store's entrance, and so we can place pictures with images of water on the wall there. A small fountain, or some other object evoking the physical presence of water, is also viable (figure 16.19).

To counter the Facing Star two-black in the combination one-two-nine, we should use water. Water will weaken the earth of two-black, bolster the strength of the Earth Base one-white, and destroy the effect of fire in nine-purple. This area is not exposed to the store's entrance; here, too, we can place water images on the wall (figure 16.19).

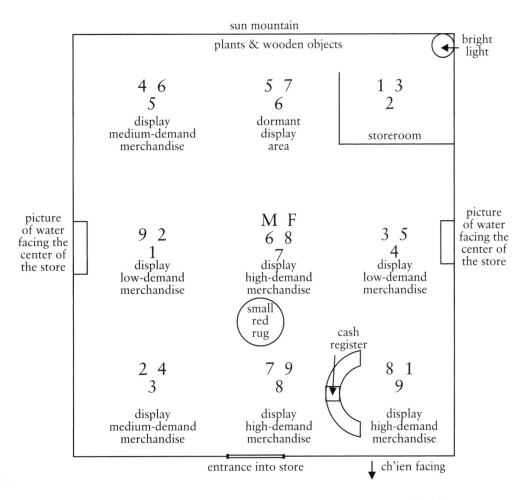

Figure 16.19 Planning the usage of space and placing countermeasures and enhancers in a store.

Enhancers. Enhancers should be situated in areas occupied by the most auspicious stars so that the benevolent effects can be augmented. I suggest that we install a red carpet at the entrance and toward the middle of the store. Do not position too many red objects in the area occupied by nine-one-eight. Although it has auspicious stars, we do not want the fire to extinguish the water energy of one-white in the Facing Star (figure 16.19).

Now do exercise 16.2.

In summary, these are the points to remember when you are generating the geomantic charts for retail spaces:

- You need to generate geomantic charts for the retail building as well as for the store itself.
- The front facing of the retail building is the side that gives the impression that it is the front.
- The front facing of the shop is the side where the store entrance is located.

- The Three Combinations chart and the Combination of Ten chart do not apply to the geomantic chart of the retail building, but they do apply to the geomantic chart of the shop, provided that all the palaces are included in the retail space.
- The Three Combinations chart and the Combination of Ten chart apply to the geomantic chart of the street-front retail site, provided that all the palaces are included in the space.

- Conditional interactions do not apply to retail spaces.

In this chapter, our focus has been on small and medium-size retail businesses. The feng-shui of large retail businesses is more complex and is beyond the scope of a do-it-yourself project. If you need to evaluate the feng-shui of department stores, specialty superstores, supermarkets, restaurants, movie theaters, car dealerships, and the like, you should employ the services of a feng-shui expert.

BOX 16.1

THE SHOPPING PLAZA AS A SPECIAL CASE OF STREET-FRONT RETAIL SITES

The feng-shui of a store located in a shopping plaza is evaluated in the same way as that of a street-front retail site (see pages 352–359). If you look at figure B16.1, you will see that the shopping plaza is simply an enclosed area consisting of access roads and shops. A store located against the convex bend of a curve in the access road is no different from one that is situated in the convex bend of a winding street. Similarly, a store positioned at the end of a T junction inside the shopping plaza is no different from a shop placed at the same type of junction in a city block.

The feng-shui of the pattern of the access roads within the shopping plaza is evaluated in the same way as that of city streets. A plaza with convoluted access roads is analogous to an area of the city with mazelike streets. Thus, all the principles that determine the selection of a street-front retail site apply to the selection of a retail space within a shopping plaza.

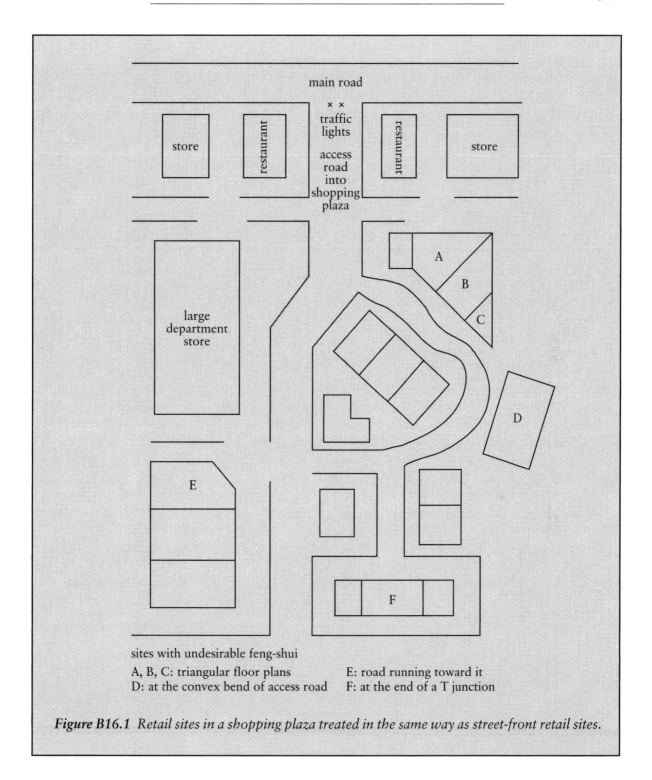

Figure B16.1 *Retail sites in a shopping plaza treated in the same way as street-front retail sites.*

EXERCISES

EXERCISE 16.1

Evaluate the feng-shui of the street-front retail sites (good, bad, or neutral) shown in figure 16.20 and give reasons for your choice. Units 1 and 2 are partially worked examples.

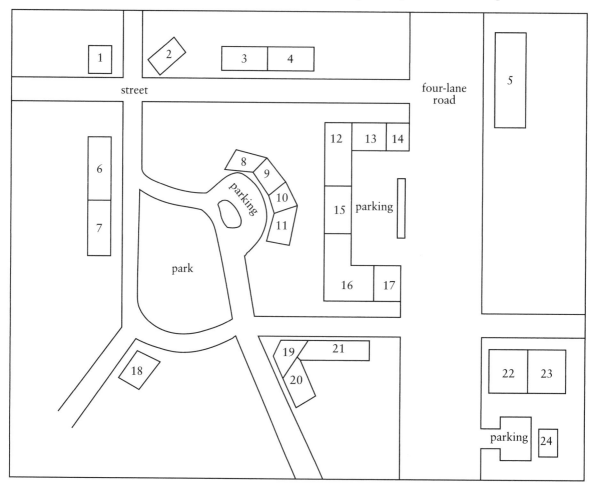

Figure 16.20 Evaluating the feng-shui of street-front retail sites.

- *Unit 1 has bad feng-shui because it is at an intersection.*
- *Unit 2 is bad because it faces an inter-section.*

(Continue with the analysis.)

EXERCISE 16.2

Evaluate the feng-shui of the shopping mall retail sites (good, bad, and neutral) shown in figure 16.21 and give reasons for your choice. The mall was completed in the fifth cycle, and the facing direction is wu. Remember that you need to evaluate a site relative to such features as escalators and walkways as well as its location within the Nine Palaces of the mall.

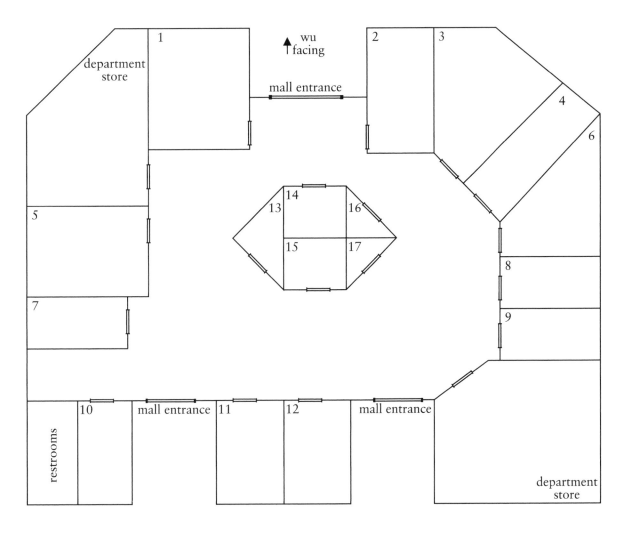

Figure 16.21 Evaluating the feng-shui of retail sites in a shopping mall.

EXERCISE 16.3

Select the retail site with the best feng-shui from exercise 16.2 and plan the usage of space in the store. You should include the installation of countermeasures and enhancers in your plan. Assume that the entrance to the store can be shifted along its front-facing direction but cannot be moved to the other directions.

ANSWERS

EXERCISE 16.1

- Units 3 and 4 are good; they are at a distance from intersections.
- Unit 5 is bad. It is at an intersection with a road running straight toward it, and it lies along a road with fast traffic.
- Unit 6 is bad because a road runs straight toward it.
- Unit 7 is good. It is positioned away from an intersection and lies in front of a park.
- Units 8–11 are all good. They are protected by the parking lot and the island. The circular parking lot also gathers benevolent energy and tames wild energy.
- Units 12, 13, 15, and 16 are good. They are protected by the parking lot, which gathers benevolent energy and tames wild energy, and they also face a park.
- Units 14 and 17 are bad: they are too close to a busy road.
- Unit 18 is bad because it is at an intersection.
- Unit 19 is bad. It faces diagonally into an intersection with a road running straight toward it, and it is hemmed in by two roads.
- Units 20 and 21 are good: they are set back from the intersection.
- Unit 22 is bad because it is at an intersection.
- Unit 23 is good: it is away from the intersection.
- Unit 24 is good. It is protected by the parking lot, which also gathers benevolent energy and tames wild energy.

EXERCISE 16.2

This is the geomantic chart:

wu facing

| 2 1 | 6 5 | 4 3 |
| 4 | 9 | 2 |

M F

| 3 2 | 1 9 | 8 7 |
| 3 | 5 | 7 |

| 7 6 | 5 4 | 9 8 |
| 8 | 1 | 6 |

tzu mountain

Superimposing the chart onto the building, we derive the following stars:

- 4/1/2—department store and unit 1
- 9/5/6—unit 2
- 2/3/4—units 3 and 4
- 3/2/3—units 5 and 7
- 5/9/1—units 13, 14, 15, 16, and 17
- 7/7/8—units 6, 8, and 9
- 8/6/7—unit 10
- 1/4/5—units 11 and 12
- 6/8/9—department store

Here is the assessment of the units:
Unit 1—neutral

There is one positive aspect—the fact that the Facing Star is one-white. There is one negative aspect. The unit is adjacent to the main entrance of the mall.

Unit 2—bad

There are two negative aspects. Note that its entrance is near the entrance to the mall and the interaction of 9/5 forebodes illness and obstacles.

Units 3 and 4—bad

There are two negative aspects. The entrances open diagonally, and the interaction of 2/3 fosters disharmony.

Unit 5—bad

There is one positive aspect, in that this unit is in a sheltered part of the building. There are, however, two strong negative aspects—the Facing Star / Earth Base combination 3/2, which portends disharmony, and the sharp edge of a wall pointing at the space.

Unit 6—bad

There is one positive effect—the fact that the Mountain Star is eight-white. There are also two strong negative aspects. The shape of the space is triangular, and the sharp edge of a wall is pointing at the space.

Unit 7—bad

There is one positive aspect, in that the unit is in a sheltered part of the building. There is one strong negative aspect: the combination 3/2 promotes disharmony.

Units 8 and 9—good

There are two positive aspects. These units are in a sheltered part of the building, and there is a small positive effect carried by the Mountain Star eight-white.

Unit 10—neutral

There is one positive aspect—the combination 8/6, which is associated with health, prosperity, and good fortune. There also is one negative factor. The unit is too close to the mall entrance.

Units 11 and 12—neutral

There is one positive aspect, a small residual positive effect carried by the Earth Base one-white after the Facing Star four-green has

been used to cancel the Mountain Star five-yellow. The negative aspect is that the unit lies too close to the mall entrance.

Units 13, 16, and 17—worst

There are three negative aspects: the doors open diagonally, the shape of the space is triangular, and the combination 5/9 is malevolent.

Unit 14—worst

There are three negative aspects. The doors open toward the mall entrance, the combination 5/9 is malevolent, and the unit is not protected from the main entrance to the retail building.

Unit 15—bad

There is one strong negative aspect, in that the combination 5/9 is malevolent.

EXERCISE 16.3

In exercise 16.2, there are two good units—8 and 9. Both units have mao facings.

	8 4		3 8		1 6	
	4		9		2	
			M F			
mao	9 5		7 3		5 1 yu	
facing	3		5		7 mountain	
	4 9		2 7		6 2	
	8		1		6	

Although the existing positions of the store entrances of both units are in undesirable locations (3/5/9), the problem can be solved by shifting them to the squares 8/9/4 (the stars of celebration) or 4/4/8 (the stars of health, prosperity, and luck). There are three excellent squares in units 8 and 9 in the mall—4/4/8, 8/9/4, and 9/8/3. There are no seriously troublesome areas, and the other squares are either neutral or quite good, making it easy to plan the usage of space in the store. After weighing all the factors, I would choose unit 8 or 9.

These are the points to note when planning the usage of space in the store:

- Place the cash register in the most auspicious spots (4/4/8, 8/9/4, and 9/8/3) facing other auspicious areas.
- Position the dominant merchandise in the auspicious areas—4/4/8, 8/9/4, and 9/8/3.
- Situate the secondary merchandise in the neutral or fairly good areas—2/6/1, 7/1/5, 1/7/2, and 6/2/6.
- Install countermeasures to neutralize the unfavorable areas—5/3/7 and 3/5/9.
- Install enhancers (red-colored objects) to magnify the effects of the benevolent stars in 4/4/8. Do not place red-colored objects in the areas with nine-purple, however; they will aggravate the fire element.

This concludes the introductory course to traditional Chinese feng-shui.

In this book, you have learned how to work on simple feng-shui projects for personal use. Understanding the materials and completing the exercises in the book do not make you an expert in the practice of the Hsüan-k'ung school of feng-shui, just as knowing how to wire a switch does not make you a licensed electrician. If you run into conditions that you feel are beyond your skill, you should obtain the services of an expert feng-shui practitioner. With the information you have acquired from studying this book, you will be able to evaluate the credibility and skill of professional feng-shui consultants should you need their help.

A P P E N D I X

THE NINE CYCLES DIAGRAMS

---

*Note: You may wish to photocopy the diagrams
on the following pages and have them in front of you
while you are studying the text or trying out the exercises.*

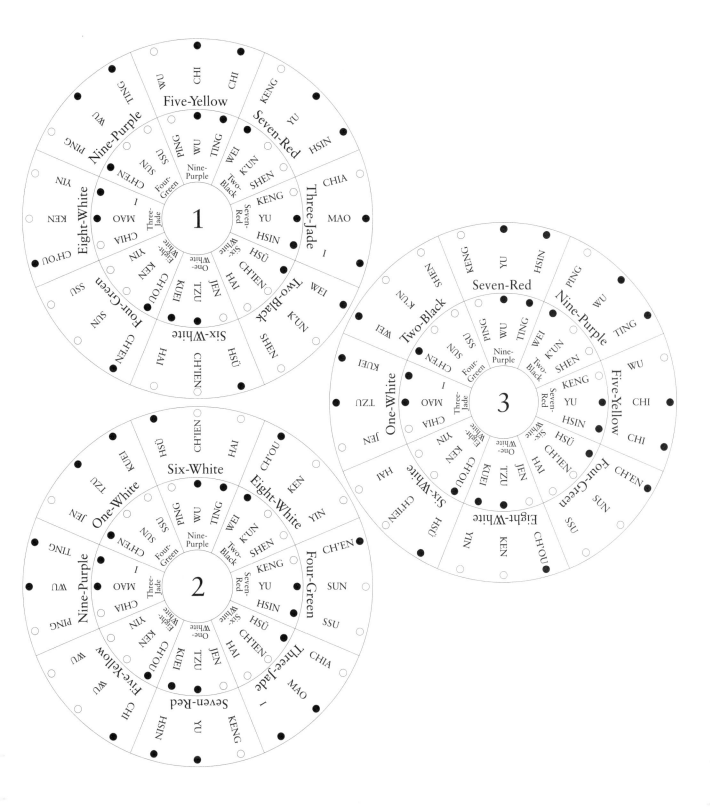

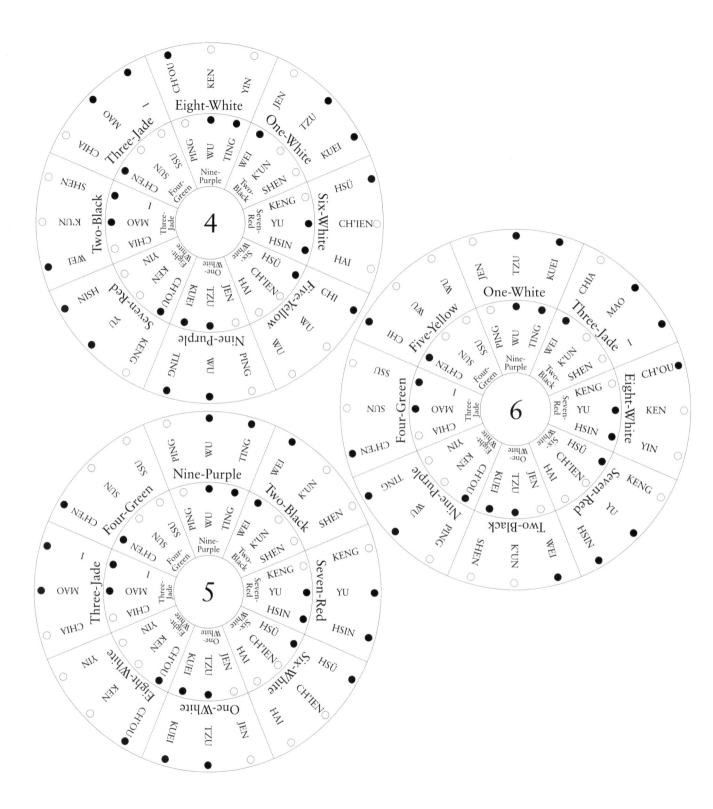

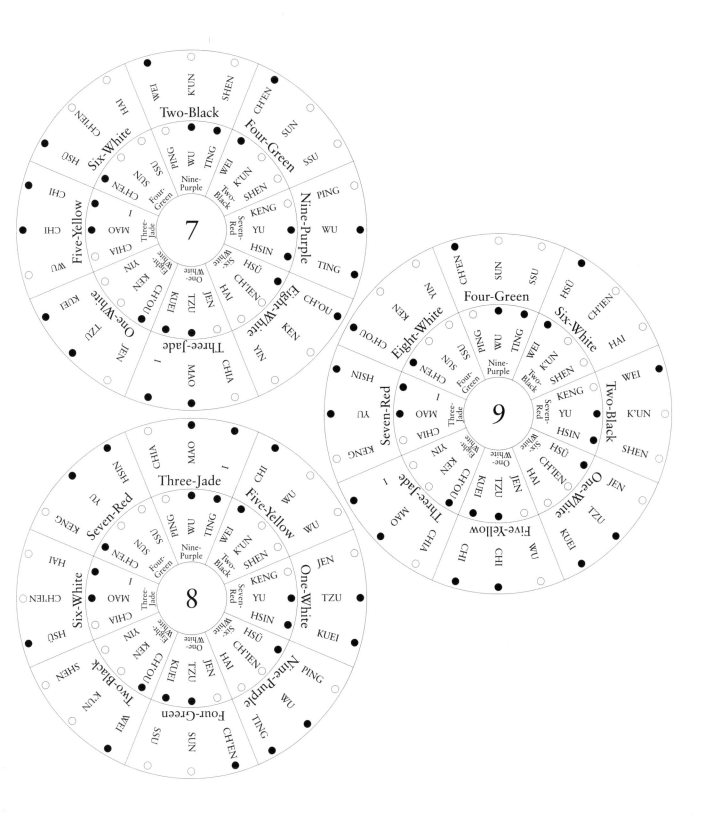

I N D E X

Illustrations, diagrams, and photographs are indicated by italics

life, the Taoist view of reality, and the nature of enlightenment to the training of the body and mind, communication, and the importance of personal freedom.

A Master Course in Feng-shui
This fully illustrated, comprehensive workbook is designed primarily for homeowners, renters, architects, and business owners who want to put feng-shui to practical personal use.

Nourishing the Essence of Life
Eva Wong presents and explains three classic texts on understanding the Tao in the macrocosm of the universe and the microcosm of the body that provide an excellent overview of the three traditional levels of the Taoist teachings—Outer, Inner, and Secret.

Seven Taoist Masters
History and legend are interwoven in this folk novel that both entertains and instructs. Written by an unknown author, *Seven Taoist Masters* is the story of six men and one woman who overcome tremendous hardships on the journey to self-mastery.

The Shambhala Guide to Taoism
This guide to the spiritual landscape of Taoism not only introduces the important events in the history of Taoism, the sages who wrote the Taoist texts, and the various schools of Taoist thinking, but also gives the reader a feel for what it means to practice Taoism today.

Tales of the Taoist Immortals
The stories in this book are of famous characters in Chinese history and myth: a hero's battle with the lords of evil, the founder of the Ming dynasty's treacherous betrayal of his friends, a young girl who saves her town by imitating rooster calls. The tales included here—which often have a moral behind them, are both entertaining and provocative.

Teachings of the Tao
Although the Tao cannot be described by words, words can allow us to catch a fleeting glimpse of that mysterious energy of the universe that is the source of life. The readings in this book are a beginner's entrée into the vast treasury of writings from the sacred Chinese tradition, consisting of original translations of excerpts from the Taoist canon.